Contradictions in Conservatism

Dr. Brian R. Farmer

PublishAmerica
Baltimore

First printing

ISBN: 1-4137-6905-5
PUBLISHED BY PUBLISHAMERICA, LLLP
www.publishamerica.com
Baltimore

Printed in the United States of America

Table of Contents

Chapter 1
Introduction

At mid-Twentieth Century, noted scholars Henry Aiken (1956), Daniel Bell (1960), and Morton White (1956) were arguing that ideology was no longer as important as it once was. What these scholars and others essentially argued was that rational analysis was taking the place of ideology in politics and that there had been an exhaustion of political ideas in advanced industrial democracies that had culminated in acceptance of welfare-State capitalism. There would still be political conflict for sure, but the basic idea that government intervention into the free market was necessary for steady and even growth, and that social action was a proper realm for government at least to some degree, had been accepted by all mainstream political parties. For example, in 1936, Democrat Franklin Roosevelt campaigned on continuation of the New Deal while his opponent, Republican Alfred Landon, essentially campaigned on continuation of the New Deal as well, but he would do it more efficiently and without deficits (Nash et al., 2001). For the purposes here, whether the New Deal could be administered more efficiently and without deficits is beside the point. The fact is that both parties were essentially accepting the New Deal programs as within the proper scope of government responsibility, and major ideological divisions over the proper role of government had been minimized.

In contrast to the ideological congruence of the two major Parties during the Great Depression, the ideological congruence of the two major Parties in the early 21st Century appears to have greatly eroded. Since the emergence of

Ronald Reagan in the 1980s and continuing through the present with the administration of George W. Bush, it is the argument of this author that the Republican Party and conservatives in general in the United States have been driven more by ideologies than by pragmatism and sound analysis, thus destroying the ideological congruence that had developed from the Great Depression until the Vietnam War era. Furthermore, the ideologies that have driven America's "conservative revolution," whether it be the "Reagan Revolution," Newt Gingrich's "Contract with America," or the present follies of the George W. Bush administration, are ideologies that have been pursued many times before throughout human history with disastrous results. For example, the doctrine of laissez-faire, preached so sanctimoniously in conservative circles, proved only to lead to worker exploitation, income inequality, monopoly capitalism, unsafe products, and environmental degradation during the Gilded Age of late 19th Century America. Laissez-faire capitalism is the world of company stores and company scrip, the world of Upton Sinclair, the world of Charles Dickens, and the world of great suffering for the masses. Conservative efforts to eliminate the role of government in the free marketplace are essentially efforts to return America to the 19th Century when 1/3 of the meat packed in Chicago was unfit to eat, when the standard water supply for American factory workers was an open barrel, and when 50% of children died before the age of five (Farmer, 2003).

Similarly, the church-state blend espoused by the Christian Coalition wing of American conservatism has proven itself to be flawed repeatedly throughout human history, whether one is discussing the Taliban in Afghanistan, or the Catholic Inquisition of Medieval Europe. To blend Church with State is to return to the time before the American Revolution when colonists in Virginia were whipped for heresy and Puritans in Massachusetts were executed for witchcraft. It is a return to the days when scientists were threatened with death if their discoveries conflicted with the teachings of the leaders of religion, and citizens were condemned to death for "heresy," or simply for thinking differently. Essentially, a return to a church-state blend is a return to the Eighteenth Century system that the authors of the Constitution abandoned. Those that espouse and preach these ideologies are essentially ignoring these lessons of history as well as empirical data and theoretical flaws in the ideologies themselves, as will be explained in the pages that follow.

In most American government textbooks there is not a chapter dedicated exclusively to ideology. This omission is somewhat befuddling since

Americans obviously are guided politically more by ideology than by facts and knowledge, because in order to be guided by facts and knowledge, it is a prerequisite that one must first actually "know something." One need go no further than "Jaywalking" on *The Tonight Show with Jay Leno* to come to the conclusion that most Americans are generally ignorant on political issues and know very little in terms of actual historical and political facts. Night after night, Leno asks some of the most basic questions such as: Who wrote the "Declaration of Independence?" or who wrote the "Gettysburg Address?" only to get responses such as "Britney Spears" or "Puff Daddy." While it is true that Leno's comedy is unscientific; empirical studies of public political and historical knowledge tend to support the same conclusion one might reach from watching Leno's antics. In other words, when it comes to politics, Americans in general are seriously deficient even in some of the most basic aspects of political knowledge. For example, in a national assessment test in the late 1980s, only a third of American seventeen year olds could correctly locate the Civil War in the period 1850-1900; more than a quarter placed it in the 18th Century. Furthermore, 14% credited Abraham Lincoln with writing the Bill of Rights and 10% credited Lincoln with the Missouri Compromise (which would have been quite an accomplishment for someone who was eleven years old at the time). Finally, 9% named Lincoln to be the author of *Uncle Tom's Cabin*. While this knowledge of history is abysmal, performance on questions concerning current affairs yield equally poor results. In a 1996 public opinion poll, only 10% of Americans could identify William Rehnquist as the Chief Justice of the Supreme Court. During the 1980s, the majority of Americans could not correctly answer whether the Reagan Administration supported the Sandinistas or the Contras in Nicaragua and only a third could place Nicaragua in Central America (Schudson, 2000, 16).

This does not mean, however, that the American public necessarily knows less than their leaders. In 1956, President Eisenhower's nominee as Ambassador to Ceylon was unable to identify either the country's prime minister or capital during his confirmation hearing. In 1981, President Reagan's nominee for Deputy Secretary of State, William Clark, admitted in his confirmation hearings that he had no idea how America's allies in Western Europe felt about having American nuclear missiles based there (Moore, 2002, 88). For his part, George W. Bush once referred to the Kosovars as "Kosovians," argued that the United States should "keep good relations with the Grecians" and confused a Slovenian foreign minister with

DR. BRIAN R. FARMER

the country of Slovakia (Miller, 2002, 198). Perhaps most revealing, however, was Bush's statement in Glamour Magazine during the 2000 Presidential campaign where he confused the Taliban in Afghanistan with "some band" (*Glamour*, 2000).

This is not to say, however, that American schools have gotten worse, or that Americans are more ignorant than they have been in the past. In 1945, for example, 43% Americans polled could name neither of their U.S. Senators. In 1952, only 67% could name the Vice President, and in 1945, only 92% knew that the President's in the United States is set at four years (Schudson, 2000, 16). With this type of ignorance, it is perhaps surprising that Democracy in America has worked as well as it has. If there are so many Americans that are evidently ignorant of even the most basic historical and political knowledge, (as the surveys suggest), then they must be making their political decisions based on something other than knowledge. That something is ideology.

Ideology

Ideologies are belief systems through which people view and interpret reality. In the words of Milton Rokeach (1972), "Ideology refers to more or less institutionalized set of beliefs—the views someone picks up." Ideologies are not reality, but instead produce simplified versions of reality for those that view the world through ideological frameworks. Ideology interprets and explains what is wrong with society in simplistic terms and provides simplistic prescriptions purported to solve all societal ills. In general, people are very good at identifying someone else's ideology and noting the flaws in their precepts, but people may not even recognize that they are normally just as ideological themselves. In the United States at present, there are scores of differing ideologies, some mainstream, and some on the political "fringe." The fringe ideologies, such as Nazism, are easily recognizable as ideologies by the masses and generally scorned for their "heretical errors" and deviations from social mores and accepted norms.

Consider, for example, the Lilleth character (the wife of Frazier) on the TV situation comedy *Cheers*. The Lilleth character is a satirical portrayal of radical feminist liberation ideology, an ideology that does exist as a political "fringe" ideology in the U.S. The character is humorous to many because real-life versions of Lilleth, or persons that at least share some of the characteristics of Lilleth's ideology (author of the book, *Women Good, Men*

Bad), have been known to many of us. For instance, at Texas Tech University (where I was previously employed), there was once a petition by female faculty members and students to remove the word "Ladies" from the door of the female restroom facilities and replace it with "Women." To the petitioners, "Ladies," was a term that symbolized male domination of women. To others, it was merely a term that directed them to the proper restroom that had little or no symbolic value.

Another fringe ideology that the majority of Americans recognize as an ideology is the radical black liberation ideology. Pop culture has parodied this ideology in innumerable ways, from Damon Wayans' "Homey the Clown" character on *In Living Color*, to Chris Rock's "Nat X" character on *Saturday Night Live*, the comedians have viciously lampooned an ideology that essentially holds (in the words of Rock), that "the white man did it to me." The routines are humorous to many because the majority of Americans recognize the ideological flaws and they have recognized approximations of those flaws in the ideology of a real person.

All ideology, however, is not so benign. If we consider racist Nazi ideology, for example, we will find that the ideology simplistically teaches that, "all of the world's problems" are created by "subversive Jews" and other minorities. The simplistic solution of the Nazis in Germany in WWII therefore included the genocide of Jews and others that the Nazis considered societal "problems" with the result that ten million people died in the Nazi death camps. Nazism, of course, is only a fringe ideology in the United States and therefore does not appear to be a dangerous force in American politics at the moment. It should be remembered, however, that Nazism was only a fringe ideology in Germany as late as 1928. The fact that the Nazis came from political "nowhere" to assume power in Germany five years later, and then overran Europe within a dozen years, is a testimony to the mobilizing power of ideology. If American politics has become more ideological in recent years rather than more practical, then it has also become more dangerous.

Conservative Political Ideology

Samuel Huntington (1957) argues that conservatism is best understood not as an inherent theory, but as a positional ideology. According to Huntington, "When the foundations of society are threatened, the conservative ideology reminds men of the necessity of some institutions and the desirability of the existing ones" (Huntington, 1957, 455). According to

Huntington, ideological conservatism arises from the anxiety that develops when people perceive that valuable institutions are endangered by contemporary developments or proposed reforms and the awareness that perceived useful institutions are under attack then leads conservatives to attempt to provide a defense of those institutions. Huntington (1957, 456) explains that because "the articulation of conservatism is a response to a specific social situation…the manifestation of conservatism at any one time and place has little connection with its manifestation at any other time and place." In other words, conservatism is an extremely situational ideology and conservatives at one time or another have sought to conserve just about every institution ever invented, from monarchies, to aristocracies, to slavery, to tariffs, to free trade, to capitalism, to religion, to the defense of communism in the late 1980s in the Soviet Union.

Conservatism, however, is forced to be selective concerning what traditions and legacies must be retained and which ones may be discarded. In what Edmund Burke referred to as the "choice of inheritance," one may expect disagreement even among conservatives as to which societal institutions are absolutely essential and must be preserved, which ones may be altered and how, and which ones should be abolished completely (Muller, 1997, 31).

In one diverse form or another then, conservative political thought has existed throughout recorded human history. For example, the Pharisees, Chief Priests, and Teachers of the Law mentioned so disparagingly in the Gospels of the New Testament were by Huntington's definition conservatives bent on retaining long-standing societal institutions against the new teachings of Jesus of Nazareth. Similarly, some of the enemies of Mohammed in the 7th Century that preferred to retain existing traditions instead of the new teachings of Mohammed were certainly also conservatives.

The term "conservative" itself, however, dates to 1818 as the title of a French weekly journal, *Le Conservateur*, that was purposed to "uphold religion, the King, liberty, the Charter and respectable people" (Muller, 1997, 26). If President George W. Bush is inserted for the word "King," and "Constitution" is inserted for the word "Charter," then one may see that the fundamental elements of conservatism in France in 1818 are still present in the U.S. in the 21st Century. Other aspects of conservative thought that have remained constant throughout the centuries are presented below.

Transcendent Moral Order

In spite of the diversity of institutions that conservatives throughout the centuries have sought to defend, a set of assumptions and themes behind conservatism have endured. Among those is the assumption that there exists a transcendent moral order to which humans should attempt to conform society (Kirk, 1982). Conservatism therefore tends to be skeptical of new and abstract theories that attempt to mold society to a new morality because the existing order arose and exists as it does due to its consistency with the transcendent and true morality. Consequently, any theory of a "new" morality represents "immorality" or it would have already emerged through the human experiences of the ages. In the United States of the 21st Century, conservatism has therefore opposed the "abstract theories" of communism and socialism as well as feminism, civil rights, gay rights and "liberal" welfare programs.

Negative View of Human Nature

Conservative ideologies typically emphasize human imperfections and depravity, especially those of common individuals. Typically, humans are viewed as naturally bad, selfish, uncooperative, and incapable of honorable behavior unless coerced. Christian religious conservatives tie the negative view of human nature to the doctrine of original sin in the Bible, and argue that human nature has been flawed ever since sin first came into the world in the Garden of Eden. In this perspective, it is impossible for humans to be good without divine assistance (Muller, 1997). It is also because of this belief in a flawed human nature that conservatives also view human attempts to create a "just society" through reason, as Plato prescribed in *The Republic*, as unrealizable. Consistent with their theme of humans as flawed beings, conservatives typically argue that there are limits to human knowledge and this fact should act as a limit on attempts at societal innovation. Consequently, governments of humans lack the wisdom and knowledge necessary to intervene in the free market in order to remedy poverty or inequalities without producing unintended negative consequences (Quinton, 1978, 17). Similarly, "ideal utopias" prescribed by subsequent philosophers (such as Karl Marx, for instance) are impossible. In the words of conservative political theorist Glen Tinder (1989, 23), "To pursue the ideal of perfect justice is to ignore our fallenness."

Instead, conservatives argue that change, if it is merited, should take place gradually, come from experience, and occur within the bounds of existing customs and institutions. Societal change most certainly cannot be derived from abstract theories contained in a prescriptive rule book. As such, conservatives distrust intellectuals, whether sociologists, political scientists, historians, psychologists, or economists, who would reform society based on intellectual arguments (Kirk, 1986, 13-20).

Focus on Order

Conservatives are skeptical of a society without constraints on the "fallen humans" and argue that institutional measures must be taken to ensure order. Conservatives can therefore be expected to clash with liberals over the expansion of rights and the utility of existing institutions (such as Church) that conservatives view as necessary to control human passions and disorder. In the words of Edmund Burke in Reflections on the Revolution in France, "the restraints on men, as well as their liberties, are to be reckoned among their rights." Burke therefore argued for retention of customary moral rules even if those rules had not been subject to rational justification. After all, flawed human reasoning would be unlikely to rationally determine definitively whether customary mores were rationally justified or not. Even if such things could be known, conservatives' low regard for ordinary humans leads them to believe that most people would lack the time, energy, and intellect to reevaluate societal mores anyway. Therefore, conservatives argue that humans have a duty to abide by existing societal rules in most cases (Muller, 1997, 11). Edmund Burke argues that because the dissolution of the social order would also destroy the societal institutions by which human passions are restrained, the individual has no right to opt out of obligation to the State and community (Muller, 1997, 11).

In spite of the low view of common humans and the negative perception of human nature in general, in an apparent contradiction with their view of human nature, conservatives typically argue that there are elites, cultural, political, and economic, who know better than others and should make the decisions for society (Muller, 1997, 18). John Adams, for example, spoke of the existence of a "natural aristocracy" that anyone could join by virtue of merit or ability (Dunn and Woodard, 1991, 62).

12

Emphasis on History and Existing Institutions

Conservatives place a major emphasis upon history and the history of human institutions. For conservatives, the survival of a human institution throughout history, whether it be religion, marriage, aristocracy, or the free market, proves that the institution itself must serve a human need (Kristol, 1983, 161). The need that is met by the institution may not necessarily be the need for which the institution was created. For example, the practice of the burial of deceased human bodies may have arisen for purposes of sanitation; however, the institution of the funeral and burial serves a purpose of aiding the psychological well-being of the living. That humans at any given time may not recognize the utility of an existing institution is a reflection of the human limitations of the critics rather than the institutions themselves. The ongoing existence of the institutions themselves is sufficient to indicate their superiority in meeting human needs.

Conservatives typically point to the family as the most important societal institution, but a major emphasis is also placed on religion. Conservatives typically defend religion under these pretenses and ignore the fact that religion from time to time throughout human history has been the cause of much discord and oppression. For conservatives, it is less important whether religion is true or false, and more important that it offers humans hope and thus helps to diffuse discontent that could disrupt the societal order (Muller, 1997, 13).

Skepticism of Altruistic Efforts

Conservatives typically oppose liberal moral "do-gooders" and scoff at the efforts of those who attempt to improve the lives of those less fortunate. In general, conservatives argue that such efforts only encourage laziness and dependency among the recipients. Furthermore, conservatives again argue that such efforts have unintended and unforeseen negative consequences. For instance, a government welfare program that increases aid based on the number of children in a family may be designed to eliminate malnutrition, but would be expected by conservatives to lead to the birth of more welfare-recipient children as people take advantage of the larger government stipend. Conservatives typically view income inequalities as legitimate and natural and therefore attempts at redistribution to the poor are not only "casting one's pearls before swine," but also a violation of the natural order (Muller, 1997, 18).

Role of the State

The role of the State in conservative thought is for security and the protection of property and the free market. Conservatives therefore emphasize a strong military and favor other coercive measures, such as police, to ensure order, the security of property, and the efficient operation of the free market. The State is also expected to protect and support the important societal institutions of Church and family.

Diversity and Conservative Ideology

As previously discussed, conservatism in general is an extremely diverse area of political thought, and American conservatism is no exception to this rule. While some facets of conservatism as well as some individual conservatives themselves are more ideological than others, it is certainly a fact that most American conservatives are driven by ideology rather than analysis, whether it be one coherent ideology or a combination of several. In the words of Winston Churchill concerning conservatism, "It is stirred on almost all occasions by sentiment and instinct rather than by worldly calculations"(Quoted in Manchester, 1983, 3). Similarly, Clinton Rossiter argues that the American conservative "feels more deeply than he thinks about political principles, and what he feels most deeply about them is that they are a gift of great old men" (Rossiter, 1982, 74). If conservatism is ideologically driven, then it is important to understand those underlying ideologies within the diverse body politic that makes up American conservatism.

There are three dominant ideologies in the United States: Classic Liberalism, Traditional Conservatism, and Reform Liberalism. These three ideologies form the core of the two major political parties and the ideologies are generally reflected in the major parties' platforms and prescriptions. Classic Liberals and Traditional Conservatives tend to be Conservative Republicans, while Reform Liberalism is the dominant ideology in the Democratic Party. Conservatism is also home to a pair of important fringe ideologies, Libertarianism and Conservative Extremism that have become worthy of discussion as well in the post-Oklahoma City Bombing era. These ideologies and their contradictions will be discussed in greater detail in the following chapters.

Chapter 2
American Political Socialization, Theory, Values, and Beliefs

Political Socialization

Political Scientists assume that political attitudes, values, and beliefs are learned. This, however, is only an assumption. It is certainly within the realm of possibility that there is a gene that determines whether individuals are liberal or conservative. If that is the case, then the conservatives are perhaps in trouble, because those "liberal" scholars in charge of genetic research will surely find that gene and eradicate the one that turns people into republicans. Until then, however, we will continue with our perhaps flawed assumption that political attitudes and beliefs are learned, rather than innate.

If we assume that political attitudes are learned, then the process of forming those political attitudes becomes a major focus. This process of forming political attitudes is termed as political socialization, and there is an immense body of scholarly research that deals with this subject. In these studies, scholars have determined through the analysis of the political attitudes of adolescents that these attitudes essentially develop during the "formative years" between ages eleven-fifteen (Hyman, 1959, Lane, 1959, 216-219, Adelson and O'Neil, 1970). Survey research conducted on children at the beginning of the formative years (age 9-10) reveals that children normally do not have a coherent political perspective prior to age eleven.

Children may know whether they like a particular President, etc., but they are generally unable to respond with any coherent ideological pattern when they are posed with more veiled and in-depth questions that cause one to think about policy without familiar labels.

Similar survey research on persons at age sixteen, however, reveals that by age sixteen people normally have developed coherent political attitudes and that the core ideology around which those attitudes revolve may not change substantially throughout the rest of their lives. In other words, whatever political perspective people have adopted by age sixteen may be the basic political perspective that they hold to for the rest of our lives. This being the case, it becomes very important to understand the elements that work to shape political attitudes during those formative years between the ages of eleven-fifteen.

Socialization Agents

Parents and Family

Parents and Family are widely considered by scholars to be the most important political socialization agents in society. This conclusion is supported through empirical research that has revealed a strong correlation between the political attitudes of parents and those of their children (Hyman, 1959). When both parents are strongly leaning conservative, research suggests that there is approximately a 90% chance that their children will have similar political views. The same thing can be said for those who are strongly leaning liberal. In cases where the parents are of opposing political persuasions, there appears to be a weak tendency (56%) for the political attitudes of the children to be consistent with the political attitudes of the father rather than the mother. There is some dispute among scholars as to why this is, with some scholars arguing that people purposefully socialize their daughters differently than their sons and thus make their daughters less political. Consequently, children are more likely to adopt the politics of their father, who is the more political of the two parents. If this is not the case, and the different political path of daughters/mothers is not a genetic gender difference, then the difference must be explained through other socialization agents.

Peers

Scholars have identified numerous psycho-social characteristics that are inherent among youth. Endemic to the politically formative stage in the life cycle (ages eleven-fifteen) is the need to have a high affiliation with peers and a preference for the affiliation with peers to that of family and adults (Csikszentmihalyi and Larson, 1984). As such, peers are most certainly important socialization agents during the formative years; however, the research suggests that peers are less important as a *political* socialization agent than parents and family due to the low place of politics in the hierarchy of priorities among adolescents during the formative years. During adolescence, individuals tend to focus their conversation more on relationships and youth activities as well as sports, music, and academic pursuits. Politics generally occupies a lower priority than these other items; hence, the impact of peers as a political socialization agent during the formative years is somewhat muted.

School

School, of course, is also an important socialization agent since it is at school where people interact for about seven hours per day during the formative years. During these formative years, however, schools normally must reinforce attitudes learned in the family and community and are not therefore generally "radical" socialization agents.

The reasons that schools tend to reinforce conservative family and community values can be traced to the traditional public school structure. Typically, local school boards (the official policy-making bodies for the schools) are elected. Persons that are not residents of the school district are normally ineligible to run for school board, meaning that the members of the school policy-making body are drawn from within the community itself. Being that these board members are drawn from within the community, it follows that their values are likely to reflect those of the community from which they were drawn—especially when they are democratically elected. In general, democratically elected officials at any level must reflect the values of the electorate or their electability becomes questionable. In general, democracy and the government it creates will reflect the character of its people and school boards are certainly no exception to this "rule." It takes perhaps some rather fantastic mental gyrations to conceive of a democratic system where conservative voters routinely elect school board members that espouse radically different value systems than those of the voters. It also follows that if these school board members stray too far from family and community norms, they are simply unlikely to be elected. Secondly, if radical individuals do somehow win the election and then attempt to implement ideas that are outside of societal norms, they will most likely find themselves at odds with the community and voted out during the next election. Teachers within the school district operate under similar constraints since their livelihood is controlled by elected school board officials and indirectly by the electorate itself. As a consequence, most teachers at the primary and secondary level dare not stray too far from the norms of the surrounding community.

For example, in New York City in the 1990s (a city that Bill Clinton carried twice in Presidential elections and in a State where Hillary Clinton is a Senator) a teacher was fired for his association with a group known as NAMBLA. NAMBLA is known in full name as the "North American Man/ Boy Love Association," a group that advocates sex between adult men and young boys. The slogan for the group is "sex after eight is too late" and the said reference is not to eight o'clock in the evening (Etzioni, 1994, 11). It turns out, evidently, that those "liberals" in New York City (that twice voted for Bill Clinton) did not want a potential pedophile teaching in their schools any more than do those "conservatives" in rural America and the NAMBLA member was terminated from his position as a New York City educator. Evidently, opposition to pedophile teachers is a bit nonpartisan in character and also bridges the gap between urban and rural politics.

So who are those "liberal" teachers in public schools indoctrinating children with "radical" ideas anyway? In most communities, the majority of teachers will be from within that community or from another community within a hundred-mile radius of that community. For example, in Amarillo Texas where I reside, the school with the largest representation of graduates in the Amarillo Independent School District is West Texas A&M, the closest four year school to Amarillo, located in Canyon, Texas, about fifteen minutes from my residence in Amarillo. Similarly, the city with the largest representation of students at West Texas A&M University is Amarillo. Finally, the majority of teachers in the Amarillo Independent School district live in—you guessed it—Amarillo. In other words, a typical teacher in the Amarillo Independent School District is likely to be someone who went to school in Amarillo or somewhere near, attended a University near Amarillo, and now teaches and resides in Amarillo. Such a person is unlikely to have values themselves that are far from the norms of the community since they themselves are essentially products of that community. Consequently, their norms and values typically reflect those of the community of which they are a part. This is not to say that there are not some teachers that do not reflect the norms of their community; however, such individuals will face pressure to keep radical deviations from the norms of the community to themselves under threat of reprisals.

For example, in very socially conservative towns in the "Bible belt," regardless of one's personal position on gay rights and the 14th Amendment, it might be wise for any public school teacher to refrain from enthusiastically pushing a gay rights agenda in the public school system unless that teacher very much enjoys parental confrontation. If, for example, a public middle-school government teacher were to argue that under the 14th Amendment, "equal protection under the law" and equal "privileges and immunities" cannot be denied to all persons "born or naturalized in the U.S.," that teacher would certainly be correct. If that same teacher followed that Statement by pointing out that the 14th Amendment protections apply to gays because they, like heterosexuals, may be "born or naturalized in the U.S.," that teacher is still correct, but also could possibly expect mild parental confrontations. If, however, that teacher made the decision to take the argument a step further so as to say that "equal protection" and equal "privileges and immunities" require that the government recognize gay marriage (marriage being a "privilege" extended to heterosexuals, but not homosexuals, and thus a 14th Amendment equal privileges violation), one might expect that teacher to be on the receiving end of some more serious parental confrontations. Discussions of the matter between the parents and school administrators as well as between school administrators and the teacher are perhaps likely to follow. Most teachers prefer to avoid this type of unpleasant confrontation and thus keep their discussions closer to societal norms.

If, however, this hypothetical teacher took the argument even one step further and argued that "equal protection" and equal "privileges and immunities" in the 14th Amendment require that gays must be able to adopt children (after all, heterosexual couples enjoy this privilege), one might envision that not only would all parental hell to break loose, but there may be lawsuits, vandalism, a terminated contract, a media event, and a prayer vigil of 24 elders from the local church outside that teacher's door. Even the most "radical" teachers normally want to avoid this type of confrontation with community, not to mention the unemployment that may follow. What this illustrates is that public school teachers are very much constrained by the values of the community in which they teach, and teachers may vary seriously from the norm only at their own peril. As a consequence, "radical" political ideas are more likely to be learned somewhere besides the public schools.

Media

Another group of major socialization agents that have been accused from time to time of imparting radical ideas on America's youth are the mass media. Survey data reveal that the vast majority of conservatives believe that the mass media in the U.S. is pushing a radical left agenda. Furthermore, most Americans believe that the media is very influential in shaping political attitudes (Janda et al., 1992).

This view has been supported somewhat by empirical research. For instance, much attention was given to a study of the impact of television and Kindergarten children in the 1980s (Singer and Singer, 1981) where two groups of children watched two different television programs (Batman and Mr. Rogers' Neighborhood). In this study, children that watched adventure shows such as Batman began to exhibit more aggressive behavior in an apparent imitation of what they had viewed on television. Conversely, the children that watched Mr. Rogers' Neighborhood did not exhibit similar aggressive social behavior, suggesting that the media has the power to influence social behavior.

If, however, the media are incredibly effective as an ideological socialization agent, and if the media are overwhelmingly liberal as some have charged, then why are all Americans not liberals? One can only conclude that the media are either ineffective as an ideological socialization agent or the media are not in fact pushing a liberal agenda. Instead, scholars tend to argue that the media are more important in setting the political agenda, but less important in the formation of ideology or partisanship (Janda et al., 1992). In other words, the media are effective at determining what Americans will be debating, but they are not so effective at shaping individual opinions one way or the other surrounding that debate. John Steinbruner (1974) argues that the human mind is programmed with decision mechanisms that screen out information that the established set of responses in the brain are not programmed to accept. In other words, people tend to psychologically tune out messages that conflict with preconceived notions or things that they believe to be true. For example, in the 1990s, a story hit the media concerning logging in the Pacific Northwest that was threatening the habitat of the Spotted Owl. Liberals (typically more pro-environmental protection) protested the logging that threatened the habitat of this endangered species while conservatives protested the protection of the owl at the expense of business and human needs. In either case, the media presentation of the story placed the spotted owl on the political agenda, but individual reactions to the story were pre-programmed based on ideological predispositions and arguments conflicting with individuals' pre-programmed responses were tossed aside. This being the case, Media are severely limited as a socialization agent as people typically filter out messages with which they disagree and follow their pre-programmed ideological responses.

Proliferation also hinders the Media as a political socialization agent since those in the formative years may simply select out political information from their personal media spectrum. Young persons in their formative years (eleven-fifteen) are in many cases less likely to be watching CNN or CSPAN than MTV and VH-1. This is a phenomenon that has developed within the last thirty years, however. For those that "came of age" prior to the 1970s many only had three television channel options, and during the State of the Union Address, those options were reduced to one as all three networks carried the President's speech. In contrast, the adolescents of the 21st Century may have scores of TV channels and can stay tuned to the mass media 24 hours a day and still tune out political information in its entirety if they so desire. There is perhaps little that one can gain in the way of political information from an evening of Ozzy Ozzbourne and Anna Nicole Smith.

Workplace

The workplace often has been cited as a political socialization agent, and its impact on the formation of political labor movements is of obvious importance since individuals may spend more waking hours in the workplace than with friends or family. The workplace, however, has a number of limitations as a political socialization agent. First, the impact of the workplace is hindered because the workplace experience is generally post-formative in character. In other words, if the formative years for political attitudes are eleven-fifteen, the impact of the workplace is seriously lessened since most individuals do not enter the workplace until age sixteen. As a consequence, by the time that an adolescent becomes employed for the first time, that person's political attitudes largely already may be set.

This is not to say, however, that the workplace cannot be politically influential. In general, the political socialization power of the workplace increases when there is little diversity of function in the workplace and workers work in close proximity with one another. Labor Unions have exploited such situations for political socialization for over a century, but the socialization power of the workplace even under these conditions is difficult to separate from socioeconomic factors that tend to greatly influence political attitudes.

Religion

Religion has become increasingly political in orientation since the late 1970s (especially Protestant Fundamentalist Churches), under the influence of individuals like Jerry Falwell and Pat Robertson, who tend to mix religious beliefs with political concerns. Additionally, there appears to be a strong correlation between Protestant fundamentalist beliefs and political conservatism (Kellstedt and Green, 1993). For a number of reasons, however, empirical research has been somewhat less conclusive than one might think.

First, effectiveness of religion as a political socialization agent is difficult to determine because its impact is so difficult to separate from family influence during the formative years. In other words, most adolescents in the formative years between ages eleven and fifteen generally attend church (if they attend at all) in the accompaniment of their parents. As a consequence, it is difficult to determine if the impact on their political attitudes that one may attribute to church is actually attributable to church, or attributable primarily to parents. Obviously, one might expect the church to have some impact among those who attend regularly, but how much? Where can the line be drawn between church influence and parental influence? To compound the problem further, typically, conservative parents often take their children to a conservative church that teaches the same conservative politics that the parents teach at home. In such situations, it is difficult to determine where church influence begins and parental influence ends (Kellstedt and Smidt, 1993).

Another factor that makes the impact of religion difficult to determine is the uncertainty of the causal order. While empirical research shows that fundamentalist Protestants are much more likely to be conservative than

Catholics and non-fundamentalist Protestants, whether or not it is their religions that have shaped their political views is unclear. In other words, do people become Republicans because of what is taught in fundamentalist churches, or do people choose conservative-leaning churches because they are already conservative themselves and therefore choose churches that are consistent with their already-held political views (Kellstedt and Green, 1993)?

Another factor that hinders the impact of religion as a socialization agent is the degree to which people pay attention and understand the political messages. In the words of Welch et al. (1993), "In view of the many mechanisms that intervene between communicator and target audience—inattention, selective perception, distortion—it is unwise to assume that church members perceive clearly the messages intended by the clergy." In other words, it is difficult for the preacher to politically influence the congregation if no one is listening. It is perhaps worth mentioning again, that political attitudes are generally formed between the ages of eleven and fifteen. Is this the age where people pay attention to the preacher in church?

American Values and Beliefs

The United States is a very pluralistic society with many diverse groups and beliefs. As such, there is perhaps no political issue where Americans display unanimity and there is no coherent set of beliefs that one could indisputably call "American political theory;" however, there are a number of areas where Americans exhibit general trends in opinion surveys. Additionally, some of those trends are rooted in a long history of relatively consistent American political behavior. Some of the more important and salient of those beliefs and behaviors will be discussed below.

Individualism

Perhaps as important and salient as any other American trend is that the U.S. is a very individualistic society. Essentially, the role of the individual in American society tends to take precedent over the State. This perspective grew out of the writings of John Locke, from whom the founding fathers' borrowed heavily in writing both the *Declaration of Independence* and the Bill of Rights. The Lockean individualist perspective grew out of the Age of Enlightenment and the struggle of the American Colonists in the 18th Century to release themselves from Monarchical rule. Lockean individualism can be seen in countless facets of American society, from lax laws of incorporation, to expansive criminal rights, to the icons of pop culture (Bellah et al. 1985).

In general, Americans want to be able to conduct their business and their private lives without governmental interference. In this, Americans are not necessarily exceptional; however, it is the degree to which Americans will go to ensure that they are "let alone" that is indeed exceptional. Robert Bellah et al., (1985) summed up the American individualist perspective by stating that Americans believe that "Anything that would violate our right to think for ourselves, judge for ourselves, make our own decisions, live our lives as we see fit, is not only morally wrong, it is sacrilegious." As a consequence, murderers walk free on the streets in America because policemen violated their due process rights. Similarly, the air in Houston Texas is the dirtiest in the country because a recent Governor was so lax in enforcing environmental laws (viewed as government interference that violates the rights of people to do business) that air pollution in Houston is now worse than in cities much larger, such as Los Angeles (Begala, 2002).

Also in Texas, under that same Governor, laws requiring individuals to wear motorcycle helmets were repealed because such restrictions are viewed as violations of the right to personal choice. This is in spite of the fact that few would argue that motorcycles are safer without a helmet. Instead, it is obvious that the prospect of millions of Texans riding around on motorcycles without helmets has a negative impact on society as a whole. After all, society as a whole will eventually pay indirectly for the medical bills for thousands of motorcycle riders who were injured while riding without helmets. Society will do so through the higher taxes needed to compensate for the increase in bad debts at county hospitals because of the increase in serious head injuries that necessarily follows the repeal of a motorcycle helmet law.

Texas, however, is not alone in its staunch individualism. Individualism is so pervasive in America that many popular heroes, both real and fictional, have strong individualist streaks. Movie and television police dramas, for instance, for decades have been dominated by individualistic police characters that must "do things their own way." From Clint Eastwood's "Dirty Harry," to Peter Faulk's "Columbo," to the ever-changing cast of "NYPD Blue," the fictional police hero typically must work outside of standard operating procedures, if not from outside of society as a whole, in order to produce the results necessary for positive reform of society. The celluloid police hero is perpetually in trouble with the well intentioned and intelligent, but "by the book" lieutenant for gross violations of department rules, and it is common for our hero to even be suspended or voluntarily go into temporary "retirement" so that he can continue to chase villains unrestrained by anti-individualistic rules.

As it is in American fiction, so it also is with American non-fiction heroes. Non-fictional individualists in America often enter politics and become Senators (ex-Vietnam-POW John McCain), Governors (ex-Navy Seal and Professional wrestler Jesse Ventura), and even Presidents (ex-mercenaries and war heroes Theodore Roosevelt and Andrew Jackson). All of the above fit the mold of "Rambo" or "Dirty Harry" in that they tended to march to the beat of a "different drummer" and retained their individualistic attitudes after they moved into the public arena to attempt societal reform.

At any rate, this elevation of the individual at the expense of the common good is very common in the U.S. and certainly more common in the U.S. than in Eastern societies. In Eastern cultures, such as in Japan and the Middle East, greater emphasis is placed on society as a whole rather than on the rights of individuals. These societies are known in political science terms as "holistic" societies where the common good tends to take precedent over the rights of individuals (Nakane, 1986). Examples of holistic behavior include the Japanese Kamikaze pilots in WWII and the suicide bombers of al Qaeda. In both cases, it is certainly not the good of the individual suicide bomber that is elevated, since the bomber dies, but theoretically, the death of the suicide bomber benefits the societal common good. In the case of Japan in WWII, the sacrifices of the Kamikazes were intended to prevent an American invasion and thus preserve the whole of Japanese society. In the case of al Qaeda's suicide bombers, the purpose is to please Allah and therefore benefit the common good through Allah's blessings (White, 2001). In either case, the suicide bomber is analogous to a honeybee that stings a human that threatens the hive. The bee dies shortly after the sting, but the death of that bee may save the entire hive if the threat is driven away. Americans tend not to have to have such a honeybee mentality. As a consequence, the Kamikaze attacks of WWII and the suicide-bombers of al Qaeda are very difficult for individualistic-thinking Americans to understand. At any rate, the Kamikazes of WWII struck a major blow to American morale. Similarly, al Qaeda's attacks of 9/11 left many Americans not only outraged, but also bewildered.

Another important facet of American individualism is self-reliance. Alexis De Toqueville (1835) in his classic work, *Democracy in America*, noted that Americans insist on always relying on their own judgment rather than on "received authority" in forming their own opinions and that Americans tend to stand by their own opinions regardless of the positions of authority figures. In other words, Toqueville argued that Americans tend to be those "don't confuse me with the facts, my mind is made up" type of people, or at least they were in 1831. This reliance on self and aversion to "received authority" helps create a situation where common persons can rise to high positions in America; however, it can also create a climate where common Americans distrust their political leaders and refuse to follow those with greater knowledge.

Individualism has another down side as well. Since Americans generally believe that individuals should rely on themselves rather than on society as a whole, among many Americans there is a lack of empathy for societal "losers" and a tendency to view the societal underclass as "those who have failed to take the necessary initiative to take care of themselves." As a consequence, there is a social stigma associated with government aid to the poor or welfare. For example, during the Great Depression of the 1930s, an estimated 50% of Americans that qualified for government relief programs did not apply in order to avoid the social stigma of being "on the dole" (Brinkley, 2003).

A further problem with American individualism is that individualism often conflicts with traditional societal structures such as church, which also have broad support in American society. For example, some American individualists choose to engage in sex outside of marriage, some abuse alcohol, some engage in homosexual relationships, some join nudist colonies, some smoke marijuana, and some pierce their bodies and get tattoos. Which of these activities are legitimate government interests and which are matters that should be left to individual discretion and choice are matters of debate in and of themselves. On exactly where such lines should be drawn, there is no complete consensus.

Another very American political belief related to individualism is the belief that politics and government are justifiable and honorable only to the extent that they improve the human condition. In this perspective, governmental institutions may be disobeyed or abolished if they overstep their bounds and disparage people's rights without a clear and present gain in the public good. These principles can be found in the *Declaration of Independence,* where Thomas Jefferson and the founding fathers claimed that the purpose of government is the preservation of rights and that any government that destroys such rights should be abolished. As such, individual liberties are only limited by clear cases of the public good and the rights of others. For example, the Second Amendment guarantees the right to bear arms; however, in the interest of what al Qaeda has proven is a clear case of the public good, the right has been forfeited at airports. Similarly, students may not exercise their rights to bear arms by pointing those guns at the professor because such activity violates the professor's (an individual's) rights to "life, liberty, and pursuit of happiness." In other words, the right of one person to keep and bear arms is curtailed where the rights of another begin.

American Conception of Equality

Equality in the American political mindset is a multifaceted concept that is among the most important in American political thought. The roots of the American views of equality arose out of the "age of enlightenment" that influenced American founders such as Thomas Jefferson. The American view of equality is reflected by Jefferson in the *Declaration of Independence* where he asserted, "all men are created equal." Although Jefferson's intention may have been merely go assert that the American people were equal to the English people at the time and therefore entitled to the same status under law, the concept has grown as the Nation has matured in its Democratic journey. Obviously, Jefferson's "all men are created equal" did not include blacks since Jefferson himself was a slave owner, but Americans later took Jefferson at his words rather than his deeds. As Alexis de Toqueville (1835) pointed out in his classic work, *Democracy in America*, equality has a long tradition in America beginning with a great equality that existed among the immigrants that settled the shores of the original American colonies. In the words of Toqueville (speaking of New England), "the germs of aristocracy were never planted in that part of the union." Toqueville goes on to explain that the American laws of inheritance that abolished the English tradition of primogeniture and installed a system where all children shared equally in inheritance eliminated the English economic system based on landed gentry and inheritance and replaced it with a more merit-oriented system. When the experience of settling the American frontier, another great equalizer, is added to that already egalitarian culture, what emerged is a culture that is in some ways greatly egalitarian. Then there is that experience at Jamestown where everyone was equally starving and only 60 of 2000 immigrants survived from 1607-1609 (Brinkley, 2003). I guess I said that wrong. It looks like about 97% were equally dead.

Among the ways that Americans conceive equality is "equality of opportunity" (Fowler and Orenstein, 1993). Americans generally believe that everyone should have an equal opportunity to succeed, especially in economic life. The concept of equal opportunity takes for granted that results will vary greatly depending on talent, drive, health, inheritance, and of course, just plain luck. The important thing is not that some will achieve more than others, but that all have the opportunity to achieve. It should be stressed that this equality of opportunity is only an ideal and never will be completely achieved in reality. Clearly some have a better chance at becoming a millionaire or President than most of us because they might have a father that was a millionaire or President himself.

Another facet of equality that is stressed by Americans is political equality (Fowler and Orenstein, 1993). The concept of political equality includes the rights of all people to participate in government and the political process. Political equality also includes equal treatment under law. Like equality of opportunity, political equality is an ideal that Americans strive toward; however, complete political equality remains elusive. For example, aggregate statistics reveal that black men typically receive harsher sentences for the same crimes as compared to other groups in society (Farmer, 2003). Some of this inequity is undoubtedly tied to economics, and African Americans as a group still earn significantly less in income per capita than the general population. A lack of income translates into poorer quality lawyers, which evidently also translates into jail terms. Once again, political equality is only an ideal that Americans are constantly striving toward, but like other facets of equality, has not been realized to its fullest.

A third major facet of equality in American political thought is the concept of the equal value of each individual human life. This concept is embodied in Jefferson's "All men are created equal," but it also has a basis in the Christian value-system that is so pervasive in American society that stresses the concept of "equality before God." Apostle Paul in Galatians 3:28 argued that "there is neither Jew nor Greek, slave nor free, male nor female, for you are all one in Christ Jesus." The point Paul was trying to make here is that everyone is equal in the good Lord's eyes, regardless of gender, ethnicity, or economic status. One example in current American society is that organs for those who need transplants are not theoretically awarded to the highest bidder or to one ethnic or gender group over another, but instead based on who needs them the most. In other words, the heart patient that is closest to death is the one that goes to the top of the list for a transplant, regardless or ethnicity, gender, or economic status.

One aspect of equality that Americans in general clearly do not embrace is the concept of equality of condition. This is the Marxist idea that all human beings, regardless of intellect, education, etc., should be equal in terms of their material possessions. Americans reject such an idea as "communist," but the idea itself did not necessarily originate with Marx. Plato, for instance, told his pupil Aristotle that, within any organization, no one should earn more than five times as much as the lowliest worker. Similarly, early Christians in Jerusalem evidently adhered to equality of condition according to the book of Acts (2:44-45) where it is Stated that they "had everything in common. Selling their possessions and goods, they gave to anyone as he had need." For emphasis, the writer of Acts includes the story of Ananias and Sapphira (5:1-11) who deceitfully kept back a part of their property for themselves rather than donating it to the entire church community. The deceitful couple is then immediately struck dead by the Almighty for their actions.

Americans, in contrast, generally reject such "share the wealth" plans, believe that "life is what you make it," and do not see any problem with CEOs making hundreds of millions of dollars while others make minimum wage as long as each had the "equal opportunity" to be wealthy. According to a poll published in American Enterprise magazine in 1990, only 29% of Americans thought it was the government's job to reduce income differentials. In contrast, 60-70% of Britons and Germans and 80% of Italians and Austrians indicated that reducing inequalities was part of the government's job (*Economist*, 1994). As a consequence, American society has been measured by the Brookings Institution, Rand Corporation, Lynn Karoly, and World Bank, as the most unequal (in terms of income) of all developed industrialized democracies (*Economist*, 1994). It is also in spite of economic studies, such as that of Torsten Persson and Guido Tabellini in the June 1994 issue of *American Economic Review*, that suggest that income inequality may be harmful to economic growth. In the Persson and Tabellini study of 56 countries, the analysis revealed a strong negative relationship between income inequality and growth in GDP per capita. Similar results have been produced by the Institute for Public Policy Research (*Economist*, 1994).

American Conception of Justice:

Justice has been a subject of politics and government from the earliest codifications of law and political science. Plato uttered this "first question" of political science as a simple interrogative offered in *The Republic* when he presented a discussion of "What is justice?" Similarly, if we turn again to the Bible, we find that the cry of the prophets (Jeremiah, Micah, and Ezekial) in the ancient Jewish Scriptures was for "God's justice." The prophets sought justice for the poor, the suffering, the widows and orphans, and for the enemies of the Jews. Americans, of course, have their own conception of the answer to Plato's original question and their own version of "justice" that they cry for. The American conception of justice includes the multifaceted American conception of equality discussed in the section above. In other words, if people are denied equal opportunity, Americans generally perceive it to be unjust. Similarly, most Americans now tend to view the denial of equal treatment under law or the denial of equal political rights to be an anathema to justice. Additionally, if organs needed for human transplants were allocated to the highest bidder rather than based on needs or were reserved for "whites only," most Americans would view the situation as unjust. Justice, however, is not synonymous with "equality" in American thought even though equality plays a major role. The other facet of justice where there is widespread agreement is the concept of justice as "just desserts."

The idea behind the concept of "just desserts" is that each individual receives his or her rewards based on merit. In other words, if an individual works very hard to finish at the top of the class (and also scores in the 98th percentile on the MCAT), then there is a very good chance that person may be accepted to Medical School somewhere prestigious such as Harvard. If that same individual continues to work hard and finishes at the top of the class at Harvard Medical School, then perhaps that person can continue to study and become a top specialist. In American society, the medical specialist in our example is likely to become very wealthy, far wealthier than most fellow citizens. Americans in general, however, do not object to our hypothetical medical specialist's wealth. After all, our specialist worked and studied very hard to achieve success and the wealth is merely the "just dessert" or proper reward for his/her hard work. The basic idea of just desserts in this case is that as long as the opportunity existed for all of Americans, it is fine if those that achieved it become extremely wealthy.

In contrast to our medical specialist example and other examples of Bill Gates-style "meritorious success," there are literally millions of others in America that achieve very little monetary or material success. Consider, for instance, the case of the homeless person that lives in a refrigerator box, does not work, and spends most of every day consuming alcohol. There is a large group of Americans that would consider the homeless State of our "alcoholic" to be his "just dessert." Since our "alcoholic" doesn't work and drinks too much, he therefore doesn't deserve any condition better than his homeless State. His activity in life (or lack of it) "merits" no better condition (or at least it does not in this perspective).

One major impact of the American view of justice as "just desserts" is that it tends to hinder liberals in their efforts to reduce income inequalities. For instance, when the Federal Government filed anti-trust suits against Standard Oil at the beginning of the 20th Century and against Microsoft at the end of that same century, many Americans opposed the government action because John D. Rockefeller and Bill Gates had "earned" their wealth. Conversely, the idea of justice as "just desserts" tends to erode support for "welfare" programs because individualists tend to believe that the "lazy" poor people are responsible for their own poverty and therefore do not "merit" the government assistance.

American Conception of Freedom

Freedom, like justice and equality in the American conception, is another multifaceted concept; however, there is not complete unanimity in American politics on exactly what are the meanings of "freedom." According to Fowler and Orenstein (1993), the American conception of freedom generally includes political freedom, civil liberties, economic freedom, and other particular freedoms listed in the U.S. Constitution. Each of these aspects of freedom will be discussed below.

The concept of "political freedom" is essentially the liberty to participate in government and politics. Unfortunately, universal political freedom was not originally guaranteed in the original U.S. Constitution (the subject was left for the States to determine) and the next 180 years of American history following the writing of the Constitution included a protracted struggle of the disenfranchised to gain full participation rights. Landless Americans, women, minorities, and young persons aged eighteen-twenty-one would eventually all gain full participation rights by 1971, but it certainly was not without a struggle. Whether one is discussing participation rights for women, or for minorities, or for non-property owners, those with full participation rights gave up their exclusive on those rights to those who demanded participation only grudgingly. Once the struggle was won, however, there were little sentiments for repeal. Since 1971, when the 26th Amendment extended participation rights to age eighteen, for instance, there has not been a concerted movement on the American political scene to return to disenfranchisement of persons eighteen-twenty or any other particular group. Thus, at least for now, the struggle for political freedom appears to be settled. The struggle to get people to exercise that freedom (if American low voter turnout is any indication), however, is another matter.

A second facet of the American conception of freedom is the concept of civil liberties (Fowler and Orenstein, 1993). Civil liberties include the right to be treated with respect as a citizen with equal privileges and equal treatment under the laws. The idea is that there should not be one law in America for the poor and another for the rich, nor a law for the men and another law for the women, nor is there one law for whites and another for blacks, but all are treated equally under law regardless of class, gender, ethnicity, etc. Like political freedom, the struggle for civil liberties has permeated American history. Unlike political freedom, however, the struggle over civil liberties is permanent and ongoing. For instance, courts and legislative bodies have been struggling with Affirmative Action for over three decades and the entire concept remains both unevenly applied and controversial. Gay rights activists argue that gays are "born or naturalized" in the U.S. and therefore receive equal rights or "privileges" under the 14th Amendment. Thus, gay rights groups push for the "privilege" or "right" to marriage between same-sex couples. Simultaneously, the Christian Coalition maneuvers to counter the expansion of rights and privileges for gay Americans claiming that gays may be born in the U.S., but gay sexual activities conflict with the teachings of the Bible and therefore their rights and privileges should be limited.

Civil liberties, however, like the concepts of equality and justice, are only ideals and have not been fully realized in American society. American society is replete with groups and individuals (gays again come to mind) that argue (rightly or wrongly) that they have been denied equal privileges.

A third facet of freedom, as it exists in the American conception, is the idea of particular freedoms. Particular freedoms are essentially those listed in the Constitution, such as right to remain silent, right to a speedy and public trial, freedom from unreasonable search etc. Particular freedoms also include liberties that have been constructed by the Supreme Court, such as the right to privacy, that are not specifically enumerated in the Constitution. Most of the disputes over these types of freedoms (When is speech protected? What is "excessive bail?" etc.) are eventually settled by those very same Courts.

The final piece of the American conception of Freedom is economic freedom, or the freedom to choose one's own economic course in terms of occupation and freedom/control over one's own assets. In other words, Americans generally believe that individuals should be able to choose their own occupation (as opposed to being born into it as in the Indian caste system). Furthermore, there generally should be no limits hindering occupational choice based on gender, ethnicity, or religion. In other words, laws limiting blacks to employment only in agriculture or domestic servitude (such laws did once exist in the American South) are viewed as limits on freedom and antithetical to the "American way." Furthermore, parents may encourage their children to choose one occupation over another, but the final decision remains with the individual rather than the parent.

Similarly, there are no legal restrictions on how Americans may spend (or misspend) their assets (although, once again, there were once laws in the U.S. that penalized blacks for "misspending their income"). Complete control over one's own assets may mean that one may live in a poor neighborhood, yet own a luxury car, a television satellite dish, and expensive jewelry. While these types of spending patterns may be condemned by some as inappropriate allocations of one's assets, they are certainly a legal economic choices.

Political Obligation

The concept of political obligation refers to duties and responsibilities that one has in society regardless of preference. For instance, in Texas individuals are obligated to "stop and render aid" at the scene of an accident if they are the first on the scene, regardless of personal preference for doing so. Americans are also obligated to pay taxes, serve on juries and generally obey the laws of the land. Political obligation is generally lightly regarded in the U.S. (as compared to some other developed democracies such as Germany, Japan, and the United Kingdom) and obligation is generally only required upon the consent of the individual. For example, Americans may opt out of obligations to serve their country in combat by claiming conscientious objector status and asserting that their religion precludes such behavior. The boxer Muhammad Ali is perhaps America's most famous conscientious objector in this regard. Ali opted out of combat duty in Vietnam in the 1960s because he claimed that his peaceful religion, Islam, prevented him from combat duty. Ali, however, is not alone in his "low view" of political obligation. For instance, only approximately 40% of Americans typically show up for jury duty when summoned, even though Americans say they believe in trial by jury "of your peers" in opinion surveys. Similarly, during the Vietnam War, thousands of Americans shirked their obligation to serve the military by fleeing to Canada. The list of leading American political figures that did not serve in Vietnam is long, but includes Presidents Bill Clinton and George W. Bush, former House Speaker Newt Gingrich, frequent Presidential candidate Pat Buchanan, and radio talk show host Rush Limbaugh. According to Begala (2002) and others, President George W. Bush did not even fulfill his obligations in the Air National Guard. Pat Buchanan, who is evidently now an avid jogger, did not go to Vietnam because of his bad knee (Franken, 2003). Rush Limbaugh was exempt from service due to his Peridontal Cyst (Franken, 2003). One can surmise from this that Americans are evidently not overly rigid concerning political obligations. Perhaps this is why President Carter responded a few years after the Vietnam War by pardoning the "draft dodgers." Obviously, this means that failure to seek military service (or to even shirk it) does not mean future political failure for American politicians.

Nature vs. Nurture Debate

Thus far in this chapter, basic areas where Americans are in some sort of general agreement have been the subjects of discussion. When it comes to the character of human nature, however, there is nothing approximating a consensus, and instead there is a deep divide among Americans related to ideology and partisanship. The "great schism" is essentially over the basic "good" or "bad" character of human nature. There are two dominant views that will be discussed below.

The first of these two views is the realist "nature" view. Realists believe that nature or genetics play a dominant role in determining human behavior and argue that humans as a group are naturally bad and uncooperative. As such, humans require coercion in order to ensure proper behavior. For example, the posted speed limit on Texas highways is 70mph. Many individuals drive near the speed limit, but tend to set the cruise control in their vehicles two to three miles per hour over the speed limit. Obviously, these individuals know that 72mph is over the speed limit because there are "Speed Limit 70" signs in Texas every few miles. The realist perspective can easily explain this deviant behavior. In this perspective, drivers know the speed limit, but being "bad" by nature, intentionally break the rules and go over the speed limit anyway; however, they do so by miniscule amounts because the Department of Public Safety Officers (State Police) will generally not issue citations for two to three miles per hour over the speed limit, but can be expected to do so for violations in excess of five miles per hour over the posted limit. That being the case, in the realist conception, people can be expected to cheat a little on the speed limit because they are "naturally bad," but may avoid cheating enough to invoke coercion (fines). In other words, people engage in criminal behavior (driving 72mph in a 70mph zone) because they are essentially "bad" by nature. As such, education, rehabilitation, counseling and the like are useless. The only thing "bad people" understand is coercion; therefore, criminals should be fined, incarcerated, flogged, and/or executed depending on the severity of the crime. Realists tend to be politically conservative and their prescriptions tend to be coercive in character (incarceration, corporal punishment, and executions for serious law violators) (Martinson, 1974, 22). In the words of President Ronald Reagan, "right and wrong matter; individuals are responsible for their actions; retribution should be swift and sure for those who prey on the innocent" *(Justice Assistance News,* 1981, 1).

In foreign policy, realism normally translates into diplomacy by force. Statements such as "force is the only thing they understand over there" are consistent with the realist perspective and the idea that the U.S. could work through international organizations such as the UN is anathema to realism. In the realist perspective, it would be unwise to "negotiate" with other world leaders such as Saddam Hussein because they can't be trusted. In foreign policy as well as domestic, coercion then becomes the chosen policy tool.

Roots of realism can be seen in the American Judeo-Christian heritage. The prophet Jeremiah (17:9) declares that "The heart is deceitful above all things and beyond cure," obviously suggesting that humans are naturally bad. Similarly, Jesus is quoted by Matthew (7:19) as saying "For wide is the gate and broad is the road that leads to destruction, and many enter through it," once again suggesting that the majority of people are basically bad.

A quick read of almost any newspaper in America on any given day may act to vindicate the realists. One glance at American crime statistics suggests that there does indeed appear to be a lot of bad out there. Furthermore, some deviant behavior, such as that of Jeffrey Dahmer, who killed people and ate them, simply cannot be learned from anyone in society and reflects a depraved nature of humans. For a larger historical example, who on earth with even rudimentary knowledge of the Holocaust could conclude that human beings are basically good?

In contrast to the realist view is the idealist "nurture" view that is generally viewed as the "liberal" view of human nature. Idealists believe that human nature is mostly a product of environment. Idealists have a more positive view of human nature, arguing that humans are naturally good, it is just that some are corrupted by society. Since all behaviors in this perspective, both good and bad, are learned; Idealist's prescriptions tend to be education-oriented (law violators are given counseling, rehabilitation, and other educational treatment programs). Idealists defend their positions by noting the innocence of human newborn babies. Perhaps very few individuals can hold a newborn baby in their own arms and declare that the newborn infant is inherently evil and in need of salvation. Society, however, obviously corrupts these wonderful, innocent children and turns them into something else long before adulthood. After all, after children learn to say Mama and Dada, the next word many parents hear from their children is likely to be "mine."

So which perspective is correct? Is it the realist or idealist? Actually, humans are not as uncomplicated as either perspective might suggest, and instead all people are products of a combination of both genetics and socialization. Realists clearly must admit that socialization or learning does impact human behavior. Otherwise, there is no reason to listen to Dr. James Dobson's "Focus on the Family" because if children will turn out good or bad based on genetics and it is impossible to fight this human "nature," then all parenting is wasted effort. This is hardly the position taken by Dobson and "Focus on the Family." Dobson's Focus on the Family ministry openly supports conservative politics; hence, it is obvious that American conservatives mix some idealism with their realism. The same may be said for those "liberal idealists" who argue for stiffer penalties for hate crimes and didn't exactly call for compassion and counseling in the case of the race-motivated dragging death of James Byrd in Jasper, Texas.

The real question then is not whether nature or nurture both play a role in behavior, but instead concerns which factor is more dominant in behavior: Nature or Nurture? This question is the subject matter of the movie "Trading

Places" from the 1980s starring Eddie Murphy and Dan Akroyd. In the movie, a pair of wealthy, Wall Street brokers, make a bet concerning human nature and they use Murphy and Akroyd as their game pieces. Essentially, one broker bets that he can take an unemployed black street beggar (Eddie Murphy), whom he sees as the victim of his environment, and turn him into a wealthy Wall Street broker. He also bets that a wealthy white Wall Street broker (Dan Akroyd), would become a penniless begging criminal if he were thrown into the environment of the street beggar. In the movie, Murphy (the beggar) becomes a wealthy broker and Akroyd (the broker) becomes a criminal when they are cast into their opposite environments, thus supporting the "nurture" view. "Trading Places," however, is only a movie and it has little bearing on reality. Or does it? The debate rages.

Chapter Three
Classic Liberalism

Classic Liberalism

Classic Liberalism is one of the dominant ideologies within both conservatism and the Republican Party of the early 21st Century. Classic Liberalism, however, is very different from current liberalism and should not be confused with "liberals" within the contemporary Democratic Party. Classic Liberalism is essentially the "liberalism of 1776" that was espoused by Thomas Paine, Thomas Jefferson, Benjamin Franklin, and many of the other leaders of the American Revolution. In 1776, "liberal" generally meant a belief in representative government, the free market, and greater equality under law. The "equality" component in 1776, however, should not be overstated. Women and minorities, as well as landless white men, were generally prevented from political participation in 1776 by the laws of the States in which they lived. Furthermore, there was no provision in the Articles of Confederation (or later the Constitution of 1789) that provided for universal suffrage. That being the case, the "representative" government that the Classic Liberals espoused in 1776 was largely representative only of land-owning white males. This limiting of political participation to white male property owners is certainly not considered "liberal" by today's standards, but it was very "liberal" in 1776 when the international norm was rule by autocratic monarchy.

The ideas of Classic Liberalism have their roots in the Age of Reason that produced John Locke, Baron Charles de Montesquieu, and Adam Smith, who published *Wealth of Nations* in 1776 during the American Revolution. The ideas of Locke on "natural rights" may have been as influential on the thinking of the American founding fathers as the ideas of any other political theorist. Similarly, Adam Smith is not only considered a major contributor to the ideology of the founding fathers (and Classic Liberalism), but he is also considered perhaps the "godfather" of free market capitalism, which is as essential to liberalism as limited, republican government.

In *Wealth of Nations*, Smith argued that society should be organized around a limited, representative government and a free marketplace. In this Classic Liberal construct, people pursue their own self-interest within a set of rules that maximizes personal freedom and the free marketplace. The aggregation of all individuals working to secure their own self-interest is what drives economic growth. All society, rich and poor alike, benefits from individual competition in the free market. In Smith's conception, great capital accumulation by people seeking wealth is a benefit to society as a whole. The wealthy capitalist will both consume and invest excess capital, thus creating economic growth and employment for the working classes as well. As a consequence, the natural actions of the wealthy with their capital will end up benefiting not only the wealthy, but society as a whole, and the situation of the poor and working classes will improve along with that of the rich. In the words of Adam Smith, "a rising tide lifts all boats."

Leaders in the Classic Liberal framework, both political and economic, arise based on merit and competition. Theoretically, the "cream rises to the top," meaning that the best, hardest working, and brightest will achieve the most economic and political success.

Wages and prices in the Classic Liberal framework will be determined according to Adam Smith's "invisible hand" of supply and demand. The free market also determines which goods will be produced in what quantity, and how and to whom those goods will be distributed. In general, if demand exceeds supply, prices will rise, but if supply exceeds demand, prices will fall. In this construct, labor is treated as just another commodity. If there is an oversupply of workers in any particular sector, wages in that sector can be expected to fall; consequently, workers will abandon that sector for a higher-paying sector of the economy and wages will improve in the sector that has been wage-depressed. Similarly, if there is a sector of the economy that is labor-short, wages will rise in that sector and thus attract workers and eventually place downward pressure on the inflated wages in that economic sector.

Government for Security and Order

The role of government under the Classic Liberal construct is to provide the security and order necessary for the efficient operation of the free market. If the free market does not have sufficient security and order, the entire free market system may collapse or become chaotic (Hoover, 1994). The situation in Iraq after the fall of Saddam Hussein may be a case in point.

Free Trade Benefits All Countries

Another major tenet of Classic Liberal ideology is a belief that free and unfettered trade benefits all countries (Smith, 1776). Classic Liberals argue that countries should trade for goods (import) where they hold a comparative disadvantage and export goods where they hold a comparative advantage. Included below is a hypothetical figure to illustrate the Classic Liberals' arguments that trade benefits all countries. In this fictitious construct, each country shifts labor into industries where they hold a "comparative advantage" and shifts labor away from industries where they hold a "comparative disadvantage." The countries then each trade their excess "comparative advantage" goods for the goods they need to meet their shortfall in goods where they hold a "comparative disadvantage." After the trade, both countries are better off economically than they were before trade took place. In our hypothetical model, the United States has a comparative advantage with Mexico in the computer industry due to a better education system and a better-developed high-tech sector, but Mexico has a comparative advantage with the United States in citrus-growing, due to a climate in some parts of Mexico that is more suited to citrus fruits. In such a scenario, if the United States can shift labor away from citrus-growing, where it is less efficient, to the high-tech sector, then the U.S. can produce an excess of computer products that can be traded to Mexico in exchange for the citrus that it is deficient. The shift of labor out of citrus-production to the high-tech sector would obviously produce a citrus shortage in the U.S. if it were not for the fact that Mexico could easily meet America's citrus needs by shifting workers out of their own high-tech sector (where they are less efficient) to the citrus-growing sector (where they are more efficient). Mexico should then produce a citrus surplus that could be traded to the U.S. in exchange for computer goods to meet the needs of their deficient high-tech sector. The fictitious scenario below in Figure 1 illustrates how both the U.S. and Mexico can economically advance through trade.

Figure 1: Free Trade Example: U.S./Mexico Citrus for Computers

Hypothetical worker output per hour:

	U.S.	Mexico
Computers	9	4
Citrus	3	2

U.S. Output per 100 Workers		*Mexico Output per 100 Workers*
Computers	900	400
Citrus	300	200

U.S. Shifts 10 Workers to Computers		*Mexico Shifts 20 Workers to Citrus*
Computers	990	320
Citrus	270	240

Trade

U.S. Exports 80 excess Units of Computers to Mexico->
<-Mexico Exports 30 excess Units of Citrus to the U.S.

After Trade

	U.S.	Mexico
Computers	910	400
Citrus	300	210

In our fictitious construct displayed above in Figure 1., both the U.S. and Mexico increase their wealth by shifting labor to economic sectors where they hold a comparative advantage and engaging in trade for products where they hold a comparative disadvantage. Classic Liberals are quick to focus on the fact that models similar to those in Figure 1 are suggestive of universal economic benefits for free trade.

Problems with Classic Liberalism

Perhaps the most glaring problem for Classic Liberalism is found in the very nature of the free market "merit system" itself. In other words, by its very nature, the free market creates income inequality because humans are not all endowed with equal talents and abilities. Furthermore, the free market does not provide an equal reward to all talents and abilities. To acknowledge that there is a last, is also to acknowledge that there is a "first" and therefore to acknowledge inequality. Classic Liberals, therefore, whether knowingly or unknowingly, acknowledge that the free market creates income inequality through their argument that the best and most talented will succeed through competition. It follows that if the societal "cream rises to the top," as Classic Liberals so argue, there must also be a bottom, and the least talented in society or societal "scum" can be expected to fall to the bottom and stay there. This social "scum" does not necessarily consist of criminals or moral degenerates, but instead includes those that lack the talents monetarily rewarded by society. For example, the janitor may work just as hard today as the physician, and his job may even be more physically demanding, but janitorial services are not the services that are rewarded greatly in the free market; hence, the janitor earns much less than the physician due to the laws of supply and demand.

Even Adam Smith (1776), the godfather of free market capitalism, recognized this fact and argued for some luxury taxes and redistribution of wealth to the poor. Although Smith is also famous for arguing that a "rising tide lifts all boats," evidently a rising tide does not lift all boats equally. In fact, it appears that some boats have holes and tend to do a good titanic imitation in the "rising tide." According to Herrnstein and Murray (1996), the best predictor of individual economic success is ACT scores; hence, those that score very well on standardized tests (supposedly smart people) tend to do very well economically, while those that score poorly on standardized tests (supposedly less-smart people) tend to experience much less economic success. Herrnstein and Murray essentially argue (not without controversy) that the "intelligence" measured on such tests is genetic; therefore, the best and brightest succeed in the free market because they were born with greater talents, while the "dimmer bulbs" tend to fail because they were born with less mental capacity (which is hardly their fault). As a consequence, as the United States became increasingly free-market oriented during the Reagan-Bush years, income inequality in the U.S. also increased and the real buying power of the working class and poor simultaneously declined adjusted for inflation. Furthermore, since income inequality also has been linked to slower economic growth, the inequality may have the long-term effect of harming even the wealthy through slower economic growth (*Economist*, 1994). If that is the case, then not only does the unfettered free market not benefit everybody, it appears that it might actually harm society as a whole.

Mergers and Monopolistic Capitalism

A further problem with Classic Liberalism is that the free market often leads to merger-mania and monopoly capitalism. Karl Marx argued that capitalism contains the seeds of its own destruction. Marx argued that capitalism contains a constant pressure for expansion driven by the profit motive and capitalists therefore will attempt to increase their market share, in turn creating downward pressure on both wages and prices. Essentially, the capitalists will try to increase sales and market share by cutting prices. Consumers will then purchase more from the capitalistic enterprise with the lower prices, thus increasing the sales and market shares of the merchants with the lower prices. In order to turn a profit at the new lower prices, however, the merchants must cut their costs, meaning that wages will be cut for the laborers within the organization. The low-price merchants' competitors will attempt to regain the lost market share by retaliating with reductions in prices (and therefore wages) of their own. In order for the first discounting merchant to regain the market advantage that had been gained from the original price-cutting, prices (and therefore wages) must be slashed again. In turn, the lower wages in the marketplace lead to a diminished buying power of the workers and eventually to a decline in the aggregate demand for goods since the workers earning less must therefore consume less. The decline in demand then leads merchants to again cut prices to increase sales, and wages again are cut to ensure a profit. In the Marxist framework, the scenario continues in a downward implosive spiral until capitalism collapses.

Obviously Marx's theory leaves a few items unexplained since capitalism has not imploded in the time since his 19th Century writing. Therefore, Classic Liberals delight in concluding that Marx's theory was void of substance. That said, there does appear, however, to be at least a grain of truth in Marx's arguments. One need only look at the American economy in the late 19th Century where John Rockefeller had a monopoly on oil, Andrew Carnegie a monopoly on steel, and the E.C. Knight company a monopoly on sugar manufacturing, to see that American capitalism had moved toward monopoly capitalism in numerous sectors and that the economy was beset with tremendous income inequality. The situation was not corrected until the Federal government under Theodore Roosevelt (and later William Howard Taft and Woodrow Wilson) intervened into the free market and broke up the monopolies.

Furthermore, a quick glance at the changes in the American economy since WWII reveals that the 19th Century economic scenario may be repeating itself again. For example, a visit to any antique car museum (often better known as the faculty parking lot) will reveal the movement in the American automobile industry away from competition toward an oligopolistic, if not monopolisitc, market. Whatever happened to Hudson, Packard, Rambler-Nash, Studebaker, Maxwell, and Stanley Steamer of the early 20th Century? In 2003 they are all gone, and all that remains are the "Big Three" American automakers. To make matters even worse, it is unclear whether Chrysler still should be considered an American automaker at all since the corporation is now controlled by the German company, Damler-Benz.

The American retail business is in similar shape. Montgomery Wards, Woolworth's, and Gibson's Discount Centers all seem to have gone the way of the Stanley Steamer. Even Kmart is on the skids in the face of the WalMart retail department store "monopoly." Furthermore, just like Marx predicted, wages in the retail department store industry have dropped precipitously since the 1960s. In the 1960s, workers in American Department Stores were likely to be full time employees with benefits packages, but in 2004, Department Store workers are often part time employees with low wages and minimal benefits packages. It appears that competition in the retail department store industry has driven down wages and prices to the point where few persons in the industry can actually make a living and the industry appears to be moving toward monopoly capitalism (Wal-Mart), just like Marx predicted.

Tyranny of the Majority

Another problem with Classic Liberal ideology is that the free market allows for tyranny of the majority. American history is replete with supporting examples, including, but not limited to, slavery, Jim Crow laws, and the denial of equal opportunity to women. In 1956, 80% of Texans voted for a non-binding referendum that would have made inter-racial marriage illegal. On that same ballot, 80% of Texans voted for two other measures that were designed to prevent school integration. One might argue that the U.S. has advanced since these times of oppression of minorities, but more recent examples suggest that the majority would still exact its tyranny on the minority if there were no Constitutional protections.

For example, some communities in the United States would perhaps vote to disenfranchise gay Americans were it not for Constitutional protections. A case in point was made in 1998, when a mayoral candidate in Springdale, Arkansas, stated as part of his campaign that he favored the placement of a road sign on the outskirts of Springdale with the words "No Fags" printed on it. The campaign stirred a controversy that revealed the willingness of many in the Arkansas community to strip gay Americans of their Constitutional rights. In Fayetteville, the municipality that borders Springdale, the City Council voted six to two to adopt a resolution that prohibited city officials from discriminating against applicants for city jobs based on their sexual orientation or familial status. Fayetteville Mayor Fred Hanna vetoed the resolution saying it was divisive and "contrary to the public interest of the citizens of Fayetteville." The City Council then voted to override the veto during their May 5, 1998 meeting. This prompted a group opposed to the resolution to begin collecting signatures to bring the matter to a public vote. The measure was put on the November 3, 1998 ballot and the measure was defeated with 7811 (57.7%) voting against and 5731 (42.3%) voting for the resolution to prevent discrimination based on sexual orientation (*Northwest Arkansas Times*, 1998). In short, it appears that a solid majority in Fayetteville Arkansas favored discrimination against homosexuals in municipal hiring in 1998. It is perhaps unlikely that Fayetteville is completely unique. If there were no Bill of Rights and no powerful national government behind that Bill of Rights protecting gay Americans, there might be nothing preventing the majority from exercising their tyranny over the homosexual minority in Fayetteville. A government with such power is inconsistent with the "limited government" aspect of Classic Liberalism.

Inequality of Opportunity

Similarly, the free market may create, or at the very least allow, inequality of opportunity. Once again, the examples of Jim Crow laws and the informal system of discrimination in employment against minorities and women prior to the institution of Affirmative Action are testimonies to the inequality of opportunity that often exists in the free market society. These inequities were only remedied through government intervention into the free market in a manner (Affirmative Action) inconsistent with the "limited government" creed of Classic Liberalism.

Unsafe, Unhealthy, and Immoral Products

The free market also allows for unsafe, unhealthy, and immoral products. For example, prior to the intervention into the free market by Theodore Roosevelt with the Federal Meat Inspection Act, it was estimated that one-third of the meat sold in America was unfit to eat, and any number of contaminants, including animal feces and urine, commonly could be found in meat sold in the U.S. (Nash et al. 1998). Upton Sinclair (1906) created a political firestorm with his documentation of the unsavory conditions in the Chicago meat packing industry at the turn of the Century in his novel *The Jungle*. Sinclair described spoiled hams treated with formaldehyde and sausages made from rotten meat scraps, rats, and other refuse (Nash et. al, 1998). The presentation in Sinclair's work was so graphic that it caused President Roosevelt to push for policy change. Roosevelt's initial reaction to Sinclair's book is well captured by one of his White House servants at the time (quoted in Carson, 1997, 75):

Tiddy was reading Upton Sinclair's novel, toying with a light breakfast an' idly turnin' over th' pagesiv the'new book with both hands. Suddenly he rose fr'm th' table, an'cryin': I'm pizened,' begun throwin sausages out iv th' window. Th' ninth wan sthruck Sinitor Biv'ridge on the head an' made him a blond. It bounced off, exploded, an' blew a leg off a secret-service agent, an' th' scatthred fragmints desthroyed a handsome row iv ol' oak-trees. Sinitor Biv'ridge rushed in, thinkin' that th' Prisidint was bein'assassynated be his devoted followers in th'Sinit, an discovered Tiddy engaged in a hand-to-hand conflict with a potted ham. Th'Sinitor fr'm Injyanny, with a few well-directed wurruds, put out th'fuse an'rendered th'missile harmless. Since thin th' Prisidint, like th' rest iv us, has become a viggytaryan.

Thousands of other Americans had similar (though less violent) reactions to that of Roosevelt in 1906 upon reading Sinclair's novel; consequently, Sinclair's book created a groundswell of support for government regulation of food products that continues through the present. Meat, of course, is not the only food item that is regulated by the government. Consider, for a moment, the rodent droppings that might be present in cereal without government regulations? Then consider that Classic Liberals (today's free market republicans) argue against "government regulation of business" because it hinders the ability of businesses to make a profit. Now consider that these "anti-regulatory" Republicans currently control both houses of Congress and the White House.

Tainted food, however, is not the only product problem allowed by an unregulated free market. Child pornography, for example (Included here as an example of an immoral product) would evidently also be rampant in an unregulated free market since such materials appear to be still available even in the current "regulated" market. The laws of supply and demand that govern the free market mean that for every vice for which there is a societal demand, the market will produce a supply. Consequently, the unregulated market will have prostitutes, mind and body destroying drugs, and pornographic books and films. Obviously, even the regulated market has all of these things, but one would imagine that the problem should be worse without government regulations.

In addition to allowing products that violate public morals, the unregulated free market allows profits to unscrupulous businesses that will sell all manners of products and make all kinds of false claims under the motive of profit. This was the case before government got involved in the business of regulating such things, and it still is. Consider the following article from 1905 (quoted in Nash, 1998).

Gullible Americans will spend this year some seventy-five million dollars in the purchase of patent medicines. In consideration of this sum it will swallow huge quantities of alcohol, an appalling amount of opiates and narcotics, a wide assortment of varied drugs ranging from powerful and dangerous heart depressants to insidious liver stimulants; and, far in excess of all other ingredients, undiluted fraud. For fraud exploited by the skillfullest of advertising bunco men is the basis of the trade.

So it was in 1905 prior to government regulations, but the general trends appear to have continued somewhat even with government regulations. For example, the marketers of a food supplement known as "Enzyte" claim that their product will enlarge penis size up to 41%. Advertisements for Enzyte State that "87% of women secretly revealed they wouldn't mind if their partner had added size. Enzyte can take you there." There are also similar products on the market that are purported to increase the size of women's breasts. Evidently, little has changed since the Pure Food and Drug Act of 1905, and advertisers still make questionable (if not just plain false) claims despite the "big government over-regulation."

Free Market Dislocations

A further problem with Classic Liberalism is that the market produces harsh dislocations and hardships such as unemployment. In truth, all unemployment is not due to the fact that there are some lazy people that do not want to work. Instead, investment in the free market can be expected to produce new technologies that have the negative result of displacing workers. For instance, many a wagon wheel manufacturer was put out of work in the early 20th Century after the introduction of the automobile. Similarly, the ice man that delivered blocks of ice to private residences was quickly put out of work after the invention of electric refrigeration. In either case, the unemployment that resulted had nothing to do with the willingness of people to work, and everything to do with free market-driven changes in technology that displaced workers.

Problems with Free Trade

Another facet of Classic Liberalism that is fraught with problems is the Classic Liberal doctrine of free trade. This is not to say that free trade may be all negative, and indeed it is not; however, it is also far from a panacea. For example, the laws of comparative advantage may shift employment in any given country to low wage industries. In our fictitious free trade example presented earlier, for instance, Mexico would shift labor into citrus farming while the United States would shift labor away from citrus farming and into computers. Obviously, the shift of workers in Mexico from the high tech sector to citrus agriculture would involve a shift from a higher wage industry to a lower wage industry and thus depress wages, consumption, and growth in Mexico as well as technological advancement. In general, empirical studies suggest that more workers in the agricultural sector in any country seems to correlate more with economic underdevelopment, than with development, thus the long term impact of such a shift due to free trade may be negative (Wheeler and Muller, 1986).

A further problem with free trade is that it often leads to dependence on unreliable foreign sources for goods. For example, the OPEC oil embargo of

1973 sent oil prices soaring and contributed to double-digit inflation in the United States. The embargo did not end until Henry Kissenger made a visit to the Middle East to warn the Saudis that the U.S. would not tolerate a continued embargo; hence, the embargo ended thirty days later, but not before significant economic upheaval (Jones, 1996).

Chapter 4
Traditional Conservatism

Negative View of Human Nature

The second major conservative ideology prevalent in the Republican Party in the late 20th and early 21st Centuries is known as Traditional Conservatism. Traditional Conservatives tend to espouse the negative view of human nature and a low view of the average person's intelligence. In other words, Traditional Conservatives tend to be "realists" that tend to view humans as naturally bad, uncooperative, untrustworthy, and often just plain stupid. As a consequence, Traditional Conservatives tend to view government and politics (both permeated with those corrupt and dull-minded people) with great skepticism (Hoover, 1994). After all, if people are naturally bad, they can be expected to be extra bad when they are entrusted with political power. The popular saying that "power corrupts, but absolute power corrupts absolutely" is consistent with Traditional Conservative ideology.

Traditional Conservatives view the current society as in decay, depraved, and decadent. The government within that society in the here and now is equally flawed, but the government and society of the past are viewed as virtuous, and glorious. As such, Traditional Conservatives have disdain for current politicians such as the "immoral" Bill Clinton who is a product of the current flawed society (Schumaker, Kiel, and Heilke, 1997).

Traditional Conservatives also tend to demonize their enemies. Whether the enemy is Bill Clinton or Saddam Hussein, the enemy is not only despised, but demonized, dehumanized and condemned not only as a political opponent, but as evil by very nature (Berlet, 1998). A very good example of such "demonization" is Osama Bin Ladin's ability to portray America as such an evil infidel that God will be happy with his "martyrs" for flying airplanes into buildings and killing thousands of innocent people. Osama Bin Ladin and his followers are the Traditional Conservatives in the Islamic world. A closer look at Traditional Conservatives in the U.S. reveals some striking similarities. For example, the web site of Westboro Baptist Church in Topeka Kansas (www.godhatesfags.com/) denounces homosexuals not only as "workers of iniquity" and "abominable," but also includes a memorial celebration of the number of days that Matthew Shepard (a gay man murdered by exposure in Wyoming) "has been in Hell." In such a mindset there is only good and evil, white and black, with us or against us, and no "grey areas" or anything in between. Osama Bin Ladin and the Taliban are obviously fabulous examples of this ideology, but then so is the Westboro Baptist Church in Topeka.

The negative view of human nature espoused by Traditional Conservatives also translates into low social trust. As a consequence, Traditional Conservatives tend to favor rule through coercion, and advanced security measures through a strong military, a strong police force, and an emphasis on personal self-defense. A strong military is necessary because foreign entities cannot be trusted not to attack. A strong internal police force is needed because the "naturally bad" humans will not otherwise behave. Measures for personal defense, such as the right to bear arms, are required for the same reasons (Schumaker, Kiel, and Heilke, 1996).

Policies for dealing with crime are slanted heavily toward retribution and punishment, with incarceration and corporal and capital punishment favored over rehabilitation programs. Essentially, since humans are naturally bad, the only thing they might understand is pain (Territo, Halstead, and Bromley, 1989). The Traditional Conservative view on punishment is reflected in numerous passages in both the Koran and the Bible. In the words of Mohammed in the Koran, (5:38) "And the man who steals and the woman who steals, cut off their hands as a punishment for what they have earned." Similarly, Moses writes in Exodus 21:23-24 "If there is serious injury, you are to take life for life, eye for eye, tooth for tooth, hand for hand, foot for foot, burn for burn, wound for wound, bruise for bruise."

In spite of the negative view of human nature and the disdain for government and politics of the present, Traditional Conservatives have an extreme reverence for symbols, institutions, and history, both religious and patriotic (Schumaker, Kiel, and Heilke, 1996). Traditional Conservatives in the United States generally view the U.S. as the greatest country in the history of mankind, the American form of government the greatest ever invented (if not handed to us directly from God himself), and those that criticize the American form of government are not just critics, but an abomination that should be shipped out of the country. Furthermore, the great figures of history, Lincoln, Washington, Jefferson, Franklin, etc., were endowed with brilliance, leadership, wisdom, integrity, and virtue that simply cannot be matched in our present time. The point is that these historical figures are placed on a pedestal and the "revisionist" historians that would write things such as the accusation that Jefferson slept with his slaves or that George Washington was not a great general, but also had a mistress, are not only wrong (the DNA evidence on Jefferson and Sally Hemmings being invented by those liberal scientists), but are also just plain evil people that should be silenced. Furthermore, the mere suggestion to the Traditional Conservative that the First Amendment protects burning the flag as an exercise of free speech is absolutely preposterous. For the Traditional Conservative in the U.S., America could never be wrong, and those who might say otherwise are not true Americans.

Return to a Better, Vanished Time

A major goal of the Traditional Conservatives is to return society to a mythical, better, now vanished, time (Hoover, 1994). To clarify, the "mythical, better, now vanished, time," is not mythical in the mind of the Traditional Conservative. To the Traditional Conservative, there was indeed once a time of virtue, but today's society has strayed from the original founding principles. What is needed is a return to those original principles and virtues. As a consequence, Traditional Conservatives in the U.S. can be expected to frequently call for a return to "what the founding fathers intended." In religion, Traditional Conservatives tend to hearken back to the original principles supposedly in place when the religion was founded. For Traditional Conservatives in fundamentalist Protestantism, this tends to mean a return to "The Bible" or the principles of the "First Century Church." For the Taliban, the call is a return to the Koran and the practices of Mohammed in the 7th Century AD.

In order to return society to that "better, vanished, time," Traditional Conservatives believe that a "good government" resembling that of the past can be reconstructed as long as it is directed by "good people" with the correct set of values and correct ideology. In the Traditional Conservative mindset, there are indeed "those who know best," and it is those people who must be put in place to rule (Hoover, 1994). For the Traditional Conservatives of radical Islam, this means rule by Islamic Clergy. For the Traditional Conservative Christians of the Middle Ages, this meant rule by the Pope and the Catholic Church. For the Traditional Conservatives of the United States in the last several decades, this means that "good Christian leaders" should be elected. As a consequence, the Christian Coalition distributes voter guides that instruct prospective voters as to which politicians are Christians (conspicuously all conservative Republicans) and which are not. In this vein, Tim LaHaye, an influential Traditional Conservative due to enormous sales of his fictional *Left Behind* series, also argued for the election of "pro-moral, pro-American, and Christian" politicians in his 1980 book, *The Battle of the Mind*. In this ideological rambling, LaHaye argued that what America needed was "pro-moral leaders who will return our country to the Biblical base upon which it was founded" (LaHaye, 1980, 36). In other words, LaHaye is calling for a return to the mythical better, vanished, time. LaHaye (1980, 39) added that the American system of separation of powers and checks and balances was borrowed directly from scripture. LaHaye then exhorts "Bible-believing pastors" to encourage their congregations to vote. LaHaye is not, however, evidently in favor of voting for all of those who call themselves Christian since he also mentions that there is a "well-known parallel between the social positions of the Methodist Church and the Communist Party" (LaHaye, 1980, 164). In the appendix to his book, LaHaye includes a questionnaire for submission to political
candidates that is intended to determine whether they are moral and Christian. Questions include "Do you favor the passage of the Equal Rights Amendment?" "Except in wartime or dire emergency, would you vote for government spending that exceeds revenues?" "Do you favor a reduction in Government?" (LaHaye, 1980, 164).

Government to Keep Order and Correct Human Weaknesses

The purpose of government in Traditional Conservatism is to keep order and correct human weaknesses (Hoover, 1994). Classic Liberals are congruent with the Traditional Conservatives on the "keep order" function, but they are greatly at odds with Traditional Conservatives on the "correct human weaknesses" function. Whereas Classic Liberals are generally less concerned with the regulation of homosexual behavior, abortions, alcohol, drugs, pornography, and other "human weaknesses," Traditional Conservatives make these not only areas of government responsibility, but areas of focus. For example, Traditional Conservatives in the United States in the last several decades pushed for laws to end abortions and favored laws against sodomy, pornography, prostitution, alcohol, and other human "weaknesses." Similarly, under more extreme forms of Islam in the Middle East, families may stone to death other family members that have "dishonored" the family. In other words, if an unmarried woman gets pregnant, the family members may stone her to death for this dishonor to the family (*Economist*, 2003). Not to be outdone by the Muslims, Old Testament laws in the Bible call for executions of those who curse their parents, commit adultery, sodomy, or have sex with animals (Leviticus 20:9-15). Furthermore, in the case of sexual relations with animals, not only the human must be put to death, but the animal involved in the sex act must be killed as well (Leviticus 20:16-16).

The use of government to "correct human weaknesses" by Traditional Conservatives is tied to their views of moral absolutes. To Traditional Conservatives, there most definitely *are* moral absolutes and they can most definitely and definitively identify those moral absolutes (Hoover, 1994). As a consequence, it is irresponsible to allow people the freedom to do things that are morally wrong and therefore harm society. Freedoms, including academic freedoms, are therefore limited to these "basic truths" or moral absolutes (Hoover, 1994). Generally, Traditional Conservatives have a source for their moral absolutes, and that source is very likely to be a religious book. In the Middle East, the vast majority of the people are Muslims; hence, the primary source of moral absolutes for most Traditional Conservatives in that region is the Koran. In the United States, the religion of the majority is Christianity; hence, the primary source of moral absolutes for most American Traditional Conservatives is the Bible. In either case, Traditional Conservatives call for governmental enforcement of the moral absolutes found in their Holy books. Hence, Osama Bin Ladin calls for governments to adopt sharia, the Islamic religious laws, and make those Islamic laws into governmental civil laws as well. Similarly, Traditional Conservatives in the U.S. push for the incorporation of "Bible truths" (such as anti-sodomy laws) into the laws of the U.S. and call for Federal enforcement.

Government to Support Societal Building Blocks

In furtherance of their goal to create a good and moral society, Traditional Conservatives argue that government should reinforce the main societal building blocks of church and family (Freeden, 2003). In Iran, Sudan, and Afghanistan under the Taliban, what this came to mean in practice was Theocracy or rule by religious leaders. In the United States, President George W. Bush has pushed for "faith-based initiatives" or the provision of government goods and services through religious. Traditional Conservatives in the U.S. have also fought to eliminate the "marriage penalty tax" and some States have developed new, more stringent, marriage laws that eliminate incompatibility as a "cause" for divorce (Loconte, 1998).

Opposition to Social Change

In general, the adherence to moral absolutes tends to create a resistance to social change among Traditional Conservatives (Freeden, 2003). In the United States at present, gay rights and gay marriages are merely among the latest in a series of social changes opposed by Traditional Conservatives that perhaps date back to the very beginning of human existence. Traditional Conservatives also opposed women's rights, the end of slavery, racial integration, the Protestant Reformation, and the teachings of Jesus to name a few (Yes, the teachings of Jesus. The Pharisees were clearly the Traditional Conservatives of their society). In the Middle East, Traditional Conservatives currently oppose equality of the sexes, western dress, western music, western movies, and other "abominations" such as women without veils. In short, Traditional Conservatives can be expected to resist social changes unless those changes (such as those imposed by the Taliban) are a return to a discarded dogma of the past.

Problems with Traditional Conservatism

Problems of Moral Absolutism

One major problem for Traditional Conservatism is that large and complex societies do not have unanimity on what constitutes moral absolutes. No matter what one faction within society may call a moral absolute, there is always another faction in society (sometimes even other Traditional Conservatives) that will argue against such a categorization. For example, Osama Bin Ladin opposes the shaving of facial hair, but Saddam Hussein did not. Orthodox Jews are careful not to clip the hair on the sides of their heads and do not trim the edges of their beards (as commanded in Leviticus 19:27), but other Jews may trim both. Similarly, Protestant fundamentalists in the U.S. tend to condemn alcohol consumption, but the Catholic Church is a bit less condemning on the subject. Conversely, the Catholic Church opposes all forms of birth control, while Protestant fundamentalists do not. Examples of such disagreement are perhaps endless, even when Traditional Conservatives all agree on the same source for moral absolutes.

The validity of the Traditional Conservative view of morality is also challenged by contemporary Liberals in society. For example, Traditional Conservatives typically oppose all abortions, yet they also typically oppose welfare programs that address the needs of children after they are born. Liberals argue that it is incongruent for Traditional Conservatives to "care" so much for the "unborn," yet have no compassion for those that are already "born." What purpose is there to save the fetus if its destiny is to starve? How can it be absolutely immoral to abort a fetus, yet it is not absolutely immoral to oppose government support for children that already have been born. What is the basis for such an inconsistent moral judgment?

In American society, the primary source reference for most Traditional Conservatives on moral absolutes is the Bible. In the Middle East, it is the Koran. Unfortunately, it turns out that it is difficult to pin down some moral absolutes even when these religious books are the primary guides. This is partially because different Muslim and Christian sects differ on interpretation of the same holy books, but also partially because some of the moral precepts and commands presented in the Bible and the Koran are inconsistent with accepted norms and morals of 21st Century Western society.

Consider, for example, the Bible teachings on slavery, an institution generally disparaged in recent decades, which if not outright condoned by the authors of the various books of the Bible, certainly is not condemned. In Ephesians 6:5, for example, Apostle Paul commands: "Slaves, be obedient to those who are your earthly masters, with fear and trembling, in singleness of heart, as to Christ." In contrast with Paul, most Americans in the 21st Century, including most Traditional Conservatives, can be expected to oppose slavery on moral grounds. This is in spite of the fact that many of our "founding fathers," such as Thomas Jefferson, were slave owners and the "father of our country," George Washington, owned almost 400 slaves, none of whom were freed during his lifetime.

Furthermore, it is Traditional Conservatives that tend to call for a return to what the "founding fathers intended," the assumption being that the founders were such good "moral Christians" (Leege and Kellstedt, 1993). Since many American founding fathers were slaveowners, and slavery is generally condemned in Christendom in the 21st Century, Traditional Conservatives are therefore forced to adopt the position that "we must judge them by their time." To this, liberals can only applaud, since that is exactly what the liberals have been saying all along; namely, that morals are not absolute, and instead are determined by, and change with, society. Traditional Conservatives tend to counter with "back to the Bible" arguments, but the closer we inspect the Bible, the more difficult it is to find a moral absolutist position against slavery. For example, in Leviticus 25: 42-46, the God of Israel instructs the Israelites concerning the subject of slavery and condones the enslavement of non-Israelites by the Israelites. There is a bit of a double standard, however, because the Hebrew God specifically commands that the Israelites themselves may not be sold as slaves. Evidently, it is very good to be God's "chosen" people, and not so good for the "unchosen." The entire passage is presented below:

Because the Israelites are my servants, whom I brought out of Egypt, they must not be sold as slaves. Do not rule over them ruthlessly, but fear your God. Your male and female slaves are to come from the nations around you; from them you may buy slaves. You may also buy some of the temporary residents living among you and members of their clans born in your country, and they will become your property. You can will them to your children as inherited property and can make them slaves for life, but you must not rule over your fellow Israelites ruthlessly.

That slavery is clearly allowed here by the God of the Israelites is indisputable. That it is allowed for one group and not for another is also indisputable. That God isn't particularly concerned with equal rights is also apparent. That it is all pure and "moral," however, is entirely another issue. Were it found somewhere other than the Bible (such as the Koran, for instance), one suspects that most Bible fundamentalists of the 21st Century might find its teachings immoral. If, however, slavery was a fine and moral practice in ancient Israel because God allowed it, and if morals are absolute and unchanging, then one can only conclude that slavery in the present is also moral since morality is absolute and does not change (or at least it doesn't according to Traditional Conservatives).

Exodus 21: 20-21 allows slave masters to beat their slaves without punishment as long as they don't kill them. This suggests not only that slavery is fine and moral, but it is also moral to physically abuse the slaves as long as one does not go "overboard" and kill them.

If a man beats his male or female slave with a rod and the slave dies as a direct result, he must be punished, but he is not to be punished if the slave gets up after a day or two, since the slave is his property.

Once again, we can assume that most American Traditional Conservatives would find the above passage morally bankrupt if it were found in the Koran or any other source of moral precepts. One may also assume that most American Traditional Conservatives do not believe these to be moral principles that apply to Christians in the 21st Century; thus, in reality, Traditional Conservatives argue for the "moral absolutes" of the Bible, but they are very selective and contradictory concerning which precepts are "moral absolutes."

Some may argue that a presentation of the above passages in Leviticus and Exodus is "misuse" of the Bible. After all, every good Christian knows that we are no longer under the "Old Covenant" and we can therefore ignore some of the Old Testament commands such as "Remember the Sabbath and keep it Holy." Somehow, however, they never argued that we could ignore the "Thou Shalt Not Commit Adultery" command while Bill Clinton was President. Once again, the Traditional Conservatives are selective and inconsistent with their moral absolutes from the Bible. Furthermore, the argument that some Old Testament commands can be discarded contains a weakness, because if morals are absolute and unchanging, they should not change from the Old Testament to the New. Because of such arguments, however, included below are statements from the New Testament that appear to be very "uncondemning" of slavery. For example, Apostle Paul states in I Corinthians 7:20-24 that:

Every one should remain in the state in which he was called. Were you a slave when called? Never mind. But if you can gain your freedom, avail yourself of the opportunity. For he who was called in the Lord as a slave is a freedman of the Lord. Likewise he who was free when called is a slave of Christ. You were bought with a price; do not become slaves of men. So, brethren, in whatever state each was called, there let him remain with God.

In this passage, Paul is obviously telling his fellow Christians that Christianity does not release individuals from slavery. Instead, if one were a slave at the time of conversion to Christianity, that person should remain a slave. Similarly, that same apostle in Colossians 4:1 addresses slave owners with the following command: "Masters, treat your slaves justly and fairly, knowing that you also have a Master in heaven." Note that in treating slaves "fairly and justly," Paul doesn't mention anything about freeing the slaves.

As for the slaves themselves, Apostle Paul commands the following in Ephesians 6:5-9:

Slaves, be obedient to those who are your earthly masters, with fear and trembling, in singleness of heart, as to Christ; not in the way of eye-service, as men pleasers, but as servants of Christ, doing the will of God from the heart, rendering service with a good will as to the Lord and not to men, knowing that whatever good any one does, he will receive the same again from the Lord, whether he is a slave or free. Masters, do the same to them, and forbear threatening, knowing that he who is both their Master and yours is in heaven and there is no partiality with him.

Clearly, Paul does not advocate freeing the slaves in any of these passages. Instead, whether slave or free is immaterial because this world is not the one that matters to Paul. For Paul, the only thing that matters is the "next world" in the "afterlife." For the slave, he is to remain a slave upon his conversion to Christianity and be obedient to his master as to Christ. As for the slave owner, Paul does not tell him to release the slaves, but only to treat the slaves justly and fairly. Exactly what is just and fair about owning someone else remains unclear and these passages raise serious questions concerning slavery and moral absolutes. If slavery is sinful, why does Paul not condemn it? Does sin not matter in this world? Paul certainly does plenty of condemnation of sinful activity elsewhere (Galations 5:19-21 is a good example). It is difficult to conclude anything from these passages other than that Paul did not view slavery as sinful or morally wrong in itself.

Paul continues with his tacit support for the institution of slavery in the epistle to Philemon, where Paul addresses the problem caused by a runaway slave (Onesimus) who has since converted to Christianity. He tells Philemon (the slave owner) that he is sending the slave back——though he should be received as "no longer a slave but more than a slave, as a beloved brother." In Philemon 12-16, Paul states that:

I am sending him back. You therefore receive him, that is, my own heart, whom I wished to keep with me, that on your behalf he might minister to me in my chains for the gospel. But without your consent I wanted to do nothing, that your good deed might not be by compulsion, as it were, but voluntary. For perhaps he departed for a while for this purpose, that you might receive him forever, no longer as a slave but more than a slave, as a beloved brother.

Based on these writings of Paul in Ephesians, Corinthians, and Colossians, it appears inconsistent that Paul's "no longer a slave" statement in Philemon means that Paul is declaring the freedom of the slave. Instead, a logical conclusion is that the slave is returning to his former condition of servitude (the condition he was in when he was called), but he is going to be treated like a "brother" while enduring that servitude. There is no suggestion whatsoever that "owning one's brother" might be morally wrong.

Some may argue that this passage should be interpreted instead to mean that the slave Onesimus has become freed. If this is so, why is he then being sent back, since it at least infers that returning to Philemon was not Onesimus' choice, but Paul's. Further evidence that Onesimus remains a slave is found in verse 14 where Paul informs Philemon that "without your consent I wanted to do nothing." This suggests Paul recognized that it was the slave owner Philemon who has control over the destiny of Onesimus. The statement "that you might receive him forever" in verse 15 may be Paul's suggestion that because Onesimus is now a Christian brother, Philemon can now own him "forever," and it was for this purpose that Onesimus was converted! This is far from a condemnation of slavery, and this is not "old covenant" here, but New Testament and Apostle Paul, the most prolific writer of New Testament epistles. In the final analysis, if we are to hold to the "moral absolutes" of the Bible and argue that morals are constant and unchanging, it is difficult to conclude anything other than that slavery is moral and permissible for Christian believers both then as well as now. If one must hold to moral absolutes, the only other possible conclusion is that Apostle Paul was wrong, and slavery was wrong then as well as now. Accepting this position, however, calls into question the doctrines of Bible literalism and inerrancy, both central to the Traditional Conservatism of the Christian Coalition within the Republican Party.

Slavery, however, is only one example where American Christians of the 21st Century generally differ on a question of morality from that taught in the

Bible. Polygamy is another example. In the interest of space, we shall avoid going into as much detail here, but the Old Testament of the Bible is replete with polygamy that goes unpunished and unprohibited either by the Hebrew God or by the Laws of Moses. For instance, in the Book of Genesis, Abraham's grandson Jacob had two wives, the beautiful Rachel and the "sore-eyed" Leah. The story is essentially presented in such a way that one may be caused to feel sympathy for Jacob having to work an extra seven years to get the pretty one. Bill Clinton must be wondering why Christians feel sorry for anyone that gets to sleep with two women and goes uncondemned by God or society. Instead of being condemned as an immoral polygamist, Jacob is held in high esteem as a "man of God." If immorality is always condemned in the Bible, one can only conclude that polygamy is not a moral absolute, and Bill Clinton was merely born in the wrong century.

The polygamy in the Bible, however, does not stop with Jacob. King David, "a man after God's own heart," had 14 wives and 10 "concubines." Not to be outdone, David's son Solomon, "the wisest man that ever lived" had 700 wives and 300 concubines. Concubines? Perhaps Clinton should merely have explained to the Traditional Conservatives that Monica Lewinsky was not someone with whom he was having an illicit affair, but his "Biblical concubine" ala King David. While, it is true that the Hebrew God in the Bible punished King David for adultery with Bathsheba (not to mention the murder of her husband), there are no condemnations against David for his other sex partners (14 wives and 10 concubines), only for taking his pleasure with the wife of someone else and murdering her husband. In fact, God even helped David's polygamy by striking dead the husband of David's second wife (Abigail) so that David could marry her himself (1 Samuel 25:36-44). If morals are absolute and unchanging, one should conclude from the life of King David that polygamy is all fine and dandy in the eyes of the good Lord. The only other possible conclusion (if morals are absolute and unchanging) is that polygamy is morally wrong at present and that it was also morally wrong for King David circa 1000BC. Once again, Traditional Conservatives might argue that perhaps we must judge King David by his time, when polygamy was accepted. If so, however, morals are not absolute and are instead determined by society, a position that liberals espouse and Traditional Conservatives argue against.

Moral Absolutes Limit Technological Progress

In spite of the fact that society, including the Traditional Conservatives themselves, cannot agree on moral absolutes, Traditional Conservatives end up using their moral absolutism to limit academic freedom and therefore hinder technological progress. There is perhaps no greater example than the thousand year stunting of technological growth in Europe under the auspices of the Catholic Church after the fall of Rome in 410AD. During this time period, the Church monopolized learning and systematically eliminated all ideas that conflicted with the Church's official view of the Bible. The losses in science are incalculable, but the destruction of knowledge by the Church arguably set European society back almost 2000 years. Under the oppressive rule of the Church, the aqueducts, plumbing systems, and toilets (yes, toilets) established by the Romans essentially vanished and the road system established by the Romans fell into disrepair and remained so until the 18th Century. The Church taught that all aspects of the flesh should be reviled and therefore the Church discouraged washing of the body. As a consequence, the Middle Ages were fraught with epidemics partially due to poor sanitation (Ellerbe, 1995, 43-44).

In free-thinking Greece in the sixth century B.C. (prior to the Catholic Church's monopoly on knowledge) Greek scholars developed thousands of ideas that are now accepted as sound scientific principles, but were later lost after the Catholic Church gained control of knowledge. For example, Pythagoras had first developed the theory that the earth was a spinning sphere that revolved around the sun. Related to this discovery, Pythagoras concluded that eclipses were natural phenomena rather than special dispensations of Providence. Pythagoras also argued that the earth's surface hadn't always been just as it was, but that what was then sea, had once been land (and vise-versa); that some islands had once formed parts of continents; that mountains were forever being washed down by rivers and new mountains formed; that volcanoes were outlets for subterranean heat rather than surface entrances into Hell, and that fossils were the buried remains of ancient plants and animals turned into stone (Wheless, 1997). Aristarchus (220-143 BC) correctly calculated the inclination of the earth's axis at 23.5 degrees, and thus varified the obliquity of the eliptic and explained the succession of the seasons. Erastosthenes (276-194 BC) knew that the earth was round, invented the imaginary lines of latitude and longitude, and calculated the circumference of the earth at 28,700 miles 17 centuries prior to

Columbus. Similarly, Democritus developed a theory of atoms, or constituents of matter too small to be cut or divided, in 460 BC. Anaxagoras (500-428 BC) was the first to trace the origin of animals and plants to pre-existing germs in the air and "ether" more than 2000 years before Charles Darwin. Hero of Alexandria (130 BC) discovered the principle of the working power of steam and developed a steam engine 1900 years before steam engines tamed the American West (Wheless, 1997).

After the Catholic Church (read here as "Traditional Conservatives) monopolized learning with the fall of Rome, the knowledge of the ancients became lost and it would be the 16th Century before Copernicus would reintroduce the theory that the earth revolved around the sun. Galileo later made the same "discovery" as Copernicus, and in 1615, traveled to Rome to defend the Copernican theory that the Earth revolved around the sun. A committee of advisors to the Church Inquisition declared that holding the view that the Sun is the center of the Universe or that the earth moves is absurd and formally heretical. Cardinal Bellarmine warned Galileo not to hold, teach, or defend Copernican theory. In 1633, Galileo was sentenced to prison for an indefinite term for continuing to teach Copernican theory and forced to sign a formal recantation. Galileo was then allowed to serve his term under house arrest. Galileo also asserted that all objects fall at the same rate, another scientific fact denied by the Catholic Church. Galileo decided to prove his theory and ascended the Leaning Tower of Pisa from which he dropped two iron balls of different weights. When both struck the ground at the same instant, the Christians (again, read as "Traditional Conservatives") refused to accept the results of the demonstration and drove him out of the city of Pisa (Wheless, 1997). Two hundred years later in 1835, the Church finally took Galileo's works off of the list of banned books. Finally, in 1992, the Catholic Church formally admitted that Galileo's views on the solar system are correct. The apology was a few centuries late to do much for Galileo and perhaps a bit too quiet a whisper for the thousand-year constipation of progress.

Traditional Conservatives in the U.S. at present (along with the Catholic Church) now accept that the earth revolves around the sun; however, they tend to argue against Darwin's theory of evolution (which is, in the 21st Century, mainstream science and generally rejected only by Christian fundamentalists). Similarly, Traditional Conservatives in the U.S. at present tend to oppose stem cell research because they believe it violates another moral absolute. Given their track record over the last 1600 years, it is difficult perhaps difficult to expect them to be finally right this time. Moral debates aside, it is impossible to know what medical breakthroughs may be stunted by limits on stem cell research (perhaps none), but it is also possible that future historians will place those against the teaching of evolution and stem cell research in the same bin with the Trial of Galileo and the Flat Earth Society. Time will tell, of course, but the best predictor of future prospects is probably past performance, and the past performance of Traditional Conservatives in the areas of science is consistently poor.

Limits on Freedoms Misuse Resources

The limits on freedoms imposed by an adherence to moral absolutes also tend to waste, or at least misuse resources, both human and otherwise. For example, throughout human history, how many great discoveries has the human race not had because half the population (women) was told to stay home, raise babies, and raise no questions? What was lost in Afghanistan under the Taliban as educated women were told to return to their homes and to traditional "wifery?" What was lost in the United States when blacks were reduced to slavery and legally denied education? The answers to these questions, of course, are incalculable, but to argue anything other than that technological advancement was surely hindered—that takes ideology.

Sordid History of Traditional Conservatism

The adherence to moral absolutes (and Traditional Conservatism in general) clearly has a sordid history. In retrospect, the political track record of Traditional Conservatives over the centuries appears at best silly, and at worst, just tragic. At present, the Traditional Conservatives oppose stem cell research, gay rights, abortions, and the teaching of evolution (among other things). Whether or not the Traditional Conservative positions on these issues will look ridiculous in a few decades remains to be seen; however, if history is any indication, we may expect their positions to be the subjects of future ridicule.

For example, Traditional Conservatives opposed the Civil Rights movement of the 1960s. Back in those days, Traditional Conservative preachers such as Jerry Falwell preached against integration and civil rights from the pulpit (Conason and Lyons, 2000). Traditional Conservatives also opposed the women's rights movement of the 1960s as well as the women's suffrage movement of the early 20th Century. In the case of women's suffrage, protestant fundamentalists argued that God had set a side a traditional place for women in the home as man's "helper" and that place designated by God did not include politics. As a consequence, women's suffrage would lead to divorce and the destruction of the family (Brinkley, 2003, 586).

Traditional Conservatives favored the war in Vietnam and the McCarthy "witch hunts" of the 1950s as well as the "Red Scare" of 1919 and the KKK of the 1920s. The KKK of the 1920s in particular considered itself a "Christian" organization and membership was open only to White Protestants (Chalmers, 1965). Traditional Conservatives also favored Prohibition because alcohol is obviously sinful (never mind that Jesus' first miracle was in making about 180 gallons of wine at a wedding feast). Despite this fact that Jesus' first miracle was providing wine for a party, according to the *Baptist Standard* in 1917, Prohibition was "an issue of Anglo-Saxon culture versus the inferior civilization of niggers in the cities" (Gould, 1973). If one is take the Baptists at their word here and remain congruent with the Bible (where Jesus' first miracle was wine-making) one can only conclude that it must have been a segregated wedding feast where Jesus made wine for an "inferior civilization" of blacks, since he evidently doesn't want whites and their "superior civilization" to drink alcohol.

Some Traditional Conservatives even go so far as to argue that the wine Jesus made at the wedding feast contained no alcohol. In this interpretation, Jesus evidently also invented the "miracle" of pasteurization when he made the nonalcoholic grape juice so that it did not ferment and turn into wine in the Palestinian heat. Traditional Conservatives also sometimes argue that Jesus made wine instead of water because the water in the Middle East at that time was full of impurities and unsafe; hence, Jesus made wine, a safer, more sanitary drink, instead. If this is the case, and Jesus really wanted us to abstain from alcohol, then why didn't Jesus just make clean water? Evidently, he can walk on it, but he can't clean it.

Traditional Conservatives also favor prayer in schools and the teaching of "creationism," but opposed flying (if man were meant to fly, he'd have wings) in the early 20th Century (Nash, 1998). Furthermore, Traditional Conservatives opposed the abolition of slavery, favored the Tories in the American Revolution, favored the Salem witch hunts (as well as the rest of the "witch hunts" in both the U.S. and Europe), and, evidently, also favored the crucifixion of Jesus of Nazareth. Although many contemporary scholars argue that it was the Romans, not the Jews, who executed Jesus, most

Fundamentalist Christians argue that Jesus was essentially killed by the Pharisees and other Jewish religious leaders. The Pharisees, Chief Priests, and "Teachers of the Law" in this interpretation executed Jesus because he violated their interpretations of the "moral absolutes" in the Jewish Law. Clearly, the Pharisees, Chief Priests, and "Teachers of the Law" to whom the Gospels make reference were the Traditional Conservatives of the ancient Jewish society. With this historical track record, perhaps one should view anything espoused by Traditional Conservatives with great skepticism?

Unclear Who Are the "Good People"

Another major problem for Traditional Conservatives is that it is unclear just who are the "good people" that should rule. For example, the Taliban in Afghanistan certainly considered themselves to be the "good and Godly people" who were obligated to rule over the people in Afghanistan and correct societal "weaknesses." Meanwhile, most of the rest of the world denounced those same Islamic clerics as "evil tyrants" and a government that "harbored terrorists." Similarly, the Catholic Church killed thousands of people for witchcraft for centuries in Europe, but these actions are now denounced as morally wrong even by most Catholics. Furthermore, even the Catholic Church admitted that they were wrong in opposing Galileo's astronomical conclusions. Closer to home, in 2003, George W. Bush referred to the regime of Saddam Hussein in Iraq as part of an "Axis of Evil" and accused Saddam of "brutality" and of killing his own people. In the 1980s, however, the U.S. had been aiding that same "evil" dictator in his war against Iran. Furthermore, at this writing there is a ruling entity in Iraq that is still killing Iraqi people on a regular basis, but Traditional Conservatives do not view the American occupying army and their Commander in Chief as "evil." Traditional Conservatives might argue that the U.S. military only kills those "evil" Iraqis that are loyal to the "evil" Saddam Hussein (who obviously has only really been evil since his invasion of Kuwait in 1990, otherwise he surely would not have been aided by the good and moral Reagan Administration). To the families of the dead Iraqis, it probably matters little whether it was "good" Americans or "evil" supporters of Saddam Hussein that killed their family members? In the final analysis, just the fact that there are insurgents against the American occupation may suggest that many Iraqi people are unable to recognize that the American troops are good and moral. Traditional Conservatives may argue that the insurgents are evil themselves, but in any case, there certainly is no universal agreement on who is "evil" and who is not.

Finally, Traditional Conservatives themselves do not appear to be consistent in choosing their own "good" leaders. For example, the Christian Coalition argues for the election of "Christian" leaders, but Traditional Conservatives overwhelmingly supported a former Hollywood actor in his second marriage (Ronald Reagan, the only "divorced" American President) over the Southern Baptist Christian Jimmy Carter in his first and only marriage in 1980. Newt Gingrich, who led the Republicans back to power in the House in 1994, also had extramarital affairs and announced to his wife that he wanted a divorce while she was in the hospital recovering from surgery (Franken, 2003). Pat Buchanan's wife gave birth to a child two months after they were married. "Book of Virtues" Traditional Conservative Bill Bennet admitted a gambling habit in 2003 (Franken, 2003). Traditional Conservatives are not even consistent with their support for their current darling, George W. Bush. Although the Christian Coalition supported George W. Bush for President in 2000, those same Traditional Conservatives within the Republican Party in Texas just four years earlier prevented some of George W. Bush's delegates from attending the Republican National Convention because Bush was too "soft" on abortion (Maxwell and Crain, 2002). Either the Traditional Conservatives are inconsistent in separating "good" leaders from "evil," or somewhere between 1996 and 2000, "God" changed his mind on George W. Bush. Perhaps "God" just found someone he liked much less in that southern Christian family man Al Gore who stressed how he wanted to protect God's creation (the earth) from human destruction. On the other hand, perhaps "God" just wanted Bush to have at least a decade of being sober before he received divine support; hence the shift in Christian Coalition support for Bush between 1996 and 2000. Perhaps, on the other hand, "God" had nothing to do with it and the Christian Coalition is a group of inconsistent and selectively informed ideologues.

George W. Bush is also representative of the incongruence between what Traditional Conservatives say they revere in terms of the "self-made man" and "work ethic." In other words, Traditional Conservatives tend to say that they support sobriety and hard work and argue that people should be rewarded based on that hard work; however, their most recent champion, George W. Bush, actually worked very little before becoming Governor of Texas in 1995, admittedly focused primarily on alcohol consumption until the age of 40, and set a record for the number of vacation days by a President in his first year in office. By April 15, 2004, George W. Bush had made 33 trips to his ranch at Crawford, TX for recreation and relaxation. All told, Bush spent almost eight months of his first 38 months in office at Crawford, Texas (*Economist*, April 17, 1994). The previous record vacation days was held by the Traditional Conservatives' previous champion, Ronald Reagan. Conversely, Traditional Conservatives typically loathed Lyndon Johnson, Jimmy Carter, and Bill Clinton, all three noted "workaholics" during their time in the White House.

Intolerance and Demonization of Enemies

The adherence to moral absolutes also creates intolerance for those that think differently and leads to demonization of enemies. Those that think differently are not only political opponents, but "evil" individuals that may be exterminated. The very meaning of the word "heresy," for which the Catholic Church executed, tortured, and brutalized thousands for centuries, is "to think differently." Traditional Conservatives in the 21st Century that kill others because the others "think differently" include Osama Bin Ladin and the Islamic extremists that carried out the 9/11 attacks on the U.S. Bruce Hoffman (1995) argues that Religious terrorists are different than other types because they are not constrained by the same factors that inhibit other types. They see their world as a battlefield between the forces of light and darkness. Winning is not described in terms of political gains. Instead, the enemy must be totally destroyed. Hoffman argues that Holy terrorists see killing as a sacramental act and the purpose of their operation is to kill. Pointing to Islamic terrorism as an example, Hoffman argues that the purpose of religious terrorism is to kill the enemies of God. In doing so, religious terrorists demonize their enemies. This makes murder much easier because the enemies are no longer people, but are instead equated with the ultimate source of evil. Enemies are devilish and demonic and in league with the forces of darkness. It is not enough to defeat them. Instead, they must be completely eradicated. Similarly, Chip Berlet (1998) argues that the demonized enemy becomes a scapegoat for all problems and it becomes possible for the group to believe that all evil is the result of some sort of conspiracy involving their scapegoat and the evil entity.

Plot Mentality

The "Plot Mentality" is the ultimate result in this mindset where the Traditional Conservatives view the world as a cosmic struggle between the forces of good and evil (Eatwell, 1989). In this construct, the "evil" forces are always "plotting" to destroy society. The McCarthy witch-hunts of the 1950s very well fit this type of Traditional Conservative behavior. "Liberals" in the U.S. argue that the Whitewater investigation of Bill Clinton by Kenneth Starr was a similar witch-hunt. Perhaps George W. Bush's obsession with Saddam Hussein and the other individuals in the famous "deck of cards" should be similarly categorized. For Saddam Hussein's fictitious WMDs to be a threat, one had to assume that he was plotting not only to build them, but to use them against the United States. The events since the invasion (the absence of WMDs) suggest that Bush's argument that Saddam posed an "imminent threat" was nothing more than a paranoid fantasy.

In the case of Islamic terrorism, the "Plot Mentality" is a major driving force behind the actions of the terrorists. According to Berlet (1998), fanatic Muslims blame all of the world's problems on a conspiracy between the U.S. and Zionists in Israel. Religious terrorists are not necessarily seeking a "wider audience," as are other terrorists, because their play is for God, and they need no other audience.

Apocalyptic Thinking

Indiscriminate killing is aided by apocalyptic thinking (Eatwell, 1989). In the Koran, Mohammed speaks of a final judgment against evil, and a similar story is found in the Bible book of Revelation. In this conception, the Islamic terrorists are merely "soldiers of God" aiding him in his judgment, as are the bombers of abortion clinics in the United States. All deterrents to violence are rendered meaningless by the promise of a new age that invites terrorists to fight as holy warriors in a period of fanatic zeal when the deity is about to bring creation to an end. What difference does it make if a mess is made of this world if it is going to end tomorrow anyway? Furthermore, since God rewards the faithful, if innocent people are killed this morning, surely the dead will be in a better place in heaven this afternoon, so what's wrong with that? Finally, if "evil" people are killed, then this world is a better place without those evil people and the sooner that God can be aided in casting them all in Hell, the better.

There Is No "Better, Now Vanished, Time."

If there is any constant in history, it is that basic human nature does not change. As a result, almost every "time" could be categorized as "the best of times, and the worst of times." For example, in the case of the "golden age" of the United States in the early years following the American Revolution (an era often spoken of with reverence by Traditional Conservatives), a closer look reveals that all things were not quite so perfect. For African Americans at the time, most were in bondage; therefore, it seems reasonable to conclude that most African-Americans at the time would not think of the age of the American Revolution as a "golden age." All blacks were not slaves in 1776, and manumission, or legal release from servitude was widely practiced during the American Revolution. While 10,000 slaves were voluntarily freed in Virginia during the Revolution, North Carolina passed a law in 1778 to prohibit manumission. The statute assigned "countenance and authority in violently seizing, imprisoning, and selling into slavery such as had been so emancipated" (Andrews, 1995). Once again, this hardly could be construed by manumitted slaves at the time as a "golden age."

Similarly, the Native Americans of the time surely could not have thought that things were so "golden" either as they were being forced off of the land they had occupied for centuries. The Cherokee Nation signed a 1791 treaty with the U.S. that recognized and delineated their territory as a sovereign nation within the State of Georgia. A few years later, gold was found within the designated area of the Cherokee and shortly thereafter (1830), Congress passed the Indian Removal Act to move the Cherokee further West and off of the land they had been promised by the 1791 Treaty. The Cherokees appealed to the Federal government to uphold the 1791 treaty (Treaties under the U.S. Constitution could supercede other domestic laws) and the U.S. Supreme Court ruled in favor of the Cherokees, but the tribe was evicted from their homes and marched to Oklahoma along the "Trail of Tears" anyway. The only "gold" in this "golden age" for the Cherokees was found in the land that had been taken away from them (Andrews, 1995).

Major problems in America's "golden age," however, were not limited to blacks and Native Americans. Since political participation was limited, for the most part, to white male landowners, it stands to reason that all was not viewed as marvelous by the women, nonlanded men, and other disenfranchised minorities of the time. For example, Abigail Adams, the wife of one President and mother of another, wrote a letter to her husband, John

Adams, in 1776 asking him to "remember the Ladies" and not to "Put unlimited power into the hands of Husbands." Abigail goes on to declare to John "that your Sex are Naturally Tyrannical is a Truth so thoroughly established as to admit of no dispute" (Andrews, 1995). John, of course, responded by essentially ignoring his wife's pleas and helping forge a country that limited politics to wealthy white men. Perhaps this "golden age of America" should be viewed as the "better, vanished time" for wealthy white men, sexists, and racists.

Another "better, vanished time" in America that Traditional Conservatives tend to revere is the generation immediately following World War II. It was during these years that the United States had emerged from WWII as the greatest military power in the world and 60% of Americans attended church on a weekly basis, the highest religiosity of any time in American history. A closer inspection of those "golden years" of the 1950s, however, reveals that blacks were relegated to second-class citizenship in a segregated society and women were generally denied equal opportunity in the workplace. Furthermore, greater church attendance did not apparently translate into sexual chastity. Alfred Kinsey (1948) in his revealing study of American culture entitled *Sex and the American Male*, revealed at the time that 67% of college-educated males and 84% of non college-educated males had engaged in sex outside of the bonds of marriage, whether premarital or extra-marital. Furthermore, 37% of American males surveyed revealed that they had experienced some type of homosexual activity (this included mutual masturbation in these numbers) and 18% of rural American males had experienced sex with animals. It appears that the postwar period was mainly a "golden age" for those engaging in bestiality, hardly the behavior that Traditional Conservatives tend to revere.

Correcting Human Weaknesses Increases Government

Traditional Conservative ideology is essentially in conflict with itself in that it tends to call for "less government," while simultaneously calling for an expansion of government to correct human weaknesses. Prohibition, for example, was an attempt to correct a "human weakness" through government that led to expansion of governmental coercive structures such as the FBI and the Bureau of Alcohol, Tobacco, and Firearms. Similarly, if abortions and homosexual sexual activities were prohibited, as advocated by Traditional Conservatives in the U.S., enforcement would require new divisions within the FBI (if not entirely new bureaucratic entities) charged with ensuring that these "human weaknesses" are curtailed. Such an increase in government power not only conflicts with the Traditional Conservatives' own "less government" mantra, but also conflicts with the Classic Liberals within the Republican Party who do not view the correction of such "human weaknesses" as within the proper scope of government.

There is a further problem in determining exactly what would constitute probable cause to justify a search in such cases? For instance, if homosexuality is illegal, and two men are roommates and together and neighbors report to the police that it is suspicious that they have never seen women at the residence, does this constitute the "probable cause" to search or stake out the apartment for evidence of homosexual activity?

Concluding Remarks

Obviously, the problems and contradictions within Traditional Conservatism are legion and therefore the policy prescriptions that can be expected to arise from this ideology can be expected to be fraught with problems and contradictions as well. After all, this is the group that thinks witchcraft is real (hence the boycotts of Harry Potter), is seriously concerned about the sexual orientation of Tinky Winky, and spent the 1970s spinning records backwards in a fruitless search for reversed satanic messages (or at least they did so before the invention of Compact Discs forced them to hunt for witches elsewhere). The concern over gay teletubbies, though misplaced, is probably largely benign. The same can not be said, however, for the Red Scare of 1919, the McCarthy witch-hunts of the 1950s, the opposition to Civil Rights in the 1960s, the support for the Vietnam War in the 1970s, the Ken Starr investigation, or the invasion of Iraq in 2003. The dangers posed to the world by Traditional Conservatism are what make the study of ideology perhaps as important as any other subject in political science.

Chapter 5
Libertarianism

Libertarianism is a form of Conservatism that is often considered separate from the more mainstream conservative ideologies: partially because it is a bit more extreme, and partially because Libertarians often separate themselves from other forms of more mainstream Conservatism. In fact, Libertarians, unlike Traditional Conservatives and Classic Liberals, have their own political party in the United States and run their own candidates for office separate from the Republican Party, the party that is generally recognized as the party of mainstream conservatism.

Unlike Classic Liberalism and Traditional Conservatism, Libertarianism is not generally recognized as a dominant ideology in the U.S. and the Libertarian Political Party remains a small, splinter party that can be expected to garner less than 2% of the vote in National elections. This may be a bit misleading, however, since a 2000 Rasmussen Research poll (www.lp.org/organization/history) revealed that up to 16% of Americans might be ideologically Libertarian even if they tend to vote for Republican political candidates instead of those from the Libertarian Party. If these survey data are valid, it suggests that the Libertarians, though much smaller as an organized political Party in the U.S., are nonetheless of significant importance as an ideological force in American politics.

Central Tenets of Libertarianism

Libertarianism is essentially an offshoot of Classic Liberalism where the basic premises and fundamental foci have been altered from the primary focus of Classic Liberalism on the free market to a primary focus instead on individual choice. Libertarianism is in many ways similar to Classic Liberalism, but more extreme in its call for limited government, celebration of individual rights, and adherence to the free market. In the Libertarian construct, unlimited consumer choice tends to crowd out or demote other values championed by Classic Liberals and Traditional Conservatives. Essentially, Libertarians are individualist conservatives whose primary political objective is the minimization of government, and through the minimization of government, the maximization of personal freedom and choice (Hoover, 1994).

Libertarianism is a hyper-individualist ideology where Libertarians view themselves as the "true believers" in individual freedom and stress the fact that government, by its very nature, limits freedom. Individual freedom is valued above all else and it is assumed that the greater the individual freedoms, the greater the common good. A major part of the Libertarian celebration of individual freedom is the freedom and control over one's own property. For Libertarians, individual property rights are virtually inviolate and the property owners should be free to do whatever they please with their own property regardless of concerns for the common good. For the Libertarians, the freedom over one's own property is essentially an encapsulation of the common good in itself. The Libertarian position on private property is explained in detail by Robert Nozick (1974) in *Anarchy, State, and Utopia*. Nozick argues that individuals are "entitled" to their property and everything in society flows from this property entitlement. For Nozick, individual freedoms and property rights are inextricably intertwined. Consequently, individuals cannot be deprived of their rights to their property without their consent or without just compensation. Furthermore, government cannot make policies that place limitations on individual freedoms or deprive persons of their property because any governmental actions should require the consent of the individuals affected by those actions.

Libertarians also share some similarities with Traditional Conservatives, in that Libertarians tend to hearken back to a "better, vanished, time," but for Libertarians, the "better, vanished, time" is not necessarily the era of the

"Founding Fathers," but instead the time before the era of "big government" in the U.S. that is generally viewed as beginning with FDR's New Deal in the 1930s. Hence, Libertarians view themselves as "conservators" of an earlier political and economic tradition (even though that earlier tradition was really the era of Classic Liberalism and the U.S. has never really had a truly "Libertarian" era) (Hoover, 1994).

The only appropriate role of government in the Libertarian perspective is for security, especially security against threats from "without." In other words, Libertarians may favor a strong military to prevent a foreign invasion, but that is the extent of their support for governmental activities. In fact, Libertarians are likely to view the military, like other facets of government, as "wasteful" of taxpayer money and a potential danger to individual freedoms; hence, though a strong military may be necessary, it too should be subjugated to the over-riding principle of limited government (Dunn and Woodard, 1991). Some Libertarians, however, such as Murray Rothbard (1975), even argue against a large military and instead argue for the privatization of National defense. Similarly, in foreign policy, Libertarians tend to be isolationists and oppose American intervention in the affairs of other Nations. Such "globalism" can only expand the power and scope of the National government and therefore should be avoided.

In the Libertarian perspective, even security against dangers from "within" should be limited and police protections can be privatized. Optimally, individuals can arrange for their own protection either by defending themselves personally or through the hiring of private security firms (Rothbard, 1975). In other words, every avenue should be pursued to ensure that governmental police protections are kept to a minimum. Similarly, other services that one may normally think of as governmental such as education, sanitation, public health, etc. would be delivered by private entities and paid for by the users of the services. Those that do not utilize the services available would therefore not have to pay anything. In this construct, for example, the only persons that would be paying to support schools would be the students (or parents/guardians of those students) who attended the schools. Those not using the schools would pay nothing and no one would be coerced to pay anything for the benefit of anyone other than themselves. Ideally, school costs for the indigent would be paid for by voluntary gifts from philanthropists. Persons that do not attend schools nor are responsible for persons attending schools would pay nothing toward the support of education for others unless they chose to do so on a voluntary basis (Muccigrosso, 2001).

Libertarians are generally in agreement with Classic Liberals in seeking free market solutions to societal problems. In the Libertarian vision, wages, prices, employment, and distribution of goods would be properly determined by the invisible hand of supply and demand. Any government intervention into the free market for any purpose is anathema. Libertarians may admit that such a system may produce great inequalities due to inequalities of abilities; however, they generally argue that incomes that are gained from "just" processes of the free market are moral and just regardless of any inequality that may result. Furthermore, Libertarians argue that the State has no right to redistribute goods that were "justly" obtained through the free market (Schumaker, Kiel, and Heilke, 1997). In the words of Robert Nozick (1974) in *Anarchy, State, and Utopia*:

There is no central distribution; no person or group entitled to control all the resources, jointly deciding how they are to be doled out. What each person gets, he gets from others who give to him in exchange for something, or as a gift. In a free society, diverse persons control different resources, and new holdings arise out of the voluntary exchanges and actions of persons. There is no more a distributing or distribution of shares than there is a distributing of mates in a society in which persons choose whom they shall marry.

Nozick simplifies this theme with a play on Marx's famous dictum, "from each according to his abilities, to each according to his needs," and instead provides his Libertarian version: "From each as they choose, to each as they are chosen." In other words, governmental redistribution programs are viewed as violations of property rights and individual liberties and therefore unacceptable. Furthermore, any governmental solution is assumed to be inherently inefficient as well as a violation of the rights of taxpayers to do what they want with their own property. Taxes in general, necessarily must be kept to an absolute minimum (since government is kept to an absolute minimum) thus; the rights of property owners to control their own assets are maximized. Libertarians argue that the best method for remedying the inequalities produced through the free market is through voluntary action. Libertarians admit that inequalities will remain, but assume that the societal "haves" will be charitable enough to of their own volition prevent starvation among the societal "have nots." In no case can such charity be coerced by the State.

The Libertarian view of human nature is generally congruent with the negative views of human nature espoused by Traditional Conservatives. Libertarian Albert Nock (1931) for example, in his *Theory of Education in the United States*, argued that the average person was incapable of higher learning and simply uneducable. Consequently, some Libertarians take the realist position that humans are naturally bad, uncooperative, stupid, selfish, and untrustworthy. As a consequence, any government led by these "naturally bad" humans is likely to reflect the negative character of human nature. The minimization of government therefore also minimizes the problem of these bad, uncooperative, selfish, and untrustworthy individuals, having oppressive authority over others.

Unlike Traditional Conservatives, however, Libertarians do not favor restrictions on personal behavior or the use of government so as to correct societal weaknesses. In the Libertarian construct, individual behaviors will be regulated by the natural consequences of destructive behaviors. Drug abuse, for example, would not be worse because the drugs themselves are destructive and most people therefore seek to avoid drug addiction so as to improve their lives. Conversely, a minority of persons can be expected to abuse drugs, but since that situation also exists with governmental restrictions and controls, the imposition of such controls only raises taxes and limits freedom and does little to curb drug abuse. Libertarians point out that compliance with laws is for the most part voluntary; hence, coercive measures to restrict personal behavior are of little effect.

Libertarians also have a tendency to disdain written law, including the U.S. Constitution. Albert J. Nock (1936), for instance, argued that the U.S. Constitution betrayed the spirit of individual liberties embodied in the Declaration of Independence by aiding and abetting the rise of State power.

History of Libertarianism

The historical roots of Libertarianism are traced essentially to some of the same roots as Classic Liberalism and Traditional Conservatism. Libertarians, like Classic Liberals, celebrate the writings of Adam Smith and his free-market laissez-faire capitalism. Libertarians are also persuaded by Thomas Paine's (1776) argument in *Common Sense* that oppressive governments are the greatest threat to individual liberties. Libertarians, however, generally apply Herbert Spencer's (1851) essentially "social Darwinist" argument to the free market. Spencer wrote almost a decade before Darwin's *Origin of the*

Species, but it was Spencer who coined the term "survival of the fittest." Spencer believed in the evolution of society through free market competition. In this view, the market is essentially a means of "natural selection" among humans and the "fittest" are the brightest, hardest working, and most talented individuals who would achieve success in the free market. The weak, slow-minded, and lazy would fail in such a system, but this is natural and essentially unavoidable in a competitive system. Spencer also stressed (like Hobbes) that humans are naturally competitive, rather than cooperative, and free market competition is essentially the "State of nature." Spencer argued, however, that the free market competition would produce a better society in the long run even if the weak and disadvantaged were forced to suffer in the short run. In any case, Spencer eschewed any form of governmental intervention to alleviate the suffering of the less talented.

As previously stated, Libertarians generally accept the negative view of human nature from Thomas Hobbes and clearly espouse Hobbes' famous dictum, "That government that governs least, governs best," as a guiding principle. Taking the principle a step further, Friedrich Von Hayek (1944) argued that the State, even for the purpose of security, could lead to tyranny since reliance on the State would lead to a breakdown in the system of individual self-reliance on which a natural society was based. In Hayek's view, it was this breakdown of individual self-reliance and reliance on the State for security that led to the rise of the Nazis and the destruction of liberties in Germany in the 1930s. Hayek's theme that Statism is destructive to self-reliance was also central to the writings of Ayn Rand (1966), Tibor Machan (1974), and Albert J. Nock. Nock (1936, 3), argued in his *book Our Enemy the State* that "If we look beneath the surface of our public affairs, we can discern one fundamental fact, namely: a great redistribution of power between society and the State." In Nock's view, Democracy has ceased to function properly because instead of the government being directed by the people, the people were being directed by the government. These themes have continued to be central to Libertarianism throughout the present.

Nock had been a progressive Democrat and supporter of Woodrow Wilson prior to WWI, but the expansion of government power during the war caused Nock to become disillusioned with progressivism and turn philosophically in the opposite direction. Nock essentially became a Libertarian in the 1920s before there was such a movement, and argued that the blame for the depravity of humans should be laid at the feet of an overgrown and inept government and its laws. Nock published a journal in the early 1920s known as *The Freeman* that championed what would now be termed as Libertarian positions (Muccigrosso, 2001).

Nock and other Libertarians became important as a political force in the 1930s as part of the Conservative backlash against the New Deal. Nock's opposition to the New Deal and the rise of the State is detailed in his seminal work, *Our Enemy, the State* (1936). Nock juxtapositioned "social power," defined as the power of individuals and private associations, and State power. Nock and the Libertarians essentially equated capitalism with individual freedom and democracy and argued that the expansion of the State under the New Deal would be destructive to all three. Nock argued that the State by nature is exploitive, bent on confiscation of property, and exists to further the interests of one class over another. The New Deal, in Nock's conception, was a manifestation of this Statism and "antisocial" in character. As a consequence, Libertarians were part of the partnership of Conservatives in 1934 that formed the American Liberty League, an organization that was formed as a pressure group representing opponents of the New Deal. The American Liberty League condemned both FDR and his policies and compared him to the notorious authoritarian dictators of the time: Hitler, Mussolini, and Stalin (Muccigrosso, 2001). Nock (1936), and Ralph Adams Cram (1937) in his work entitled *The End of Democracy*, took the extreme position that the rise of Statism would eventually destroy both capitalism and democracy.

In 1943, Libertarian thought received a boost when Ayn Rand published her novel, *The Fountainhead*, a Libertarian work of fiction that essentially defined the human moral purpose as the unfettered quest for one's own betterment and happiness. Rand, like Nock and Cram, argued that freedom and capitalism were inextricably linked, and to drive the point home, sometimes gave public lectures while wearing a dress covered with dollar signs. Rand was passionately anti-communist and a defender of private property rights, Libertarian themes that have continued through the present (Muccigrosso, 2001).

After WWII, Libertarianism received another intellectual boost from what is known as the "Austrian School" or "Chicago School" of economics. Ludwig von Mises, an Austrian economics scholar who immigrated to the U.S. in reaction to the calamity of Naziism in Central Europe, argued against any form of Statism, whether Nazi or otherwise. Mises argued that Statism, including government economic planning and intervention, were incompatible with capitalism (Muccigrosso, 2001). Mises' younger Austrian colleague, Friedrich A. Hayek, who taught at the University of Chicago, concurred with Mises' analysis of Statism, but focused more on the "evils" of socialism. In 1944, Hayek published *Road to Serfdom*, in which he blamed the totalitarianism in Europe on socialist trends from the previous decades. Hayek argued that once the State controls portions of the nation's economy, it begins society down a slippery slope toward the complete control of society by the State. The slide toward State control would be gradual, but nonetheless ruinous to individual freedom and democracy in the end.

In the 1950s, the Libertarian anti-Statist theme was continued by Frank Chodorov, an associate of Albert J. Nock. Chodorov railed against Statism and taxation in his 1954 work, *The Income Tax: Root of All Evil*, and founded an essentially Libertarian interest group known as the Intercollegiate Society of Individualists dedicated to ending what he viewed as the dominance of New Deal Statism at American Universities. The Intercollegiate Society of Individualists distributed Libertarian and other Conservative publications on college campuses. Eventually, the organization became the Intercollegiate Studies Institute that distributes Conservative literature and publishes *Campus*, a national conservative newspaper written and edited by students. Libertarianism received another boost in the 1950s with the revival of Nock's Libertarian journal, *The Freeman*, which included contributions from Hayek and Mises (Muccigrosso, 2001).

In the early 1960s, the Chicago School of Economics grew in importance with the ascendancy of Milton Friedman, a student of Friedrich Hayek. In 1962, Friedman published *Capitalism and Freedom*, where he argued that capitalism and freedom were inextricably linked and that both are better served when the role of government is minimized. Furthermore, for what State power is necessary, Friedman argued that it was best placed at the State and local, rather than National, level. Friedman also argued against the Keynesian economics of the New Deal and disputed the claim of contemporary Liberals that the Depression could have been caused by defects in capitalism. Instead, Friedman argued that the Great Depression was the result of government mismanagement through misguided monetary policies of the Federal Reserve. Friedman was elected President of the American Economic Association in 1967 and received the Nobel Prize in Economics for his work in 1976. Friedman, however, did not limit his commentary to the economic realm and also argued for the elimination of military conscription and the implementation of a school voucher system for parents that wanted to use their tax money to send their children to private schools (Muccigrosso, 2001).

Libertarians largely remained within the Republican Party until the military conscription of Vietnam War of the 1960s that violated the Libertarians' celebration of individual "choice" as the fundamental basis for society (Tucille, 1970). As a consequence, a movement toward the establishment of a Libertarian Party as a viable alternative to the Republicans gained momentum. The American Libertarian Party began in 1971 in Colorado as a group of disillusioned Republicans and others disenchanted with the major Parties set out to provide an alternative. Libertarians were at odds with other Conservatives within the Republican Party over the issues of conscription, personal drug use, and the Vietnam War in general. Libertarians such as Murray Rothbard argued that the Vietnam War and globalist policies promoted statism and thus deprived the individual of liberty. Former Barry Goldwater speech writer Karl Hess argued that "Vietnam should remind all conservatives that whenever you put your faith in big government for any reason, sooner or later you wind up as an apologist for mass murder" (Quoted in Muccigrosso, 2001). Hess was also appalled by government efforts to coerce its citizens through Federal law enforcement agencies and compared the FBI with the Soviet KGB (Muccigrosso, 2001).

By 1980, the Libertarian Party was on the ballot in all 50 States and Libertarian Presidential Candidate Ed Clark received almost a million votes. Libertarians continued to be appalled at America's globalist foreign policies, the continued expansion of State power, and the continuation of the Cold War under Presidents Carter and Reagan. As a consequence, the Libertarian Party continued to gradually grow in size. Two Libertarians were also elected to the Alaska Legislature. Over the next two decades, the Libertarian Party grew gradually until over 300 Libertarians were serving in elected public offices across the country by 2001. In 2002, the Libertarian Party ran 1642 candidates for public office, the largest slate of candidates for office from any Third Party since World War II (www.lp.org/organization/history).

As the Libertarian movement gained steam, some Libertarians, most notably Karl Hess, a former speech writer for 1964 Republican Presidential candidate Barry Goldwater, advocated not only separation from the Republican Party and the formation of a Third Party, but separation from the community at large. Hess argued that a better society could be forged through self-reliance on the neighborhood-community level and argued that society should become decentralized into self-sufficient neighborhoods. Hess's ideas, as he outlined them in *Community Technology* (1979), spawned a separatist Libertarian community in a Washington D.C. neighborhood. Though the Libertarian community in the nation's capital was a failure within five years, the ideas of neighborhood-level self-help as strategies for fighting urban decay became adopted by the Reagan Administration in the 1980s. They are also reflected in George H.W. Bush's vision of "1000 points of light" and call for volunteerism at the end of the decade.

Problems with Libertarian Ideology

Libertarianism suffers from all of the same problems and contradictions stemming from the free market as Classic Liberalism. Essentially, the unregulated free market produces inequalities, unsafe products, environmental degradation, and profits to unscrupulous merchants to the detriment of the common good. Furthermore, there is no historical example that supports the Libertarian contention that "volunteerism" can adequately solve the problems of poverty and extreme income inequality that tend to result from the free market in a large, industrialized society. Even the small scale Libertarian neighborhood experiment in Washington D.C. in the 1980s quickly failed.

The Libertarian focus on individual security also appears to be problematic. After all, the very reason that governments are formed in the first place is because humans are unable to provide for their own security on an individual basis and all too often, a society without sufficient government becomes Thomas Hobbes' savage jungle where life is "nasty, brutish, and short." A case in point may be Iraq after the U.S. invasion when Saddam Hussein's police State was dismantled and the country quickly devolved into looting, anarchy, and violence as a result. In general, Libertarians are victims of what Jean Jacques Rousseau termed as the "Law-Freedom Paradox." Essentially, while Libertarians are correct in their assertion that law limits freedom, it also appears that there is little freedom without law.

Individualism by its very nature clashes with the restrictive positions on social issues taken by Traditional Conservatives. Libertarian individualism essentially celebrates choice as its highest value; hence, some individuals in such a system can be expected to choose activities such as homosexuality, substance abuse, abortions, and sexual promiscuity that are abhorrent to Traditional Conservatives. Consequently, the individualism and minimal government positions of Libertarians (much like those of Classic Liberals) also clash with Traditional Conservatives who would use government to rid society of activities they view as human weaknesses such as pornography, prostitution, drug abuse, homosexuality, and abortions. Ayn Rand (1962), for example, criticizes Traditional Conservatives for their failure to wholeheartedly embrace unfettered capitalism. In the words of Rand:

> The plea to preserve "tradition" as such, can appeal only to those who have given up or to those who never intended to achieve anything in life. It is a plea that appeals to the worst elements in men and rejects the best: it appeals to fear, sloth, cowardice, conformity, self-doubt—and rejects creativeness, originality, courage, independence, self-reliance.

Similarly, Libertarian pundit Russell Kirk (1982) argues that because of the Libertarians' beliefs in the "moral freedom" for individuals, they oppose restrictions on abortion as restrictions on individual freedoms. Traditional Conservatives respond with criticism of Libertarians for their lack of concern for customs, traditions, history, and societal institutions such as church and family (Dunn and Woodard, 1991). Libertarians have also been accused by Traditional Conservatives (and Contemporary Liberals), of following an ideology that is without morality due to their emphasis on individualism that essentially celebrates the "virtues of selfishness." Additionally, if all persons are selfishly seeking their own good, and no one is seeking the common good, it should not be surprising if the common good does not result since no one is actually seeking it or giving it a priority.

Libertarians counter these charges with the arguments of Ayn Rand (1961), in *The Virtue of Selfishness*, where she argued that societal moral decay was not due to selfishness, but due to a tendency to equate morality with altruism. Rand accepts the Hobbesian negative view of human nature and argues that human nature does not allow people to sacrifice for others. As a consequence, altruistic morality is a nice idea, but humans are unable to pursue it in practice. In contrast to what they therefore view as truly futile moralities espoused by Traditional Conservatives, the Libertarian view of a moral person is one that simply respects the rights of others, pursues the best things for their own lives, and does nothing that discourages others from becoming equally self-reliant. The problem with Rand's argument is that if humans are naturally bad, then they cannot be expected to live up to the Libertarian view of the "moral person," and instead can be expected to trample on the rights of others when it suits their own selfish motives.

Libertarians have also criticized Traditional Conservatives for what they view as inflexible, archaic, and authoritarian value systems and structures that they view as hindering liberty. H.L. Mencken, a writer for the *Baltimore Sun* during the 1920s and 1930s and a leading Libertarian critic of the New Deal also criticized Fundamentalist Protestant religions and rural American values. Mencken (1996), once declared that the American farmer did not belong to the human race and that the American South was ruled by "Baptist and Methodist barbarism." Obviously, such a position places the Libertarians at odds with the core support for the Republican Party.

Finally, in the minds of many, Libertarianism was effectively discredited by the Great Depression and World War II. Liberals argue that if there is any lesson to be learned from the Great Depression, it is that sometimes government intervention into the free market is necessary to alleviate free market harshness. Similarly, the World War II experience suggests that security is impossible without collective action; hence, Libertarianism is doomed to failure both in the area of security and in the areas of economic and social welfare.

Concluding Remarks

Libertarianism continues to be a growing ideological force in American politics and an important influence in the Republican Party. As the Republican Party under George W. Bush (as well as the Democrats) have continued to violate the Libertarian principles of less government, one might expect Libertarianism to continue to grow in the near future as a reaction to government expansion. Another severe free market economic downturn where Governmental solutions become popular, or another major security threat, however, may again discredit the movement.

Chapter 6
Conservative Extremism

Conservative Extremism is not a dominant ideology in the United States, but that does not mean that it is absent (it is not), or that it is impotent. In fact, the Oklahoma City bombing in 1994 by Conservative Extremist Timothy McVeigh suggests exactly the opposite. Similarly, the rise of the Nazis in Germany from an insignificant splinter party in 1928 to the control of the government in 1933 is a testimony to the power potential of Conservative Extremism as ideologies that can mobilize the masses. The World War II experience largely discredited Conservative Extremist ideologies under the names of Naziism and Fascism; however, this does not mean that Conservative Extremism might not resurface in any advanced democracy under another name, whether it be the National Front in France, or the Citizen Militia movement in the U.S. It would be foolish to accept the position that the U.S. or any other advanced industrial democracy is immune to such a movement.

Conservative Extremism, like other facets of conservatism, is not monolithic, but diverse; however, there is less common agreement among scholars about the use of terms to describe Conservative Extremism as opposed to other ideologies (Eatwell, 1989). For example, McCarthyism in the U.S. in the 1950s is quite different than Naziism in Germany in the 1930s because McCarthyism did not contain the same focus on anti-semitism. Therefore, should these movements be considered ideologically similar, or different? There is, however, a commonality among Conservative Extremist ideologies in that they tend to be viewed as ideological aberrations from the norm and there is a tendency in society at large to associate a perjorative meaning with the labels attached to the movements themselves (Eatwell, 1989).

Conservative Extremism also differs from other ideologies in that it lacks its own version of a Karl Marx or some other grand theorist to whom all Conservative Extremists turn for guidance. Adolph Hitler's Mein Kampf, most scholars would argue, does not qualify. In the words of Michael Billig (1979):

Mein Kampf is better categorized as "a mish-mash of self-serving autobiography, psychopathic hatred and prejudice, should not be considered as an intellectual work of political theory. The mystery is how such nonsense became to be taken seriously by so many people.

If there is any stream of writing to which Conservative Extremists draw their ideas, it is the writings in the pseudo-science of eugenicists, who argue that there are genetic differences between peoples and races with some races superior to others (Poliakov, 1974). Writers such as Madison Grant, in the *Passing of the Great Race*, argue that a particular race of people (normally white, anglo-saxons) is superior to all others and that race must be kept pure. In cases of intermarriage between the preferred race and those of the "inferior" races, so argue the Conservative Extremists, the children always go to the "lower case," thus diluting and destroying the "superior race." As a consequence, Conservative Extremists argue for severe immigration restrictions so as to prevent such inter-racial "mixing," and segregationist policies and apartheid-inequalities under law are championed.

Central Tenets of Conservative Extremism

Conservative Extremism, whether it be termed as fascism, naziism, or the white supremism of the KKK, is a combination of racism, nationalism, and authoritarianism that has a tendency to center on a belief in the superiority of a specific group of people (Mosse, 1964). Conservative Extremism rests on the fears of foreigners and immigrants among indigenous members of the population. The target of the Conservative Extremists' wrath and fears, however, is not always the same, because as immigration patterns change, it is not always the same "foreigner" that is being denigrated. Furthermore, the form of the Conservative Extremist hatred at differing times is similar, but the content may differ because the ideologies allow "substitutability of targets" (Billig, 1979). The Conservative Extremism of Adolph Hitler in Nazi Germany, for example, had as its basis a belief in the superiority of the German people, while the Conservative Extremism of Japan during the same time period celebrated the superiority of the people of Japan. Similarly, the Conservative Extremism of the KKK in the U.S. in the 1920s was based on the "God-given right of white protestant males" and the assumed inferiority of African Americans and other non-white, non-protestant individuals (Alexander, 1965). Conservative Extremists in the U.S., however, could easily shift the focus of their wrath from African-Americans to Latin Americans or Asians depending on shifting cultural and immigration patterns and political events. After the terrorist attacks of September 11, 2001, for instance, it would not be surprising if American Conservative Extremists designated Muslims at their new objects of veneration.

Conservative Extremists accept the proposition that different persons have different levels of talents and abilities, a point with which Classic Liberals, Traditional Conservatives, and Libertarians would agree. Conservative Extremists, however, take this principle a step further and generalize it to groups of people based on ethnicity, nationality, religion, or some other societal cleavage. In other words, Conservative Extremists generally argue that different groups of people have differing levels of talents and abilities as groups, in addition to individual differences. Conservative Extremists can be expected to view the talents of their own group as superior to those of all others, and view the world as a hierarchy of groups of peoples with their own group rightfully situated at the top. In the Conservative Extremist construct, race, ethnicity, or nationalism, is normally the motivating and unifying force and purity of the group is the guiding precept of the community.

Conservative extremist ideologies are also typically reactionary in character. The KKK for instance developed as a reaction to the end of slavery and the Southern defeat in the Civil War. Similarly, Naziism in Germany developed as a reaction to the German loss in World War I and as a response to the "threat" of socialism. Fascism in Italy under Mussolini also arose at least partially due to a perceived threat from socialism (Eatwell, 1989).

Conservative Extremism generally places a high priority on myth, and like Traditional Conservatives, the Conservative Extremists may hearken back to the symbols and heroes of a better, vanished, time as a motivating force. Conservative Extremist ideologies also typically aggrandize selected historical figures to mythical and heroic proportions. The heroes of the past are then connected to an aggressive and romantic vision of nationalism that becomes in the Conservative Extremists' vision, "the way things ought to be." The present is viewed as decadent, often with nothing to "conserve." The Conservative Extremism of Osama Bin Ladin and al Qaeda, for example, preaches the decadence of the current society, calls for its complete destruction, and hearkens for a return to the 13th Century teachings of ibn Tamiyya (Benjamin and Simon, 2002).

Typically, Conservative Extremism includes leadership by a charismatic authoritarian leader who takes on mystic, "messiah-like" characteristics. Osama bin Ladin and Adolph Hitler are excellent examples of the "charismatic leader." Without such a strong leader, the movement may not be able to gather momentum. For example, Benito Mussolini, the leader of Fascist Italy in the early Twentieth Century, once remarked, "What would Facism be, if I had not been." (Quoted in Ingersoll, Matthews, and Davison, 2001, 213). The strong leader is expected to unite the people and return society to the truer version of the past. The charismatic leader in Conservative Extremism typically becomes an authoritarian leader who not only assumes policy leadership, but also assumes a leading role in constructing and perpetuating the myths on which the ideology is based and condemning heresies (Hoover, 1994). Pursuant to these goals, Osama Bin Ladin has issued religious fatwas calling for Holy War on the West. Bin Ladin has also called for the overthrow of "apostate" Islamic rulers, such as Saddam Hussein and the Saudi Royal family, whom Bin Ladin views as straying from the principles of pure Islam (Benjamin and Simon, 2003).

A central component of Conservative Extremism is often conspiracy theory. Senator Joseph McCarthy's assertion that there was a communist conspiracy to undermine the U.S. government and American society and Adolph Hitler's assertion that the German defeat in WWI was because Jewish traitors betrayed Germany are good examples. Western culture is perhaps especially susceptible to conspiracy theories since its monotheistic Christian beliefs simplify world conflict for people into a struggle between God and Satan, or good and evil. Since in Christianity, there is a general belief in invisible forces of evil plotting against the forces of good, whether those forces be witches, demons, or the Devil himself, it is then very easy to believe that there are invisible human plots as well.

Outsiders to the Conservative Extremists' preferred group (Jews in Nazi

Germany, for example) are demonized and cast as societal scapegoats for all of the ills that beset society. Consequently, Conservative Extremists generally argue that these outgroups must be purged, expelled, or at least "controlled," if not completely eradicated in order for society to advance. The most important societal problems are attributed to the scapegoat groups and to those within the preferred group itself that have adopted the ways of the scapegoats. For example, in Nazi Germany, the German defeat in World War I was explained as a result of Jewish officers that betrayed Germany at Versailles and other German officials that collaborated with the Jewish traitors (Bell, 1986).

The conspiracy theories of Conservative Extremism help provide a common sense of identity for the Extremists themselves who view themselves as having true "revelation" as to the dark and evil forces that lurk in the world while others ignorantly ignore their warnings. The Conservative Extremists then view themselves as the last bastion of hope against the hidden evil corrupting forces that are loose on society (Eatwell, 1989).

Conspiracy theories also allow Conservative Extremists to resolve dissonance. In other words, the ideology allows Conservative Extremists to explain away any and all factual evidence that appears to be in conflict with their beliefs. For instance, a Conservative Extremist may be able to believe that the Holocaust never happened because the media and academia are dominated by Jews, liberals, and communists who have forged and perpetuated intricate lies to deceive the people (Eatwell, 1989).

Conspiracy theories in Conservative Extremism, however, do not stop with the enemy scapegoats. Conservative Extremists often see conspiracies among those in their own organization. For example, Adolph Hitler purged many a dedicated Nazi out of paranoia and Joseph McCarthy even at one time accused Republican President and hero of WWII Dwight Eisenhower of being a communist (Brinkley, 2003).

The preferred group itself becomes a central focus in Conservative Extremism and the group itself takes on a glorious, mystical, almost religious, character. For the Naziism of Adolph Hitler, the focus was on the "Volk" or German people and the nature of the group was founded on blood nationalism and sacrifice (Eatwell, 1989). In Fascist Italy, the focus was on the Nation-State itself. In the words of Mussolini (Quoted in Somerville and Santoni eds., 1963):

The State, as conceived of and as created by Fascism, is a spiritual and moral fact in itself, since its political, juridical, and economic organization of the nation is a concrete thing; and such an organization must be in its origins and development a manifestation of the spirit.

The role of the State in Conservative Extremism includes the provision of security, both internal and external; however, the State is also, in the words of Mussolini (Quoted in Somerville and Sontoni eds., 1963), "the custodian and transmitter of the spirit of the people." In other words, the role of the State in the Conservative Extremist construct includes developing and perpetuating the ideological myths on which the group is predicated. History is interpreted by the State in Conservative Extremist ideological terms and events and symbols of the glorious past of the people are linked with the people of the present. The group of the present is the manifestation of the glory of the people of the past.

Conservative Extremists place a premium on order over individual freedoms and argue that unrestrained individualism leads to chaos. Whereas Classic Liberals and Libertarians assert that the State is subservient to the individual, Conservative extremists argue that such individualism leads to conflict, disunity, and chaos. Conservative Extremists argue that such a society constructed on selfishness and conflict is an affront to order, progress, and morality (Ingersoll, Matthews, and Davison, 2001). Instead, Conservative Extremists argue that there is no freedom without order and it is in a "morally pure" and orderly society that freedom is the greatest. As a consequence, individuals essentially have no rights, but only whatever privileges are granted them by the State or preferred group entity. As a consequence, no parties, interest groups, religions, or other institutions that are deemed to conflict with the good of the preferred group (as defined by the charismatic leader or governing authorities) are allowed. The only societal groups allowed are those so designated by the governing authorities since it is they who determine what is in the interest of the common good (Ingersoll, Matthews, and Davison, 2001). The social structure that emerges is one that is termed as "corporatism," where certain societal representative groups are granted monopolies on representation for different segments of society and incorporated into the State itself.

Although Conservative Extremism shares a tendency toward authoritarianism with Leninist Communism, Conservative Extremism is in other ways antithetical to Communism in that Communism constructs a society based on class, regardless of race, ethnicity, religion, or heritage. In

Conservative Extremist ideologies, a pluralist society cannot be classless because ethnic minorities, minority religious groups, etc., cannot be placed on equal footing with the preferred group. Furthermore, class interests could be expected to conflict with group unity and may conflict with the common good. As such, it is not accidental that Mussolini's Fascists came to power in Italy at a time that the middle and upper classes feared the growing political power of Italy's Communists.

Conservative Extremism has typically contained elements of Spartan machismo and militarism and lent itself toward military adventurism. Typically, the Conservative Extremists view military conflict as inevitable and even desirable and right, since it is only "right" and "natural" that the strong and "better" people should rule over the weak (Woods 1989). Essentially, if the preferred group is to be "better" than all others, it follows that the preferred group may prove their superiority on the battlefield. By testing themselves against other groups or Nation-States, the preferred Conservative Extremist group can assess their progress in their quest to become the superior people encompassed in their own mythology. Some conservative extremists, however, may become isolationists and anti-internationalists stemming from the lack of trust for outsiders and their reverence for their preferred group (Eatwell, 1989).

Conservative Extremism also contains a strain of anti-intellectualism due to its preference for emotion over substance. If the charismatic leader is to mobilize the masses, he must move them through emotive symbols rather than sound analysis. After all, sound analysis is unlikely to support the notion of the superiority of the preferred group in the first place. Additionally, the Conservative Extremists value action as more important than ideas anyway, consequently, there is little reason to study great questions intently when faster solutions can be achieved through action (Ingersoll, Matthews, and Davison, 2001).

The anti-intellectual and "action-based" focus of Conservative extremism is echoed by political theorists Nietzsche and Sorel. Sorel (1969) argued that action was a necessary part of political activity and that "thought" was mere "rationalization." Sorel therefore called for action (including violence), not thought, as a prerequisite for overthrowing what he viewed as the hedonistic, materialistic, liberal democratic State. Similarly, Nietzsche (1969) argued that "rationalism" was bankrupt as a means for political change and that instead at rare moments an exceptional leader could emerge who could lead the people to correct societal problems.

The action is necessary because Conservative Extremists view the entire existing society as decadent and in need of total abolition and replacement with a newer, better, society (Muller, 1987). As a consequence, the typical conservative preference for minimal government is replaced by the urgent need to install the "correct" political program before the forces of darkness (often communism or socialism) completely destroy society. An ideology that has as its basis the need for abolition of an existing order is particularly inclined to stress the "spirit" of a new political order rather than its content; hence, action is placed over substance (Woods, 1989). As such, Conservative Extremism typically becomes anti-democratic in character. In this construct, democratic rights and liberties will have to be limited in order to protect the good of the preferred group. After all, democracy allows the possibility that leaders will be elected that do not subscribe to the "true light" as known by the Conservative Extremists. In order to ensure that "right-thinking" individuals of the preferred group are elected, it is necessary to limit political participation to the preferred group itself. Furthermore, rights of those that are not in the preferred group will necessarily have to be limited to ensure that those in the preferred group also occupy the preferred positions in society. As a consequence, Hitler revoked the rights of the Jews in Nazi Germany and Conservative Extremists imposed segregation and Jim Crow laws on African Americans in the American South following Reconstruction.

Problems with Conservative Extremism

Sordid History

Obviously, the largest problem for Conservative Extremism is that Conservative Extremist ideologies led to the military expansionist policies of Nazi Germany, Imperial Japan, and Fascist Italy in the 1930s with disastrous results. Rights were trampled everywhere the Conservative Extremists took over, nations and peoples were conquered against their will by the Conservative Extremist regimes and enemies of the regimes were massacred by the millions. With the Holocaust in Europe, the Bataan Death March in the Pacific, and the great calamity in general that was World War II largely blamed on Conservative Extremists by the rest of the world, Conservative Extremism was effectively discredited as of 1945. After the photographs of the Nazi concentration camps became public knowledge, the idea of the great State built on racial supremacy could no longer be innocently supported

(Billig, 1979). As a consequence, Conservative Extremist groups have been relegated to the fringes of the political spectrum with very limited support, and their Parties and ideas are typically shunned by more mainstream conservatives (Billig, 1979). Furthermore, no Conservative Extremist party has risen to power in any developed industrial Democracy in the six decades following World War II. The closest that any have come is Jean Marie LePen's second place showing in France in 2003, but Le Pen was trounced in the National Election for President against Jaques Chirac, gaining only 18% of the vote. Although LePen's second place showing is certainly significant, it is difficult to say that he was near winning an election when he lost five votes out of six.

Conflict with Classic Liberalism and Libertarianism

Although the legacy of the past is undoubtedly the biggest problem for Conservative Extremism, Conservative Extremism also has another impediment to its success in that it very much conflicts with the individualism of Libertarianism and Classic Liberalism. In Conservative Extremism, the good of the preferred group takes precedent over any individual rights. In the words of Mussolini (Quoted in Somerville and Sontoni eds., 1963, 426): "The Fascist conception of life stresses the importance of the State and accepts the individual only insofar as his interests coincide with those of the State." As a consequence, Conservative Extremist ideas can be expected to be shunned as anathema by the more "mainstream" Classic Liberals in the Republican Party as well as Libertarians who place a premium on the individual.

Conservative Extremism also created very large, powerful, and coercive States in Germany, Italy, and Japan in the 1930s. The idea of a large, powerful, and coercive State is completely at odds with the "limited government" ideals of Classic Liberals and Libertarians. Similarly, the coercive State in Germany, Italy, and Japan of the 1930s created corporatist structures, command economies, and tremendous governmental intervention into the social order to the degree that the ideology became so penetrating into human activity that even individual thought was a concern of the State. The space between public and private spheres became blurred or destroyed with the result that the State was entitled to regulate all aspects of economic, political and social life (Freeden, 2003). All of these State intrusions, whether social, economic, or political, are abhorrent to Classic Liberals and Libertarians.

Conservative Extremism also tends to break down rule of law and replace it with rule by the whim of the charismatic leader. The distinctions between legality and illegality become blurred so that ordinary citizens (especially those that do not belong to the preferred group) are unable to discern which side of the law they are on and whether or not the State is their friend or foe. This break down of rule of law is in direct conflict with the rule of law premises of Classic Lockean Liberalism (the basis of Classic Liberalism) and therefore hinders the ability of Conservative Extremists to expand their appeal in contemporary "Liberal" democracies.

Inaccurate Views of History and Reality

Conservative Extremism has also often been criticized for championing inaccurate portrayals of reality and history. For instance, Jean Marie Le Pen in 1987 all but denied the Holocaust during WWII. In the words of Le Pen:

I ask myself a certain number of questions. I'm not saying that gas chambers did not exist. I have not been able to see any myself. I have not specially studied the question. But I consider it a matter of detail in the history of the Second World War...I say that some historians are debating these questions (*Observer*, 1987).

If Le Pen's perspective were unique, then one could discount it as a function of Le Pen's individual personal ignorance and psychology. Instead, however, Holocaust denial has become prevalent in Conservative Extremist literature. For example Richard Harwood (1974) wrote a pamphlet in the 1970s denying the Holocaust entitled: *Did Six Million Really Die?* The pamphlet became widely circulated among Conservative Extremists all over the world and led to the publication of more similar works (Billig, 1979). Soon, Holocaust denial began to even spread marginally over into mainstream conservative American Politics. For instance, Pat Buchanan, a former speech writer for President Richard Nixon and frequent American candidate for the Presidency essentially denied some aspects of the Holocaust in an article he wrote in the *New York Post* in 1990. In this article, Buchanan discusses what he termed as a "Holocaust Survivor Syndrome" that involved what he labeled as "group fantasies of martyrdom and heroics." Buchanan went on to deny that people were killed in Nazi death camps from toxic fumes produced by diesel engines and pumped into sealed rooms, thus essentially denying known historical facts while simultaneously displaying an ignorance of diesel engines. More recently, what is becoming a "tradition" of Holocaust denial continued with the publication of Arthur R. Butz (2003), book entitled *The Hoax of the Twentieth Century: The Case Against the Presumed Extermination of European Jewry*. The title itself pretty much tells the reader all that one needs to know.

The denial of the Holocaust, as incredible as it may seem, is not merely an attempt to rewrite or deny one isolated event in history, but is part of the "plot-mentality" paranoia that tends to afflict Conservative Extremists. The Holocaust denying extremists are essentially arguing that recorded history is a lie and a myth that has been fed to the people as part of a global plot, in this case by the Jews who control the media, the Universities, and, in their view, just about everything and everyone else. The Conservative Extremists in this case view the whole world as hopelessly duped, while they alone possess the wisdom and understanding to see through the plot for what it is (Billig, 1979). To the rest of the world, however, the plot-mentality Conservative Extremists merely appear to be either stupid, or ignorant, or mentally unstable, or all three.

Concluding Remarks

Whether it be African-American Jesse Owens winning a sprint, African-American Joe Louis winning a boxing match, or Soviet tanks rolling into Berlin, Adolph Hitler was faced with constant reminders that his myth of Aryan supremacy was in reality just that: nothing but myth. Obviously, the inglorious deaths of both Hitler and Mussolini did little to perpetuate the myths of their superior leadership. In essence, all racial superiority myths and leader-cult myths are doomed to failure because all groups of humans and all human leaders suffer from human flaws and imperfections, not to mention their own mortality. Those flaws and imperfections are easily exposed when challenged, thus eventually revealing the Conservative Extremist myths for what they are. The only real question is how many people can be deceived by the myths for how long. Unfortunately, in the cases of Germany, Italy, and Japan in the 1930s, it was too many people for too long, and the result was the death of millions.

Chapter 7
Conservatism and Environmental Policy

Environmental policy making, like other policy areas, does not occur in a vacuum, but is greatly impacted by the political environment. In the case of environmental policy, a major element in the political environment that influences policy making is ideology. In general, "liberal" Democrats tend to favor greater environmental protection at the expense of economic gains while "conservative" Republicans tend to sacrifice more of the natural environment in the interest of economic advantage. American environmental policies reflect this political struggle. Democratic control of Congress combined with renewed public environmental awareness in the 1970s to create an environmental revolution. The environmental Revolution of the 1970s placed responsibility for environmental regulation with the Federal government where it largely still resides. The Revolution also created a national political climate that was favorable to environmental protection that has not entirely abated.

Similarly, Republican control of the Presidency during the 1980s and Congress in the latter half of the 1990s produced an anti-regulatory backlash at least partially purposed to limit Federal regulation of the environment. The general feeling of Republicans was that Federal regulation had been too comprehensive and that it had produced detrimental effects on commerce. In general, political leaders in contemporary democracies are largely held responsible by the public for the State of the economy (Prewitt et al., 1991). Consequently, political leaders often can be expected to be more zealous in securing a robust economy than in preserving the environment, and this is reflected in the anti-regulatory ideologies within the Republican Party. Furthermore, the American public does not always consider environmental concerns the most important problems facing the U.S. For example, a 1998 Poll asked respondents to list the most important issues facing the nation. Only 2% listed the environment. Similarly, only 1% of respondents in a January 1995 Gallup poll considered the environment to be the "most important problem" facing the U.S. (Bosso, 2000, 56-57). These numbers should in part explain the Republican anti-environmental backlash.

Federalism and Environmental Policy

In the area of environmental policy, as in many other policy areas, there has been a flow of power away from the States and toward the Federal government in the latter half of the Twentieth century. Prior to the 1970s, the determination of air and water standards and the enforcement of those standards were left to the States. These State programs were largely ineffective because States not only lacked the resources and expertise to design and enforce such standards; they were also reluctant to impose effective environmental constraints for fear of losing industry to other States. It was generally feared (with reason) that strict environmental standards in a State might induce industries to locate in other States where environmental standards were less constraining and less costly. Consequently, in the 1970s, Congress assumed much of the environmental authority that previously resided in the States (Kneese and Schultze, 1975). The Congressional assumption of environmental responsibility, however, was a violation of conservative ideology that prefers State, rather than Federal responsibility.

Environmental policy is very conducive to centralization at the Federal level since environmental problems cross State boundaries. For example, the Mississippi River touches the borders of ten States in the U.S. If Louisiana, at the mouth of the Mississippi River and down river from the other nine, passed the most stringent environmental laws in the U.S. concerning pollution of the Mississippi, the laws would be completely ineffective in remedying pollution of the River if the nine other States bordering the Mississippi up river were not equally diligent. Obviously, no one State of the ten can unilaterally keep the Mississippi clean and the intervention of a larger entity (the Federal government) is necessary to ensure that the River is not polluted. Similarly, the very rural State of Delaware cannot have clean air if the very urban out-of-State cities of Washington and Baltimore to the West and Philadelphia to the North do not take measures to ensure clean air. Dirty air from D.C., Maryland, or Pennsylvania does not turn around and go back when it flies over the Delaware border. As a consequence, the conservative calls for a return to State, rather than Federal authority in environmental regulation are doomed to failure.

The interstate nature of some environmental problems (namely, air, water, and solid waste pollution) has led to Federal preemptions of State authority in numerous areas. The Clean Air Act, Clean Water Act, and CERCA are all cases where the Federal government has preempted State authority to create a minimum national standard. Under these acts, States are given the flexibility to impose tighter environmental standards than the minimum required by the national government and in such cases State action supplants national action; however, if the States do not act, then the national government will do so (Wells, 1996, 28). Consequently, in addition to the Federal EPA, there are agencies with jurisdiction over environmental protection within each State. The Federal structure has led to great variations in environmental laws from State to State reflecting the local politics of each State. States must submit enforcement plans to the EPA for their approval. Upon EPA approval, States may then administer their own environmental programs; however, if a State fails to meet Federal standards, the EPA may take over enforcement responsibilities in that State and impose penalties on the State.

In recent years as the Federal government retreated from aggressive environmental regulations due to the Republican "Revolution." Furthermore, The State role in environmental protection may expand even further in the near future due to the ruling of the U.S. Supreme Court in *New York v. United States* (112 S.Ct. 2408, 2428, 1992) that struck down a provision of the Federal Radioactive Waste Policy Amendments Act of 1985. The Court ruled that Congress could not "commandeer" the legislative and administrative processes of State governments and could not "coerce" States into enacting regulations for the disposal of its own waste. Since "coercion" of State governments in the area of environmental protection has been common practice by the Federal government prior to the *New York v. U.S.* case, the ruling has the potential effectively alter the State-Federal relationship in such a way that States must assume more responsibility for environmental protection. Thus far, the Executive Branch has not adhered strictly to the ruling, but if it does in the future, the result will undoubtedly be different environmental standards in different States and downward pressure placed on environmental regulations in the States as businesses threaten to flee to the States with the least stringent environmental standards. A collection of fifty "least common denominator" policies that no one really wants are the likely results.

Anti-Environmental Interest Groups

Given the trade-off between the environment and virtually all economic activities, a myriad of business groups are often working in opposition to the political efforts of pro-environmental groups. Mining companies can be expected to oppose strict land reclamation laws that force them to return land to its original condition after mining operations have ceased. Oil companies can be expected to oppose laws that increase their responsibility for cleanup in cases of oil spills and other oil-related environmental degradation. Automobile manufacturers can be expected to oppose tighter emission controls. The list of economic interests that stand to lose in the face of tighter environmental regulations is as broad as the scope of the economy. Consequently, the budgets and memberships of environmental groups are dwarfed by the size of their business opposition. If all of these business groups (who tend to be decidedly conservative) get their way and environmental regulations are reduced, the result can only be environmental degradation.

A good illustration of what happens when big business conservative anti-environmentalists get their way is the case of Texas and the Clean Air Act of 1971. When the Texas Clean Air Act was passed in 1971, existing power plants, refineries, and chemical plants were "grandfathered" and exempted from compliance with the law. By 1998, these grandfathered industrial facilities were responsible for 36% of Texas' air pollution, as much ozone pollution-causing chemicals as eighteen-million automobiles (Miller, 2002, 172). This thirty-year trend of exemptions from environmental laws in Texas has resulted in Texas being rated last of the 50 States in environmental protection (Maxwell and Crain, 2003). Under conservative governor George W. Bush in the 1990s, Texas had the nation's highest volume of air pollution, with the highest ozone levels of any State. Furthermore, Texas was the nation's leading source of greenhouse gases, accounting for 14% of the U.S.

total while boasting only 7% of the U.S. population (Miller, 2002, 168).

As if that is not enough, to these business-oriented anti-environmental groups opposed to environmental regulation should be added ideological conservative "Property Rights" groups that lobby for compensation for property owners when government environmental regulations adversely impact a property's fair market value. A prime example of such an environmental regulation opposed by these groups would be a governmental action that designates an area a "wetlands" and assigns it protection that precludes commercial development, thus preventing the owner from its full commercial potential (Bosso, 2000, 60).

Finally, ideologically conservative "Wise-Use" groups have arisen, especially in the American West, that oppose the protection of natural habitats against hunting, fishing, grazing, mining, logging, and other commercial and recreational uses. "Wise-Use" groups are typically Libertarian in their outlook, skeptical of government, and in favor of unlimited property rights for property owners. Some "Wise Use" advocates believe that Federal environmental laws are part of a "conspiracy" to restrict property rights (and rights in general) that will eventually lead to military occupation of the U.S. by the United Nations (Bosso, 2000, 61). This is obviously a shining example of the "plot mentality" that pervades the more extreme conservative ideologies. On the surface, these groups would appear to be "fringe" groups that are unrepresentative of most Americans; however, Wise-Use groups have significant success in Western States. No less than five Republicans on the House Committee on Resources in the 105th Congress were members of a "Wise-Use" group called People for the West that purported to have 23,000 members (Ferry, 1997).

Congress and Environmental Policy

Since the "environmental Revolution" of the 1970s, Congress has been a primary instrument for the formulation of environmental policy. Congressional leadership in environmental policy is anathema to "States rights" conservatives despite the fact that Congress is empowered under the U.S. Constitution to regulate interstate commerce, and commerce power implies that Congress may also regulate environmental concerns, since environmental protection and commerce are so inextricably linked. Congress also is responsible for appropriating the funds that are necessary to implement environmental policy and therefore may create bureaucratic agencies and charge those agencies with environmental policy administration. Congress then has a duty perform oversight roles over the executive agencies that they create for environmental protection. In short, Congress is empowered by the Constitution to make laws governing the environment, establish and oversee a set of government agencies to enforce the rules, and authorize either the Federal Courts or some other Federal agency to hear claims and enforce its rules. Given these Congressional powers and responsibilities under the U.S. Constitution, popular movement and new public environmental awareness of the 1960s quickly focused on Congress and transformed itself into Congressional action in the 1970s.

Congress assumed a leadership role in environmental policy with bipartisan support in the 1970s through the enactment of a flood of environmental legislation that reflected public concerns over the environment. The "environmental decade" of the 1970s began with a splash on January 1st, 1970, with Republican President Richard Nixon's signing of the National Environmental Policy Act (NEPA). This Act requires Federal agencies to consider environmental factors in agency planning and decision-making and analyze and report on the environmental impacts of their activities. In essence, the act makes all Federal agencies responsible for environmental protection. In order to ensure that Federal agencies would be in compliance with NEPA, Congress created the Council on Environmental Quality to exercise environmental oversight over the Federal bureaucracy and advise the President on environmental compliance (Paniccia, 1996, 15).

Also in 1970, Congress passed the Occupational Safety and Health Act, which created the Occupational Safety and Health Administration (OSHA). OSHA is not only concerned with workplace safety, but was also empowered under the Act to regulate toxic chemicals in the workplace that could endanger the health of workers such as asbestos and cotton dust (Shabecoff, 1993).

In his State of the Union message of 1970, Republican President Nixon broke with conservative ideologues and business groups and declared that air and water pollution legislation would be the cornerstones of his environmental policy. Nixon correctly sensed that the mood of the voting public at the time was in favor of greater environmental protection (Crispino, 1996, 29). Congress shortly thereafter passed the Clean Air Act (CAA) in 1970, which authorized the Federal government to establish National Ambient Air Quality Standards (NAAQS) to limit levels of pollutants in the air. All areas of the United States must maintain ambient levels of atmospheric pollutants below ceilings established by NAAQS (U.S. Department of Energy. 1996).

The environmental "revolution" of 1970 was topped off in December of that year by the creation of the Environmental Protection Agency (EPA), again at the direction of the Nixon Administration. The EPA was created through a reorganization of 15 existing Federal health and regulatory agencies from five different departments that were combined to form one new agency that was to become the Federal government's most important tool in the fight against environmental degradation. The EPA was immediately charged with promulgation of the Clean Air Act and established NAAQS for six different atmospheric pollutants. The EPA also banned DDT within 120 days of its creation (U.S. Department of Energy, 1996).

After the creation of the EPA, Congress passed a series of laws that expanded the agency's responsibilities. The EPA was charged with not only establishment of environmental guidelines, but also with explanation of environmental laws. identification of environmental hazards, education of the public in the areas of environmental protection, and enforcement of environmental standards (U.S. Department of Energy, 1996).

The expansion of Congressional and Federal Bureaucratic responsibilities in environmental protection was abhorrent to Conservative "laissez-faire" and "States' rights" ideology. As a consequence, Congressional initiative in environmental protection during the 1980s became much more subdued due to the election of conservative Republican President Ronald Reagan and a changing political climate that became more conservative and anti-regulatory in general. President Reagan and his followers consequently initiated a retreat from environmental protection by the Federal government driven by their laissez-faire "anti-regulatory" ideology. During the first two years of Reagan's leadership, the budget for the Council on Environmental Quality was reduced 50% and the EPA budget was cut 29% (Paniccia, 1996, 17). Federally sponsored research programs in the areas of alternative fuels and solar energy were discontinued, and White House officials made it clear that environmental regulations already on the books were not going to be vigorously enforced (Sale, 1993).

Despite these Reagan-Revolution anti-regulatory efforts of the 1980s, Congress, with a majority Democratic House of Representatives, proved to be firmly entrenched in environmental protection. Part of the reason for this is due to continued public demands for Federal intervention in major cases involving environmental degradation. For example, in 1985, essentially during the middle of the Reagan era, a Harris poll revealed that 80% of Americans supported the Federal environmental regulations and standards that existed at the time (Sale, 1993). Despite some definite shifting of political winds and conservative rhetoric to the contrary, it appears that what the American people wanted was not "less Federal government regulation" in the area of the environment, even if "less Government in general" remained the banner of the day.

One of the most important methods of policy evaluation is analysis of expenditures. Through examination of governmental budgets, one can at least understand how resources are being allocated and make some reasonable assessment of policy directions and trends. Although it is obvious that spending in any policy area does not necessarily equal success, it is also obvious that success is rarely achieved without some allocation of resources to the problem. Environmental problems are no exception. Since the environmental "revolution" of the 1970s, Federal spending on environmental programs has remained fairly constant, but was reduced during the conservative Reagan backlash.

In 1975, Federal agencies involved in environmental protection were appropriated $21.618 billion (in 1998 dollars). In 1985, during the Reagan backlash, that figure dropped 6.5% to $20.213 billion (in 1998 dollars). Specifically, "areas pollution control" declined 17% and "water infrastructure spending" declined 37% (United States Office of Management and Budget, 1999).

Conservatives tend to argue that due to government "waste," the government may accomplish the same tasks even if its budget is cut; therefore, whether or not the government is accomplishing its objectives with the reduced budget is another subject that requires evaluation. In one sense, evaluation of environmental policies is difficult. Essentially, one can never say for sure how dirty the air, water, soil, etc. might be without the policies that are in place. If the most important objective test of any policy is whether it improves the human condition, the questions should be asked as to whether air and water quality are improving, and whether hazardous waste sites are becoming less hazardous. If the answer to these questions is affirmative, then the question of whether the achieved results were worth the cost should be answered. The answer to this question, obviously, leaves room for a great deal of subjectivity since exactly how much environmental protection is expedient at what cost perhaps can never be answered definitively. Consequently, the political struggle between environmentalists and their opponents can be expected to continue indefinitely; nevertheless, there are empirical measures of pollution that can be utilized to assess to some degree whether the struggle to save the environment is being won or lost.

A 1995 study from the Natural Resources Defense Council concluded that 53 million Americans (roughly one fifth of the population) drank water that did not meet the requirements of the Clean Water Act. Consequently, although gains have been made in the fight against water pollution, the objective of safe water in all places for all uses has not yet been realized (Kraft and Vig, 2000, 22). Consequently, it is difficult to support the Conservatives' call for lower environmental budgets, less regulation and less governmental intervention since the "less government" approach evidently has not achieved success.

Clean water, however, is not the only area where government efforts have been found wanting. Environmental policies on solid wastes, for example, have been even less successful than policies directed at clean air and water. Cleanup of toxic waste sites on the EPA's Superfund National Priorities List (NPL) has been slow and costly. The average cost of cleanup at an NPL site has been approximately $30 million and the results often have been in dispute. As of 2000, only 509 of the 1400 NPL sites had been fully cleaned up and cleanup of remaining sites that do not meet EPA standards was expected to cost between $500 million and $1 trillion dollars and take until 2050 to complete before George W. Bush was elected President (Kraft and Vig, 2000, 22). Critics from the left argue that the cleanup has been much too slow, while critics from the right tend to argue that the cleanup has been much too costly. Furthermore, the cleanup of superfund sites has actually slowed under the George W. Bush administration. More than eighty Superfund sites were cleaned up each year during the second term of the Administration of President Bill Clinton. In contrast, in the first year of the George W. Bush administration, only 47 sites had been cleaned up and number dropped to 40 for each of the next two years (*New York Times*, 2/24/02)

In the area of global warming and the production of greenhouse gases, it is most difficult to determine precisely what the impact of Federal policies has been; however, the EPA estimates that the presence of greenhouse gases would be up to 150% higher by the year 2100 if the EPA had not imposed emission control standards. This suggests that the EPA's policies are somewhat effective, even if they have thus far failed to completely put a halt to the process of global warming (www.epa.gov/globalwarming/climate/index.html).

Perhaps the environmental gains would even be greater if Conservatives did not push for weak Federal penalties on environmental law violators. The fact that the penalties for violations are weak is born out by the fact that noncompliance with Federal regulations in some areas is rampant. In 1983, for example, the U.S. General Accounting Office (GAO) compared the actual discharges of a sample of water polluters with the permissible discharges and found that 82% of the sources studies were in noncompliance and 24% were in "significant noncompliance" (GAO, 1983). Similarly, the GAO found in 1994 that one in six major industrial and municipal sources inspected under the Clean water Act were in significant violation (GAO, 1996). Obviously, the burden to many entities for compliance with Federal regulations is more reprehensible than the costs of Federal penalties. Consequently environmentalists continue to argue that the current gains in environmental protection are insufficient and greater penalties are needed to ensure compliance. Conversely, polluting entities (read as "conservatives") continue to argue that the costs of meeting Federal standards are too high.

Chapter 8
Conservatism and Healthcare

On any given day, over 43 million Americans have no healthcare coverage at all and lack the resources to secure proper care on their own (Center for Budget and Policy Priorities, 12/22/2003). To make matters worse, due to State government budget cuts in Medicaid and other healthcare programs since the inauguration of George W. Bush in 2001, 1.6 million low-income people lost their publicly funded health insurance since January 2001 (Center for Budget and Policy Priorities, 12/22/03). Approximately 30% of U.S. citizens lack basic healthcare, and roughly 2/3 of those lacking in basic care have jobs (Waltzman, 1991). In the words of national health economist Uwe Reinhardt (1989), "Uniquely in the industrialized world…American healthcare exhibits opulent splendor and shocking deprivation side by side." This inequality in the American healthcare system is reflective of Classic Liberal free market ideology in that the free market (as discussed in chapter 2) by its very nature produces income inequality. That income inequality in a free market system then translates itself into inequality of healthcare, and this inequality of care makes American healthcare unique among Western industrialized democracies.

The American healthcare system is unique in a number of other important respects. The U.S. system is distinguished by the fact that it is more market-oriented and less governmental than in any other developed democracy, a reflection of America's Classic Liberal traditions. The American system is also unique in that Americans tend to be more adamant than those in most other countries about retaining their individual rights in relation to healthcare, perhaps most conspicuously the right to choose one's own doctor, reflective of America's conservative individualism. The U.S. system is also unique in that it has a greater percentage of specialists among its physicians, and greater investment in medical research than any country in the world, resulting in perhaps the world's finest technology as well as some of the best trained physicians in the world, but also the highest costs (Skocpol, 1992, 15-23).

This investment in medical research, along with the free market democracy and individualist ideology has created, however, a reliance on medical technology that is unparalleled anywhere in the world. American doctors have greater access to, and are therefore more likely to use expensive technology such as magnetic resonance imagery (MRI) machines, computerized axial tomography (CAT) scanners, and kidney dialysis machines. The twin results are that overall medical costs are driven upward, and those who lack the ability to pay may be denied life-perpetuating treatment.

In conflict with conservative "every man for himself ideology," however, Americans generally tend to support the notion that potentially life-saving technologies should be available to everyone regardless of costs. In a true free market system, those that could not afford healthcare would simply be denied care and die. This would be the free market "solution" to the healthcare crisis that conservatives so relish if the system were not infused with some sort of governmental intervention to distribute healthcare to the poor.

Despite this unpleasant reality, however, Americans typically remain true to their Classic Liberal heritage and believe that the free market and democracy will provide the best means to accomplish their healthcare goals. As a consequence, the healthcare system in the U.S. is predominantly a private system with nongovernmental entities providing a significant portion of the funds necessary to support the system. The U.S. and South Africa are the only two industrialized countries in the world where the governmental portions of healthcare funding are less than 60% (Reagan, 1992). Furthermore, healthcare services in the U.S. are normally provided by private entities, although community health centers and county health departments provide a small percentage of care with government employees and facilities.

Conservative Ideology and Healthcare Policy

Ideology may impact views on a myriad of subjects, the proper public/private relationship of healthcare being only one, but in the case of healthcare. ideology may have serious consequences as it constrains public perceptions and choices concerning the appropriate role of government in healthcare.

Since the American Revolution, when the republic was born at least partially out of a revolt against intrusive government, Americans have tended to embrace an ideology that favors free market solutions and opposes governmental intrusions. Healthcare is not an exception to these ideological restrictions (Stillman, 1991).

Healthcare in the U.S., however, is also big business in a free market democracy. The U.S. healthcare system employs over 500,000 doctors and millions of nurses, technicians, and administrators as part of a $1.5 Trillion industry (Pear, 2004). As such, much of healthcare policy will be shaped by competing groups (some ideological, but many with vested interests) who compete for the most favorable policies for their particular group. What is beneficial for one group may not be beneficial for another, and may not necessarily be the most beneficial policy for the greatest number of Americans. For example, one could expect doctors and insurance companies to favor universal healthcare coverage since it would mean more business for both, but doctors can be expected to oppose governmental limitations on fees while insurance companies may favor them since it is they who will ultimately pay the bills. Both healthcare providers and payers may be resistant to providing care to those who lack the ability to pay, but access to care for all Americans, regardless of wealth, may best serve the common good.

Government and Healthcare in the U.S.

The idea that healthcare is a governmental responsibility is not new. The Law of Moses found in the Bible, containing numerous provisions concerning sanitation and quarantine, is a testimony to that fact. Governmental involvement in health in North America (including government entitlements in healthcare) has also been around almost as long as European settlement in North America.

The first government involvement in healthcare in North America took place in the Massachusetts Bay Colony in 1636 when the settlement of Plymouth, Massachusetts, passed a law that stated that any soldier who was wounded by Indians would be taken care of for life by the Colony. Thus, the first governmental involvement in healthcare (and healthcare entitlement) in

North America arose out of a societal obligation to address the needs of its military veterans, an obligation that still involves North American Governments in healthcare almost four centuries later.

In the eighteenth century, governmental involvement in healthcare in North America remained a local, rather than national, responsibility, reflecting the conservative ideological preference for local, rather than national responsibility. As such, Eighteenth Century governmental involvement in healthcare was primarily directed at preventing the spread of epidemics through quarantines. The first of these efforts occurred in the Massachusetts Bay Colony in 1701 with the passage of legislation requiring the quarantine of smallpox patients.

The first governmental involvement in healthcare after the Colonies became the United States occurred shortly after the U.S. gained its independence from England, and followed the path established by the Massachusetts Bay Colony at the beginning of the 18th century. In response to a yellow fever epidemic of the 1790s, some of the States passed legislation that enabled cities to create municipal Boards of Health. The early Boards of Health were largely occupied with matters of quarantines in major port cities in efforts to prevent epidemics. Gradually, their attention spread to issues of sanitation in public baths and slaughterhouses as well as the immense volume of street refuse in the horse-drawn transportation societies (US Department of Health, Education, and Welfare, 1976, 37-38).

Similar to the situation in Plymouth in 1636, the first Federal involvement in healthcare arose out of a need to address the healthcare needs of its soldiers in the military. The initial Federal government involvement began with the Marine Hospital Service Act of 1798 that created Marine Hospitals in Norfolk, Virginia, and in Boston, Massachusetts, for the purpose of providing healthcare to sick or disabled seamen. Throughout the 19th century Federal involvement would remain limited to a smattering of mostly military related acts.

Despite this Federal involvement, during the 19th century, epidemics that were transmitted through water and food supplies were rampant. In general, people were ignorant of how diseases were spread, and as a consequence, human and animal waste was often found in drinking water supplies and factories generally provided water for their employees in the form of open barrels into which all employees dipped their unsanitized cups. Under such conditions, the city of New Orleans alone had over thirty epidemics of yellow fever during the 19th century, and epidemics of deadly diseases such as cholera, typhus, and smallpox, were common (Mckinlay and McKinlay, 1980, 3-14). The leading causes of death in 1900 were influenza, pneumonia, tuberculosis, and gastroenteritis. Infant mortality was 20% and only 50% of children lived to the age of five. Due to the high infant and child mortality rate, life expectancy was only thirty-six years for the upper classes, and as low as sixteen for some types of manual laborers (McKinlay and McKinlay, 1980).

In 1906, the publication of Upton Sinclair's *The Jungle*, which chronicled the unsanitary conditions of the U.S. meat packing industry at the turn of the century where a large percentage of the meat being packaged was unfit for human consumption, led to the passage of the Meat Inspection Act. The Meat Instpection Act in turn committed the Federal government to monitoring the quality and safety of meat sold in the U.S. The same year, (at the urging of President Theodore Roosevelt) Congress also passed the Pure Food and Drug Act, which protected the public from fraudulently marketed and dangerous foods and medications.

In 1912, President Theodore Roosevelt, made national government health insurance a major plank of his platform in the Bull-Moose party. Roosevelt failed to win the Presidency and his Bull-Moose party died with that failed bid, but the idea of government health insurance had been placed on the political agenda and would never be completely removed.

In the 1930s, President Franklin Roosevelt's "New Deal" included a proposal for government-subsidized healthcare as a precursor to the eventual development of some form of National Health Insurance. The AMA (American Medical Association) and the AHA (American Hospital Association), however, lobbied extensively to prevent any alteration of the fee-for-service model. Instead, the medical lobby, reflective of conservative ideologies, argued for a less socialistic solution and pushed Congress for Federal money for the construction of new Federal facilities (under the pretense that more facilities meant better access). As a result, the Hill-Burton Act of 1946 (or Hospital Survey and Construction Act) was passed, authorizing Federal dollars for the construction of hospitals. The purpose of the Act was to increase the number of hospitals nationwide, but especially in rural areas, essentially by providing an increase in available hospital beds all across the U.S. in an attempt to increase access to healthcare for all Americans. The Act was supported in Congress not only by both the AMA and the AHA, who were happy to get new facilities, but by Congressmen in rural areas (rural Congressmen are typically conservative) who were happy to get Federal dollars and the accompanying economic benefits in their districts (Murrin, 1996, 887).

In 1948, Democratic President Harry Truman included national healthcare legislation as part of his program known as the "Fair Deal" (Hamby, 1973). Truman viewed a national healthcare plan as a natural extension of the New Deal from the previous decade. Truman's national healthcare legislation, however, failed to pass in Congress due to opposition from conservatives ideologically opposed to another government program, the medical community who feared governmental cost controls, and the twin perceptions that American medicine was the best in the world and that the Hill-Burton Act would solve any problem that plagued nation's healthcare system.

Healthcare and health-related legislation exploded in the 1960s and 1970s with a Democratic Congress and the passage of over 70 separate Acts that were related to health. Perhaps the most important of these included Medicare and Medicaid, which were signed into law in 1965 by Democratic President Lyndon Johnson to provide government health insurance for the elderly and the indigent. With the passage of Medicare and Medicaid, Congress was primarily attempting to provide a remedy to the problem of inadequate healthcare coverage, rather than costs. Medicare is both hospitalization insurance for the elderly and a supplementary medical insurance. The hospitalization insurance is financed from a payroll tax on employers and employees and the supplementary insurance that covers physicians fees and other healthcare services is financed (1/3) through the payment of premiums by subscribers and from the Federal government's general funds (2/3). Medicaid is a joint Federal and State program that is administered by the States with Federal matching funds to cover the costs of healthcare for low-income families.

While Medicare and Medicaid helped fill a pair of major gaps in healthcare coverage, many of the other acts of Congress in the 1960s and 1970s were aimed at controlling costs or were prevention-oriented. Among the most important of these was the creation by Congress in 1972 of the Professional Standards Review Organizations, under which doctors would review the practices of other doctors to ensure that services paid for by Medicare were necessary and within customary practice in terms of costs (Goodman, 1980, 124-128). In another effort to limit costs, the following year Congress passed the HMO Act, which created Health Maintenance Organizations, and in 1974, the National Health Planning and Resources

Development Act. In 1983, the Prospective Payment System for hospital reimbursement and the Diagnostic Related Groups (DRGs) were created. DRGs were charged with determining the fair and reasonable charges for hundreds of healthcare treatments, and thus hold costs down by eliminating excessive charges by healthcare providers.

A number of other Congressional Acts were passed with either cost-controlling or prevention-oriented goals. These include, but are not limited to, the prohibition of saccharin, legislation encouraging medical school expansion, and new laws concerning clean air and workplace safety, consumer product safety laws, safe drinking water, the Noise Control Act of 1972, and the Hazardous Material Transportation Act of 1974. Much like the 1906 response to the links between poor sanitation and disease, greater knowledge concerning the links between toxic chemicals and diseases was instrumental in producing new government healthcare initiatives (Bardach and Kagan, 1982).

Escalating Healthcare Costs

The results of these efforts to control costs thus far are perhaps disappointing as reflected in the continued upward spiral of medical costs throughout the 1980s and 1990s. The healthcare situation illuminates a flaw in the conservative laissez-faire ideology. In a nutshell, healthcare does not well-fit with supply and demand free market economics due to inelasticity of demand. Public demand for healthcare is virtually unlimited, and that demand is often unrelated to costs or prices. In other words, those who are sick desire whatever treatment is available, regardless of costs; thus increased costs do not depress demand in healthcare as they would other basic goods and services. Furthermore, since in a pure free market system there would be thousands that could not afford healthcare (and therefore would not receive it), the laissez-faire conservative solution of the "free market" would essentially solve the problems by letting those that could not afford care go without it and die. This would be the conservative free-market approach, but it certainly would not be "compassionate."

It must be remembered that the healthcare industry in the U.S. is a $1.5 Trillion per year industry; hence, insurance companies, doctors, hospitals, and pharmaceutical manufacturers have vested interests in any changes in healthcare policy and therefore organize to pressure lawmakers toward policies that serve their interests. It is these "stakeholders" that perhaps have the greatest interest in the healthcare system and the most to lose if there are radical alterations to the system. Obviously, there would be significant damage to private insurance companies if the Federal government suddenly provided government health insurance to all Americans. Consequently, one could expect private insurers to oppose any initiative to create a single-payer system with government health insurance. Private health insurance companies, however, may not always oppose government intervention. For example, private insurance carriers might support measures that are aimed at controlling doctor and hospital fees; conversely, doctors and hospitals are likely to oppose such measures. The healthcare industry is a rapidly growing industry that accounts for over 15% of U.S. GNP, the largest such system among industrialized democracies; meaning, healthcare in the U.S. is also costly (Pear, 2004). The U.S. spends approximately $5300 per capita, about 55% more than Canada and almost double the per capita amount spent on healthcare by Germany and France, despite the fact that Germany, France, and Canada all have universal healthcare coverage and the U.S. does not (OECD, 2004). Not only is healthcare expensive, but the costs of healthcare in the U.S. increased much faster than inflation from 1970 through the present. In 2002 while the American economy was mired in a recession following the 9/11 terrorist attacks, Health costs in the U.S. increased 9.3% (Pear, 2004).

The reasons for the rapidly escalating costs of healthcare in the U.S. are numerous, but the most identifiable culprits are perhaps the aging of the population, the high costs of technology, the third-party payer system, increased poverty, increased inequality, and the accompanying social disorder that includes, but is not limited to, the AIDS epidemic. To make matters worse, some Congressional attempts to remedy the problems of cost and coverage have thus far been unsuccessful in accomplishing their goals. We will deal with each of these matters below, beginning with the failed government policies.

There are perhaps numerous reasons that Congressional attempts to control costs have often failed to accomplish their goals; however, some of the failure is attributable to the conflict between costs and coverage. In general, Congressional efforts to increase coverage may also have the undesirable consequence of increased costs. A contributing factor to this problem is the structure of Congress that is generally conducive to a type of interest group pluralism where policies reflect the influence of competing groups. Additionally, the American political climate generally is more favorable toward conservative, market-oriented, rather than socialistic reforms. This is somewhat problematic since it places an ideological, rather than practical, limitation on options. It is also problematic due to the aforementioned fact that the healthcare industry has a good measure of inelasticity of demand and therefore does not well fit within the free market supply and demand model. In other words, those who need healthcare can be expected to seek it when it is available without regard for costs. A good illustration of the problems of market-oriented, pluralist reforms is he Hill-Burton Act, which was implemented in 1946 for the purpose of increasing rural access to hospital care.

Hill-Burton Act and Costs

In 1951, five years after the passage of the Hill-Burton Act, a Presidential Commission on Healthcare Needs found that, rural residents, ethnic minorities, and persons with low income, were still much less likely to receive adequate medical care. Furthermore, infant mortality in the U.S. lagged behind those of other industrialized countries—including many of the States of Europe that had been ravaged by World War II within the previous decade (Murrin, 887). Clearly, five years after the passage of the Act, its primary goals had yet to be accomplished. As a consequence, the Hill-Burton Act, which had been viewed by Congress and the healthcare community as the best solution to the problem, quickly developed its critics. It was argued that the Hill-Burton Act contributed to bureaucratization and depersonalization of medical care since on-staff doctors in the hospitals sometimes replaced the functions of the traditional family doctors. Secondly, it is possible that the increased number of facilities also contributed to increased costs through an increase in unnecessary medical treatments and surgeries. The use of hospitals almost doubled between 1947 and 1974 and the value of hospital assets increased from under $6 billion to over $50 billion.

In reaction to the spiraling costs, by the 1960's the majority in Congress had come to view the Hill-Burton Act with a significant degree of skepticism. As a result, in 1964 the Hill-Burton Act was amended in an attempt to contain the expanding hospital usage and costs. The 1964 Amendments established local health facility planning councils that were purposed to survey local healthcare needs and determine whether new hospital facilities were indeed necessary. In 1966, Congress took their alteration of the Hill-Burton Act a step further and additional comprehensive health planning agencies were created to assess not only hospital needs, but other local healthcare needs as well (Thompson, 1981).

The Amendments to the Hill-Burton Act were unsuccessful, however, in containing the growth of hospitalization usage and costs, both of which continued to spiral upward during the decade following the Amendments to the Act. As a result, in 1974, Congress passed the Health Planning Resources and Development Act (HPRDA) in a further attempt to slow the growth of hospital costs. HPRDA created over 200 Health Systems Agencies (HSA's) that were purposed not only to assess health resources in their specified local areas, but also to establish sets of healthcare priorities and goals as well as establish five year plans for meeting those goals. HPRDA established National health planning guidelines that called for a maximum of four hospital beds per 1,000 persons in any community with an 80% occupancy rate. HSAs were given the authority to prevent hospital expansion in terms of bed capacity or equipment expenditures if they concluded that the expansion was not needed in their local area. Despite this unprecedented invasive authority, HSA guidelines did not result in a drastic reduction in the growth of hospital costs and usage. Resistance to HSA guidelines by the hospital community led to the approval of over 90% of requests for new hospital facilities that were submitted to HSAs between 1975 and 1980. In the final analysis, the Hill-Burton Act, even after the passage of the Health Planning Resources and Development Act, had been successful only in increasing hospital usage and costs, but not in increasing access for the poor living in rural areas (Thompson, 1981).

Technology and Healthcare Costs

Coterminously, the growth of technology in medicine and the accompanying high-tech equipment and procedures have produced rapidly escalating costs. New technological advancements essentially create their own demand. In other words, as soon as new equipment, drugs, or procedures become available, there is a tendency among both doctors and patients to rush to use them. For example, MRI machines were just introduced in the mid 1980s, but by 1990, MRIs alone cost healthcare payers approximately $5 billion for over 5 million scans performed on America's over 2,000 MRI machines. Per capita, by 1990, the U.S. had four times as many MRIs as Germany and eight times as many as Canada, a pair of "socialized medicine" systems that conservatives eschew (Pollack, 1991). The positive to this is that there are more machines available to those that need them, but the obvious negative is that costs are greatly increased.

It is possible that the U.S. has invested more in MRI machines than is necessary; however, the proliferation of the new technology can be largely attributed to competition between hospitals both to attract the most patients and the best doctors by offering the most up-to-date machinery (Pollack, 1991). Additionally, MRI machines require a major capital investment of between $1.2 and $2.5 million dollars. This rather large investment places pressure on the owners of MRIs to do as many scans as possible in an effort to recoup the investment as quickly as possible. Thus, technology will be used whenever it is available, and perhaps at times when the necessity of its use is questionable. To compound the matter further, numerous MRI "imaging centers" are owned at least in part by doctors, creating a conflict of interest when doctors receive income for the tests that they have ordered. According to Pollack (1991), the majority of "imaging centers" in both Florida and Georgia were owned by the same doctors that ordered the MRI scans.

New technologies may produce other secondary costs that are related to, but separate from, the cost of the technology itself. For example, new technologies, such as MRI machines, require the training of individuals to operate them and therefore create new labor costs within the healthcare industry. More complex equipment tends to require more intensive labor; as a consequence, the number of registered nurses per hospital patient doubled from a one to two ratio in 1972, to a one to one ratio in 1987 (Reagan, 1992, 71). Finally, new technology may also induce potential patients into undergoing medical procedures that they might have avoided in the past because new technology has created new procedures or made them safer or less invasive. When all of these factors are considered, it appears that the conservative laissez-faire approach to healthcare has only produced higher costs due to free market "competition."

Poverty and Costs

Another contributor to the high healthcare costs in the U.S. is the increasing poverty and social disorder. In the last quarter-century since the Reagan Revolution, the United States has moved away from the Social Welfare State model and closer to the laissez-faire free market model espoused by conservatives. Not surprisingly, the free market oriented approach has created a greater number of impoverished Americans and greater income inequality. Furthermore, America has not only spawned more poor, but the poor have gotten poorer. For example, during the 1980s, the wealthiest 1% of Americans experienced an 80% income increase, while the bottom 90% of the American income structure experienced an increase of only 3% (Sanders, 1997, 19). In 1973, U.S. workers were the highest paid in the world, by 1997, they ranked 13th. Adjusted for inflation, the average pay for 80% of American workers fell 16% from 1973 to 1993. Eighteen percent of full time jobs do not pay enough to enable workers to live above the poverty line. Furthermore, the U.S. now has the highest rate of child poverty of all Western industrialized democracies, with over 20% of America's children living in poverty. Life expectancy for black male children born in New York City's inner-city neighborhoods is lower than for children in Bangladesh (Sanders, 1997, 19). The infant mortality rate among blacks in the U.S. is twice that of whites. Similarly, life expectancy of whites is over seventy-five years while life expectancy for blacks is only sixty-nine.

The increased poverty has manifested itself in the form of increased health problems and therefore increased costs. American urban centers have recently experienced a rash of epidemics of treatable diseases that had virtually been eradicated earlier in this century. In 1982, sixteen babies were born in New York City with syphilis. That figure had risen to 1,017 in 1988. From 1988 to 1990, there was a 15% increase in cases of tuberculosis nationwide, with the growth primarily coming in the poverty stricken neighborhoods of urban areas. The number of measles cases in the U.S. in 1983 was only 1500, but by 1989, it had risen to 17,000 (Rosenthal, 1994, 1). These numbers indicate that urban economically underprivileged persons have poor access to medical care. For example, in order to receive treatment for a sexually transmitted disease in Washington, DC, a person has to be in the clinic before 9:30 a.m. and can expect to wait most of the day. The standard wait to schedule a pediatric appointment in inner city clinics is several months (Rosenthal, 1994, 9). Furthermore, the overcrowded nature of the inner city clinic means that the healthcare providers focus on treatment of acute illnesses and ignore routine preventive care such as pap smears, mammograms, and vaccinations. What these problems have translated into are higher inner city death rates. Only 30% of women diagnosed with breast cancer at Harlem Hospital live five years, compared to 70% of white women nationwide (Rosenthal, 1994, 9). Conservative ideology that holds that the poor should take care of themselves places downward pressure on programs helping the poor and thus resulting in healthcare problems for the poor and higher costs for all Americans.

There are other factors that exacerbate the situation as well. Crowded conditions, substandard housing, and poor sanitation all contribute to increased health problems. In a study conducted at Boston City Hospital, it was concluded that "indoor pollution" was a leading cause of high rates of asthma and other diseases among the poor. The greatest link to asthma was determined to be cigarette smoking by the children's parents (Rosenthal, 1994, 9). In the Boston study it was concluded that urban black children were twice as likely as white children to have asthma. Furthermore, blood lead levels of impoverished urban children were found to be significantly higher than the national average. It is difficult to imagine how the reductions in assistance to the poor favored by conservatives can help remedy this problem of "indoor pollution."

Poverty also has a connection with AIDS. The Congressional Commission on AIDS in 1992 concluded that socioeconomic factors and the poor access to healthcare among the impoverished were linked to the spread of AIDS. By 1993, the proportion of AIDS cases that are attributable to intravenous (IV) drug use was up to 30% in the United States. Furthermore, approximately half of all AIDS cases involved ethnic minorities (ethnic minorities tend to have lower median incomes than that of the general population). Once again, in the area of AIDS, it appears that conservative laissez-faire policies that oppose public assistance for the poor are a contributor to the high cost of healthcare.

Administrative Healthcare Costs

The majority of the costs of healthcare in the U.S. are covered by employer-provided private health insurance. Approximately 80% of all health insurance in the U.S. is employer provided (Reagan, 1992, 14). The costs of health insurance nationwide are over 25% of the average company's net earnings in the U.S. The private insurance system favored by conservatives results in greater administrative costs. Administrative costs in the U.S. healthcare system are estimated to be over 20% of the total costs, approximately double the administrative costs in Canada and Europe (Waltzman, 1991). The extra costs are related to the fragmentation of the system and its 1500 third-party payers. Insurance paperwork is so staggering that employment in healthcare administration in the U.S. increased over 40% from 1970-1990 (Waltzman, 1991).

Chronic Diseases and Cost

Still another cause of the high cost of healthcare in the U.S. at present is the prevalence of chronic diseases. Chronic diseases are those that are ongoing and incurable, and though in many cases treatable, will thus demand medical attention over long periods of time. There are numerous causes of chronic diseases; however, many chronic diseases, such as emphysema and cirrhosis of the liver, are not communicable, but rather are socially produced. In other words, the diseases are contracted either through usage of chemical substances in society such as tobacco and alcohol or, in the case of many chronic heart disease patients, through unhealthy diets (Rosengren, 1980). The conservative adherence to laissez-faire not only allows these products to be available where there is a market demand, but fails to provide governmental assistance through prevention and abuse programs.

Conservative Control of Healthcare Politics

Between 1980 and 1991, medical community Political Action Committees (PACs) contributed over $60 million to Congressional candidates. PAC contributions from the healthcare industry increased over 50% faster than contributions from other special interests during this period. Thirty percent of the contributions went to members of Congressional Committees with jurisdiction over health-related legislation. Physicians and other healthcare professionals provided 50% of the contributions, Insurance Companies provided over 30%, and the balance came from pharmaceutical companies and other healthcare providers (Kemper and Novak, 1992). Major recipients of healthcare contributions included the Chair of the House Ways and Means subcommittee, Pete Stark D-CA), the ranking Republican on the Senate Medicare subcommittee David Durenberger (R-MN), and Senate Finance Committee Chair Lloyd Bentsen (D-TX). Collectively, members of the Senate Finance Committee (the Committee with jurisdiction over Medicare) received over $200,000 from healthcare Political Action Committees (Kemper and Novak, 1992). In addition to giving directly to candidates, healthcare PACs also give generously to the two major political parties. In 1991, the list of donors giving over $17,000 to one or both of the major political parties included Aetna, Warner-Lambert, the American

Dental Association's PAC, Blue Cross and Blue Shield, Upjohn, and Glaxo (Kemper and Novak, 1992). These donors obviously have a vested interest in opposing any form of government health insurance for the general public.

With such powers opposed to "socialized medicine" or any other radical change to a system that has allowed healthcare revenues to exceed inflation rates for the last three decades, it is little wonder that the current system has remained as is. It should be noted, however, that the healthcare lobby is not without opposition. For example, labor unions have been fairly consistent in their support of a national health insurance program and the AFL-CIO launched a renewed campaign for national health insurance in 1989. Similarly, the American Association of Retired Persons (AARP) in 1989 adopted a position in favor of providing comprehensive care to all Americans, regardless of age (Bacon, 1989).

Additionally, some major U.S. corporations, including, but not limited to Ford, Marriot, AT&T, E.I.du Pont de Nemours, Eastman Kodak, Lockheed, and Northwest Airlines also joined the campaign for socialized medicine (Swoboda, 1990). To some, the political position taken by these major corporations is surprising, since big business is generally thought of as a proponent of free market capitalism; however, it should be remembered that these major corporations are currently shouldering much of the cost of private healthcare insurance that they provide to their employees. In 1989, Chrysler estimated that employee health costs added $700 to the price of each Chrysler automobile (Bacon, 1989). With similar costs born by other industries, it is little wonder that major corporations are searching for alternatives. These significant lobby interests, combined with polls that suggest that the majority of American voters support universal care, even if it means higher taxes, and the fact that 55% of Americans surveyed rated the healthcare crisis as America's biggest problem (McQueen, 1991), undoubtedly led to the decision of President Clinton to make healthcare reform a centerpiece of his 1992 campaign and a main focus early in his Presidency.

Formulating Policy Alternatives: The Clinton Plan

In an attempt to develop a remedy for America's healthcare problems, in January, 1993, President Clinton created a National Healthcare Reform Task Force chaired by First Lady Hillary Clinton. Included on the Task Force were noted healthcare experts from around the country who worked for nine months to compose the healthcare plan that eventually became President Clinton's national healthcare proposal. The Task Force was charged with evaluating all healthcare alternatives and developing the one alternative that would be best for the U.S. Among the preexisting alternatives were the healthcare systems that were already in place in other countries.President Clinton's Healthcare Reform Task Force adopted none of the "socialized medicine" models of Canada and Europe, and instead opted to retain (with modifications) the American "free market" system by the creation of a system with "managed competition."

President Clinton's proposed healthcare plan immediately met stiff opposition from those who expected their vested interests to be threatened under his plan. Undoubtedly, some of those who were likely to lose much of their share of the $800 billion U.S. healthcare industry were the midsized and small insurance companies, many of whom perceived that they would be forced out of business under what was an economies of scale based healthcare alliance system as proposed by the Clinton Administration.

The Health Insurance Association of America (HIAA), a lobby group that represents primarily midsized and small insurance companies who insured approximately one third of those covered by private insurance, immediately began efforts to thwart passage of the Clinton plan (Kosterlitz, 1994, 106-107). In a well-organized campaign that targeted small businesses and senior citizens, the HIAA argued that the Clinton plan would lead to more bureaucracy and unemployment (Kosterlitz, 1992, 707). The HIAA began television advertising in May, 1993, aimed at instilling fears in the minds of the American public concerning the Clinton plan. Playing on American anti-government and free market ideology, one particular ad warned viewers that "mandatory HMO systems" might be "the first step toward socialized medicine" (Kosterlitz, 1992, 107). In August, 1993, the HIAA initiated an estimated $15 million national television advertising campaign that showcased a fictitious, middle-class white couple named Harry and Louise who sat in their home discussing the Clinton healthcare plan. In the ads, Harry and Louise expressed the concern that under the Clinton plan, bureaucrats, not individuals, would be choosing which doctor one would use and young people would see premiums rise to compensate for reductions in rates for older Americans since all Americans would pay the same, "community" rate (Kosterlitz, 1994, 1542). Coterminous with the Harry and Louise ads, the HIAA initiated a multi-million dollar grass-roots lobbying campaign where citizens were implored to pressure their representatives to oppose the Clinton plan (Kosterlitz, 1994, 107).

The HIAA was not, of course, alone in their fight. Instead, they were joined by a host of other groups with vested interests in opposition to the Clinton healthcare plan. The AMA and the AHA (American Hospital Association) also engaged in vigorous grass roots campaigns as did the National Association of Health Underwriters and the Alliance for Managed Competition, a coalition of large insurance companies. The AMA was not opposed to universal coverage, but opposed the Clinton plan because it would place cost controls on fees and give market advantages to physicians who join HMOs. Similarly, the Alliance for Managed Competition favored universal coverage, but opposed government regulations of premiums and the purchasing alliances that could force them to lower premiums (Center for Public Integrity, 1994, 53-54). Meanwhile, small business groups, such as the National Federation of Independent Businesses (NFIB), opposed the Clinton healthcare plan because of the proposed mandates on employers to provide health coverage for all of their employees. These vested-interest groups were joined in the grass roots campaign by ideological groups such as the Christian Coalition, who opposed the Clinton plan on the grounds that it was a step away from the free market (Toner, 1994). In February, 1994, the Christian Coalition announced a $1.4 million grass-roots campaign to oppose the Clinton plan (Toner, 1994, A11). All totaled, it is estimated that over $100 million was spent in lobby efforts either in support of, or against the Clinton healthcare plan (Center for Public Integrity, 1994, 1).

Very quickly, leading Republicans in Congress announced their opposition to the Clinton healthcare plan. Then Republican Whip Newt Gingrich promised to oppose the plan and labeled it an example of costly "big-government inefficiency" (*New York Times*, 1993, E3). Similarly, Representative Dick Armey (R-TX) claimed that the Clinton plan would create 59 new Federal programs, expand 20 others, and impose 79 new Federal mandates that would mean higher taxes, reduced choice and efficiency, longer waits for care, and bigger government (*Wall Street Journal*, 1993). The Republican revolt against the Clinton plan spread rapidly and was picked up immediately by conservative political radio hosts who enthusiastically bashed the Clinton plan (Egan, 1995). Similarly, writings in opposition to the Clinton plan began appearing in mainstream media publications such as *Readers Digest* (Bennett, 1994).

In the end, the anti-reform lobby efforts proved to be successful. Although the majority of Americans had supported the principles of Clinton's healthcare plan when it was announced, by the summer of 1994, polls were showing that the majority of the public had turned against the plan. What the failure of the Clinton healthcare plan illustrates is that the sheer size of the healthcare system is conducive to the creation of powerful political entities with vested interests in the system, and that these vested interest groups will expend tremendous political energy to ensure that they retain the benefits they receive from the system. In essence, the healthcare system in its present form is a result of competition among competing groups purposed to maximize their own vested interests. In that sense, the U.S. healthcare system is a product of free market conservative ideology, but the inelasticity of demand in healthcare violates free market rules of supply and demand and increases costs.

The Free Market and Limitations on Choice

The dominant organization for the implementation of healthcare policies remains the combination of solo-practice doctors in private practice and freestanding hospitals. This organization, however, is undergoing a change in the 1990s toward alternative delivery systems. Individual practices and freestanding hospitals are being replaced by medical groups and chain hospitals. Two types of medical groups that are gaining significant market share are Health Maintenance Organizations (HMOs) and Preferred Provider Organizations (PPOs). HMOs and PPOs are part of a larger rubric of "managed care" that has come to mean imposition by third-party payers into the doctor-patient relationship. In general, this "managed care" has come about as the result of the efforts of third party payers to limit their own costs (Brown, 1985).

In 1973, in an effort to control healthcare costs, Congress passed the Health Maintenance Organization Act, the purpose of which was to introduce competition into the health services delivery system and therefore reduce costs and increase efficiency. Obviously, the HMO Act reflects the conservative free market approach as a solution to healthcare problems with its goal of free market competition.

The HMO Act specified what types of services should be provided by HMOs and required that HMOs hold an open enrollment for thirty days each year. The HMO Act requires that all employers with more than twenty-five employees offer the choice of an HMO if one is available in their area. HMOs are organized by the private insurance carriers as a method for providing services at a lower cost. HMOs include both hospitalization and physician visits as well as other outpatient care. Subscribers to an HMO are limited by the private insurance carrier to seek their healthcare from a closed set of doctors, hospitals, and other providers within the HMO. Doctors and other healthcare providers in the HMO contract with the private insurance carrier to provide treatment for a set fee. Physicians and other healthcare providers within the HMO agree to charge for their services at rates specified by the insurance provider.

The goals of the HMO Act were to provide a remedy for the twin problems of cost and coverage. Once again, however, these goals proved to be in conflict. By introducing competition into healthcare, it was believed that costs would be controlled; however, by forcing open enrollment, the HMO Act prevented the HMOs from being selective and turning away persons that pose significant healthcare risks (as the free market would dictate). Consequently, open enrollment put HMOs at a disadvantage with competitors who could be more selective and avoid covering persons that were greater healthcare risks. Once again, the true free market solution to healthcare would essentially bring the costs down by denying coverage to those that need it most and those that could not afford it. It is difficult to enjoy those lower costs when one is dead for lack of healthcare, and that is essentially what would happen to the poor and those with significant health risks without government intervention into the free market to force HMOs into coverage. Once again, the conservative "free market" ideology ignores healthcare realities.

These "managed care" systems (supposedly consistent with conservative free market principles) have not been without their detractors, even among conservatives. Doctors and patients alike often complain that the decisions that are made concerning healthcare are dictated by their "managed care" organizations. The "managed care" organizations in turn may require second opinions, referrals to specialists for certain procedures, limitations on hospital stays for particular procedures, and disagreements over whether any particular type of care is necessary (Brown, 1985). HMOs, like any other business, must turn a profit in order to stay in business. If the costs of services provided by the HMO are greater than the fees charged for the services, then the HMO, like any other business, loses money, and cannot remain in business indefinitely unless something changes. Consequently, such "meddling" in doctor-patient relationships and the removal of the physicians' exclusive prerogative to provide care is likely to continue as HMOs search for ways to realize profit.

Conservatism and Government Healthcare

Conservatives, however, have not limited themselves to producing bad policies in the areas of private healthcare. Instead, their individualistic ideology has also damaged the healthcare system by limiting governmental healthcare programs from accomplishing their objectives.

Medicaid, for example, the Federal health insurance program for the indigent, is the largest single government program in terms of public expenditures for the poor. As such, Medicaid has aided in the reduction in rates of infant mortality, cervical cancer, diabetes, and flu among the poor since its inception in 1965 (Anderson and Newman, 1982). Despite the fact that the Medicaid program was created to provide access to healthcare for the poor, only 40% of America's poor (those whose income falls below the Federally defined poverty line) qualify for Medicaid due to the Medicaid rules that allow each State government to define its own Medicaid eligibility criteria. This, of course, is reflective of conservatives' preference for State, rather than Federal authority, but clearly inconsistent with the goal of universal coverage.

Unlike Medicare, Medicaid is a "categorical" program under which beneficiaries must also receive Supplemental Security Income or some other sort of welfare benefits or must be an elderly person who has been reduced to poverty by nursing home costs (Bayer and Callahan, 1985, 539). As a result, in 1987, family income had to be less than 38% of the Federally established poverty level in West Virginia, but 82% in New York in order to receive Medicaid (Reagan, 1992, 21).

Medicaid is jointly funded by the Federal government and the States, with the Federal government picking up an estimated 57% of Medicaid costs in 1992; however, the Federal government's share increases as a State's income level decreases under the premise that a poor State is less able to afford the program. In order to receive the funds, however, each State must provide a minimum level of services prescribed by the Federal government. The greater national subsidies to the lower income States have not been sufficient to enable those States to provide much in the way of Medicaid. For example, in Alabama in 1987, a family of four was ineligible for Medicaid if its income was over $1860 per year (Reagan,

1992, 21). The result of such measures is that thousands are left uninsured.

Higher income States have also succumbed to pressure to cut Medicaid benefits in order to avoid becoming a "welfare magnet." In 1982, California restructured its Medicaid benefits with the result that 270,000 people were dropped from Medicaid rolls. The California situation well exemplifies the cost-coverage paradox once again. Michael Reagan (1992) estimates that 5,000 to 10,000 people died annually in California from 1983-1990 as a direct consequence of California's Medicaid cuts. Once again, the conservative free market "return authority to the States" approach appears only to keep down costs at the expense of allowing poor people to die.

The high costs of providing medical treatment to the poor have put downward pressure on the fees of healthcare providers and have led some doctors to refuse to participate in Medicaid. Fees paid by Medicaid have become notoriously low. For example, in 1991, physicians in New York received $15 through Medicaid for an electrocardiogram, whereas Medicare paid $45 and private insurance $100 for the same service. In 1991, only six physicians surveyed by the New York City Health Department indicated that they provided a full range of services in an area of NYC that contained over half a million Medicaid patients (Specter, 1991, 9). In general, it is clear that Medicaid or uninsured patients do not access the healthcare system until they are much sicker than the average patient, and then when they do access the system, they receive fewer tests and generally less care, all of which translates into the fact that they are more likely to die than privately insured patients.

The gap between what Medicaid actually pays and what healthcare providers normally charge is likely to be compensated for by higher healthcare costs to other payers in the healthcare system. The combination of Medicaid payment shortfalls and unsponsored care costs almost quadrupled in the 1980s, increasing from $3.5 billion to $13.2 billion, but the ability of the healthcare providers to shift costs to other payers may have been limited by new "managed care" systems that place downward pressure on fees. In the words of Michael Reagan, "Because hospitals are caught between private and public third-party payers—each insisting that it will cover costs only for its own group—hospitals, as well as physicians, are losing their ability to act as members of a healthcare community" (Reagan, 1992, 35). In other words, the doctors and hospitals are losing control over decisions concerning fees and coverage.

Cost-Benefit Analysis

There are a number of ways to evaluate healthcare policy in the U.S., but most common are the comparisons of aggregate health data in the U.S. to that of other industrialized nations. Since the U.S. spends more as a percentage of GNP on healthcare than any other developed industrial democracy, one would expect the U.S. to also have the healthiest population. Despite what is arguably the best technology in the world that has been purchased through the highest healthcare spending levels in the world, American infant mortality rates remain behind much of Europe and parts of Asia including Singapore and Hong Kong (World Bank, 2003). Similarly, the U.S. ranks only seventeenth among the nations of the world in vaccinating children against common childhood diseases (World Bank, 2003). The U.S. is also second only to Spain in the developed world in AIDS cases per capita (UN, 2003). In addition to its AIDS problem, The U.S. currently ranks 21st among the leading industrialized nations in life expectancy, and in the bottom third in maternal mortality. If the goal of the healthcare system is to create healthier Americans in the aggregate, the system appears to be in failure. In contrast, of the leading industrialized nations, Japan is 18th in spending per capita on healthcare, yet has the highest life expectancy and lowest rate of AIDS in the world. If the U.S. system is to be evaluated in terms of cost-benefit analysis, then in terms of these measures it is far from the most cost-effective.

What is revealed in these figures is that the U.S. is not necessarily the healthiest nation in the world despite spending more as a percentage of GDP on healthcare than any other nation. It is apparent that the costs of America's technological advancement have outpaced the ability of the American free-market healthcare system to adequately provide healthcare to all of its citizens. The American healthcare system has thus become the great paradox that President Clinton pledged to reform. The healthcare system abounds with the best technology and up-to-date facilities along with the world's largest collection of highly trained healthcare professionals, but the system lacks a structure of organization and finance that is adequate to provide coverage for all Americans at a cost that is comparable to that of other industrialized nations. This is despite the fact that America's administrative healthcare costs are over one fifth of all U.S. healthcare dollars and the highest in the world (Waltzman, 1991).

Rationing Healthcare

All countries ration healthcare in some form or fashion, but at present, the U.S. is the only industrialized democracy where healthcare is rationed based on ability to pay rather than need in accordance with conservative, individualist, free-market principles. As previously discussed, access to healthcare in the U.S. tends to diminish as income drops; consequently, under the current system the poor are bearing the brunt of the rationing. The debate over rationing healthcare heated up in 1984 with the publication of Henry Aaron and William B. Schwartz', *The Painful Prescription: Rationing Hospital Care*, where they argue that the only way to end the spiraling healthcare costs would be to deny healthcare in cases where the medical benefits were likely to be far exceeded by costs (Aaron and Schwartz, 1984). The State of Oregon has since decided to do just that, and is the first State to begin rationing its healthcare to the poor. Oregon decides for which procedures it will, and will not pay for its indigent population. Numerous high risk and expensive procedures are excluded, including radical chemotherapy and bone marrow transplants for children with leukemia. Similarly, many conditions that are not life threatening, such as spinal disk surgery, would not be treated at State expense. Although the Oregon plan in many cases increased access to healthcare for the poor, critics are quick to point out that in many cases the poor are denied care that is available to those with the ability to pay (Specter, 1991, 9-10).

An alternative rationing plan is offered by Daniel Callahan (1987), who argues against the practice of providing expensive medical treatments to the elderly since such care is often unable to significantly prolong life and what life is prolonged may be seriously lacking in quality. Callahan argues that resources that have been allocated to the elderly in healthcare should be diverted to the young, and that the real question should not be whether the care is available, but whether we have the obligation to use it in the case where someone has already lived a normal life span (Callahan, 1987).

There are major problems with these and any other sort of cost-benefit analysis in terms of healthcare, however. Exactly how does one place a monetary value on saving human life? For example, in the early 1990s a new type of pacemaker was developed that would prevent disorganized heart rhythms that cause sudden death. Costs, however, are over $50,000 per patient. It is estimated that there are approximately 100,000 people who need such a device at a total cost of $5 billion (Schwartz, 1992). Should we let people die if they are unable to pay $50,000? In 1980 it was estimated that providing sprinklers in nursing homes cost $86.00 for each year of life saved (Rhodes, 1980). Since the vast majority of people in nursing homes are elderly and have already lived a normal life span, should we then not place sprinklers in nursing homes? Obviously, there is no perfect system for placing value on human life, but unfortunately, the combination of unlimited demand and limited resources will force U.S. to devise one system or another. As long as America clings to its market-based system, the value of human life will continue to be determined by an individual's ability to pay rather than any other variable.

Moral/Ethical Analysis

Critics argue that the U.S. healthcare system fails in terms of moral or ethical analysis. Ethics deals with moral duty and obligation. The concept of ethics goes far beyond merely keeping one's activities legal and expands the concept of obligation to include respect for the dignity of the individual. Any assessment of the ethics of American healthcare must consider the complexity of the system with its multiplicity of providers, payers, and policymakers, all of whom face choices within the system between competing values (primarily between costs and coverage). Moreover, those involved in healthcare matters now must deal with a host of other complex issues that include, but are not limited to, genetic engineering, a plethora of new reproductive technologies, the proper use of animals in medical testing, the usage of fetal tissues in medical research, and questions surrounding the most ethical process for rationing expensive, medical life-saving equipment that we are perhaps unable to provide universally. On such issues, there no clear consensus.

Since it is clear, however, that access to care and quality of care remain linked to income (Rosenthal, 1994), it is perhaps somewhat difficult to argue that the U.S. "free market" system is the most ethical. The ethical problems in the system are clearly demonstrated by the presence of the best medical technology in the world existing side-by-side with inner-city epidemics of diseases for which there have been vaccines for decades. Critics of U.S. healthcare policy therefore see a need for principles and orientation that will enable all actors involved in healthcare policy to see the broad policy needs and implications in any given situation, rather than limiting their vision to their own interests. Too often, healthcare policymakers, whether they be healthcare policy providers, payers, or governmental policymakers, make their decisions with little consideration for the common good, instead focusing only on the good of their own organizations. For example, a policymaker for a private insurance carrier may determine that it is in the best interest of the organization to immediately terminate health coverage for employees that are laid off from their employer that provides their coverage; however, whether such a policy is the best for the society at large is open to debate.

Although it is impossible for all policymakers to consider all ethical and value choices (and some choices, such as complete nationalization of the U.S. healthcare system may be politically infeasible), it is perhaps all too easy in the current fragmented system for policymakers to close their ears to policy options that are outside of their direct interests. Numerous ethical questions concerning American healthcare remain open. Are all options actually being seriously considered? Is Congress wrong to assume that Americans will not accept some form of "socialized" medicine? Is it possible that the system remains as it is not because it provides the greatest benefit for the greatest number, but because powerful lobby groups have shaped it as it is to further their own interests? Should policy be based on what the private sector is willing to do, rather than on what we believe it should do? Finally, has ideology about the proper role of government obscured good judgment? In short, critics suggest that healthcare policy makers should factor into their decision making the larger distributive question —healthcare for whom?

Chapter 9
Conservatism and Gay Rights

In May, 1993, the Supreme Court of the State of Hawaii ruled that the denial of marriage licenses to three lesbian and gay couples violated the Equal Rights Amendment to the Hawaiian State Constitution. The Court's decision was widely viewed as a decision that could represent the first official recognition of same-sex marriages on the State level in the U.S. The case did not immediately legitimize same-sex marriages in Hawaii, however, because the Hawaiian Supreme Court remanded the case back to the lower courts for a new trial. The lower Courts were charged with determining if the State could prove a "compelling State interest in denying the marriage licenses" in such cases (ACLU, 5/15/96). While a final decision in the Hawaiian courts was not expected to be reached for several years, the news of the case touched off a firestorm of controversy and mobilized political activity both for and against gay rights throughout the U.S.

The magnitude of the decision of the Hawaiian courts was amplified by the obligations of the States under the Full Faith and Credit Clause in Article IV of the U.S. Constitution. The Full Faith and Credit Clause requires that States recognize the statutes, records, and judicial proceedings of other States. Consequently, under the Full Faith and Credit Clause, it could be argued that if one State, such as Hawaii, recognized marriages between same sex couples, then other States would be obligated to recognize those marriages as well. In other words, if the State of Hawaii were to recognize same-sex marriages, then a same-sex marriage performed in Hawaii would have to be recognized by other States.

The 49 other States responded to the Hawaiian Court decisions with the introduction of a flurry of anti-gay marriage bills aimed at releasing States from recognizing same-sex marriages under the Full Faith and Credit Clause. At present, 38 States have such "Defense of Marriage Acts" that define marriage as the union of a man and a woman (*Economist*, 2004, 29). The laws that were passed are not uniform in the different States, but tend to be of the following three basic types: Laws that declare same-sex marriages to be "null and void" or that marriage is a union between a man and a woman; laws that declare recognition of same-sex marriage from another State to be prohibited; and laws that declare recognition of any type of out-of-State marriage to be valid only if the couple could have married in the State itself (ACLU, 1996).

Social Conservative groups pressured Congress for national legislation that would nullify any potential recognition of same-sex marriages stemming from the Hawaii decision. The conservative backlash against gay marriage violates a number of tenets of conservative ideologies. First, governmental limits on marriage infringe on the freedom of choice and individualism that "Libertarianism" holds so dear. The push by social conservatives (read as Traditional Conservatives) is also in conflict with the laissez-faire ideology of the Classic Liberal wing of the Republican Party. In general, "Classic Liberal" conservatives argue for less government, and a governmental definition and regulation of marriage obviously would produce more government and more government power rather than less.

The push for national legislation defining marriage also violates the conservatives' standard argument that authority should remain in the States rather than the national government. Essentially, if a law were passed by Congress defining marriage for the States, it would essentially preempt State authority to define marriage for themselves, thus eroding States' rights.

Nevertheless, in May of 1996, a bill was introduced in Congress, known as the Defense of Marriage Act (DOMA) that would redefine marriage in Federal law as a "legal union between one man and one woman." Section Two of the Bill also provided that:

No State, territory, or possession of the United States, or Indian tribe, shall be required to give effect to any public act, record, or judicial proceeding of any other State, territory, possession, or tribe respecting a relationship between persons of the same sex that is treated as a marriage under the laws of such other State, territory, possession, or tribe, or a right or claim arising from such relationship (ACLU, 8/6/96).

In effect, Section 2 of the bill releases States from their Full Faith and Credit Clause obligations under Article IV of the U.S. Constitution in regard to State laws on same-sex marriages. Perhaps the most visible group that offered opposition to the bill was the American Civil Liberties Union (ACLU). The bill immediately came under criticism from the ACLU's Director, Laura W. Murphy, who stated that:

This goes beyond legislators saying they are not ready to accept same-sex marriages....This is an unnecessary and mean-spirited attempt by some in Congress to select out lesbians and gay men for discriminatory treatment. (ACLU, July 11, 1996).

Murphy added that in her opinion the bill did "nothing to defend marriage. . . Its only purpose and effect is to bash lesbian and gay Americans and to pick up a couple of votes along the way" (ACLU, September 10, 1996). Similarly, The ACLU's Director of the National Lesbian and Gay Rights Project, Matthew Coles, argued that there is a wealth of economic and legal benefits attached to civil marriages. It follows then, if those benefits that accompany marriage are granted to heterosexual couples, but denied to gay couples, it is a form of discrimination. Coles further argued that :

At this moment, gay men or lesbians can lose their homes to the government when a partner becomes ill, are barred from intensive care units when their partners are desperately ill, or lose everything when a partner dies because society refuses to recognize their relationships (ACLU, July ll, 1996).

ACLU opponents of the bill testified before Congressional Committees and denounced it as unconstitutional since the bill releases States from the obligations of the Full Faith and Credit Clause. Since the Constitution is supposedly "higher law" to which all others are subservient, the ACLU argued that Congress lacked the authority to circumvent a Constitutional obligation through legislation. Once again, conservatives were acting in a manner inconsistent with their own ideology. In this case, Traditional Conservatives, who revere patriotic symbols such as the Constitution, preferred to ignore the provisions found in Article IV.

Representatives of the ACLU also testified that the bill violates Equal Protection under Law for gay individuals. Essentially, the ACLU argued that under the DOMA, same-sex couples are denied all of the same recognition, responsibilities, and privileges, as other married couples. These privileges and responsibilities include, but are not limited to: bereavement or "sick leave" to take care for a partner or a partner's child; pension or social security continuation when a partner dies; the ability to keep a jointly owned home if a partner goes on Medicaid, dies, or becomes sick; joint tax returns and exemptions for primary relationships on estate taxes; veteran's discounts on medical care, education, and home loans; immigration and residency for partners from other countries. (ACLU, 8/6/96).

Countering the arguments of the ACLU were Social Conservative groups such as the Christian Coalition. These groups mounted a media propaganda campaign that favored the Defense of Marriage Act as a measure that would safeguard against the erosion of the American family. Social Conservative groups constructed advertisements and announcements in support of the Defense of Marriage Act on the basis of "morality." Social Conservative talk shows and TV evangelists used their programs as forums to warn against the "decline of morality" that is associated with gay lifestyles. The strategy of the social conservatives was to influence their Congress indirectly by convincing their constituents that the Defense of Marriage Act was in the best interest of America and morality.

Among the more pointed accusations of the social conservatives is the argument that homosexuality is linked to pedophilia. One newsletter from James Kennedy's Coral Ridge Ministries featured a photograph of young children under the headline: "Sex With Children? Homosexuals Say Yes!" It is argued in the newsletter that sex between adults and children is a major component of the gay rights movement (People for the American Way, 1/10/00).

Social Conservative groups also associated homosexuality with anti-religious demonic powers or supernatural forces of evil in clear cases of what social scientists would term as "demonization" of their enemies. According to televangelist Pat Robertson on the 700 Club, "Many of those people involved in Adolph Hitler were Satanists. Many of them were homosexuals. The two things seem to go together." Robertson further argued that "homosexuals want to come into churches and disrupt church services and throw blood all around and try to give people AIDS and spit in the face of ministers" (People for the American Way, 1/10/00). Evidently, "Jesus loves the little children, all the children of the world" only if they are not homosexuals.

The social conservative literature often portrayed the homosexuals as engaged in a covert, but far-reaching anti-religious and anti-morality plot to undermine America. Conservative activist Anthony Falzaro argued that, "Satan uses homosexuals as pawns. They're in, as you know, key positions in the media, they're in the White House, they're in everything." (People for the American Way, 1/10/00).

In general, proponents of the bill often portrayed the bill as supporting "family values." Proponents of the bill countered the ACLU's argument that DOMA violated the Equal Protection Clause by denying gays the right to marry. Instead, proponents of DOMA argued that homosexuals had the same marriage privileges as heterosexuals. By this they meant that Homosexuals were free to marry anyone they wished, as long as the marriage was to a person of the opposite sex. DOMA prevents only same-sex marriages, which would be denied equally to heterosexuals as well as homosexuals; hence, in their view both groups are treated equally under the Act.

Concurrent with the battle over DOMA, gay rights advocates had introduced an alternative bill in 1994, known as the Employment Non-Discrimination Act (ENDA) that would protect homosexuals against discrimination in the workplace on the basis of sexual orientation. The bill had languished in Congress for two years, but would finally come to a vote in Congress at essentially the same time as the Defense of Marriage Act. Gay rights groups hailed ENDA as Federal enforcement of the Fourteenth Amendment. Conversely, social conservatives argued that ENDA constituted "special privileges" for gays (People for the American Way, 2000).

On July 13 of 1996, by a 342 to 67 vote, the U.S. House of Representatives passed the Defense of Marriage Act. The Act redefined marriage in Federal law as a "legal union between one man and one woman," and thus denied recognition of marriages by same-sex couples under Federal law. A second provision of the bill created a "gay exception" purposed to relieve States of the responsibility of recognizing same-sex marriages performed in other States under the Full Faith and Credit Clause of Article IV in the U.S. Constitution. In September of 1996, the Senate also passed the bill by a vote of 85-14, and simultaneously rejected the bill that would outlaw discrimination in the workplace on the basis of sexual orientation (ENDA).

This is despite the fact that 84% of Americans in one *Newsweek* poll supported equal rights for gays in the workplace (People for the American Way, 2000). Thus, the protracted struggle of gay rights groups for the passage of ENDA concluded in defeat.

President Clinton's White House Press Secretary Michael McCurry had earlier indicated to reporters that the President would sign the legislation if it were passed by Congress. According to McCurry, the President opposed same sex marriages, but supported equal treatment in the workplace (ACLU, May 22, 1996). The announcement by the Clinton Administration that the President would sign the bill came only two days after the Supreme Court ruled that laws that single out gays for second-class status violate the basic guarantees of the Constitution. This apparent "victory" in the Supreme Court for gay rights groups was either ignored by Congress, or interpreted by Congress as not applying to DOMA. In either case, gay rights groups promised immediate Court challenge of DOMA.

The Defense of Marriage Act was signed into law by President Clinton, the same President that had made the inclusion of gays in the military such an important policy statement just three years earlier. While the apparent about-face may be related to election year politics, the President's action was a symbol to gay-rights advocates that they neither had the support of the Democratic Chief Executive nor the Republican Congress and their political opponents had indeed won this round.

With DOMA now the law of the land and same-sex marriages in effect illegal throughout the U.S., one might have expected the opposition to gay rights from social conservatives to subside and the furor over gay rights issues to die down somewhat. Nothing appeared to be further from the truth as the National elections of the 1990's came to a close with the mid-term elections of 1998. Instead of vanishing as an issue, the furor over gay rights again heated up. Candidates in search of support from social conservatives continued to propose anti-gay-rights policies as major components of their campaigns in 1998. A prime example was the mayoral race in Springdale, Arkansas, where Christian Coalition Mayoral candidate Timothy Hill declared that "Homosexuals are perverts...I will do everything I can to keep them out of Springdale." Hill promised to post a sign at the edge of town that said "No Fags in Springdale" (People for the American Way, 1/10/00).

The gay rights issue also heated up again in Congress in May of 1998 when Republican House Majority Whip Tom DeLay hosted a meeting between Republican Congressional leaders and leaders of religious right interest groups. The leaders of the religious right were pushing for more Congressional action on conservative social issues in return for their help in encouraging their members to support Republican candidates in the elections of 2000. Representative Joe Pitts of Pennsylvania was appointed to direct a "Values Action Team" that would be in charge of ensuring that the concerns of social conservatives were high on the Republican agenda. Opposition to gay rights remained a central tenet of that social conservative agenda (People for the American Way, 1/10/00).

On the other side of the agenda, gay rights advocates had been lobbying for Presidential action to secure the end of employment discrimination based on sexual orientation. Three weeks after the Republican Values Action Team was put into motion, President Clinton issued an Executive Order protecting gays from employment discrimination in the Federal workplace. Clinton's Executive Order quickly came under fire from social Conservatives. On June 15, 1998, Republican Senate Majority Leader Trent Lott compared gays to alcoholics and kleptomaniacs on the Armstrong Williams cable television talk show (People for the American Way, 1/10/00). Lott was essentially making the case that homosexuality was some sort of disease or mental illness. Also in June of 1998, a group calling themselves Log Cabin Republicans, a self-proclaimed gay Republican group, was denied a table at the Republican party's State convention in Texas. Party spokesman Robert Black called the Log Cabin Republicans a "deviant group" and equated gays with child molesters and the Ku Klux Klan (People for the American Way, 1/10/00).

The next month (July, 1998), Representative Joe Hefley (R-CO) proposed a bill that would in effect overturn Clinton's anti-discrimination executive order. Proponents of the bill argued that they were not in favor of discrimination against gays, but opposed "special privileges" for gays under Clinton's Executive Order. For example, Randy Tate of the "Christian Coalition" argues that although "Christian charity should be extended to all individuals....that doesn't mean in the public policy realm that we need to extend special privileges to individuals based on their private sexual behavior" (*Hardball*, 1998). Similarly, televangelist Pat Robertson argued that "I just don't think we should craft laws that give privileges on the basis of the way people perform sex acts" (People for the American Way, 1/10/00). Nevertheless, the bill did not pass and the anti-discrimination Executive Order was allowed to stand (People for the American Way, 1/10/00). Similarly, Representative Frank Riggs (R-CA) proposed a bill to withhold

Federal housing funds from the city of San Francisco for the purpose of discouraging the city's "gay-friendly" policies. Most notably, although same-sex marriages are not recognized in the State of California, San Francisco has an ordinance recognizing "domestic partnerships" between same-sex couples. Riggs' bill also did not pass, but received support from social conservatives (People for the American Way, 1/10/00).

Thus, the twentieth Century came to a close with discrimination against homosexuals in the Federal workplace prohibited under Federal law by Executive Order, but same-sex marriages now also prohibited under Federal law. The two policies appear to be incongruent, but the American democracy has not always produced consistent civil rights policy. The rights protected under the Constitution of the U.S. at the end of the twentieth century reflect the competing ideologies and values within society just as they did when the Constitution was written in 1787.

The twenty-first century brought America a continuation of the gay rights debate and gay marriage became a central focus of the Presidential campaign on February 24, 2004, when Republican George W. Bush asked Americans: Do you want a Constitutional ban on gay marriage? Bush asked this question despite the fact that at a speech to the Republican Governor's Association just twelve hours earlier he had argued that "voters face a stark choice between two visions of government: one (Bush's) that encourages individual freedom, the other (the Democrats') that takes your money and makes your choices" (*Economist*, 2004). Obviously, by any measure, Bush's Constitutional ban on gay marriage would take away choice from gay Americans, thus not encouraging individual freedom and instead "making their choices" for them. Just as obvious, Bush's Traditional Conservative ideology that favors the use of government to "correct human weaknesses" conflicts with his own Libertarian and Classic Liberal ideologies that place premiums on personal freedoms. Of course, Bush's Constitutional ban also violates his own "States' rights" conservative ideology, and Bush himself argued that "some activist judges and local officials will permit gay marriage in one place" (*Economist*, 2004). Never mind that "permitting gay marriage in one place" would be consistent with "returning authority to the States." It is also worth noting that Bush has criticized "activist judges" on the gay marriage issue, but Bush certainly did not criticize the "activist judges" on the U.S. Supreme Court that intervened into State affairs in a Florida election and stopped the recount mandated by Florida law so that he could gain the Presidency in the first place.

Chapter 10
Conservatism and Social Welfare

Social welfare policies, like other policies, are not created in a vacuum, but are instead shaped by competing interests and social values within society. The U.S. is primarily a free market economy with private ownership of most production, thus reflecting Classic Liberal ideology, but there is socialization of some production and services such as police, education, and the military. Social welfare is merely another policy area where much of the policies are formulated and implemented by public, rather than private entities. Social welfare policy is a mix of both public and private entities with the public sector accounting for approximately 60% of the American social welfare system.

One of the major political divisions in the U.S. concerning social welfare policy is over the proper role of government. In other words, which services properly should be socialized and which services properly should remain the jurisdiction of private entities? Intertwined with that debate is a debate over which level of government should assume responsibilities for social welfare policy.

Conservative Ideology and Welfare

Formulation of social welfare policy is also greatly complicated by ideological debates over the root causes of poverty and basic differences in social values. Political conservatives in the U.S. tend to look for market solutions to social welfare problems while political liberals tend to view government as the solution to social welfare problems they view as unsolved by the free market. Political conservatives typically emphasize individual character deficiencies as the sources of failure among the poor (slothfulness and low intelligence, for example). In contrast, political liberals tend to view poverty as the result of societal forces that are often outside of the control of the impoverished (racism, sexism, abusive households, or a lack of educational opportunities), but that can be remedied through government intervention.

Social welfare policy in the U.S. is developed amid an individualist society that places a priority on self-reliance, and frowns on one's inability to provide for one's own subsistence. Consequently, welfare itself is contradictory to the basic value system of conservative Americans, and thus the frequent subject of political attacks.

Conservatives generally argue that government intervention into the economy to correct social hardships is harmful to the economy (a violation of Classic Liberal, free market principles). The Classic Liberal wing of America's conservatives tend to view the proper role of government as one of security, and any activities that are not security-related are matters for the private sector and the free market. The use of government as the primary means for combating poverty therefore is itself controversial and central to an ideological debate over the role of government in American politics. Put simply, the U.S. is a very individualistic society, and the dominant American ethos supports the notion of self-responsibility. Under the individualist ethic, each person is responsible for his or her own well being. If an individual is unable to provide for his or her own well being, it is not necessarily the responsibility of the rest of the community to attend to those needs. Essentially, economic failure on the part of the individual is often viewed as the fault of the individual and largely attributable to a lack of effort on the part of that individual. Poverty is therefore often viewed by conservatives as a phenomenon that is individually caused, rather than produced by the free market society. In other words, the poor have less because they are lazy, lack motivation, and/or choose not to better themselves. Consequently, efforts to aid those individuals only reward the lack of effort and perpetuate laziness (Lipset, 1967). These dominant values of individualism and self-sufficiency contribute to the unpopularity of welfare programs and helped bring political pressure for welfare reform in the 1990s (Hansenfeld and Rafferty, 1989).

Traditional Conservatives also oppose many social programs that they view as contradictory with the traditional family or hinder the development of traditional family structures (Bane and Ellwood, 1994). For example, welfare benefits for unwed mothers and children born out of wedlock and Medicaid benefits to AIDS patients are viewed by social conservatives (Traditional Conservatives) as anti-marriage and tantamount to public support for immorality.

Furthermore, conservatives argue that government social programs violate sound economics by placing downward pressure on investment (and therefore GNP) since they take resources from the wealthier segments of society (that would have invested the funds) and allocate them elsewhere. Conservatives also generally oppose welfare programs because they contribute to higher taxes, which conservatives vehemently oppose. Additionally, conservatives tend to be opposed to central government power in juxtaposition to State power, hence, conservatives tend to oppose Federally directed welfare programs and favor State, local, and private efforts, at least in their rhetoric. These ideological factors, combined with the fact that welfare recipients do not have the resources necessary for a strong political power base, have created a political environment that is and has been ideologically antagonistic to welfare since 1970 (Heclo, 1994, 396).

Federal involvement in social welfare policy as we know it has been the center of controversy since its inception under the Social Security Act of 1935. Much of the debate over welfare in general is complicated by ideological views about the proper role of government and differing beliefs concerning the impact of welfare on the behavior of recipients. In general, liberals believe that there is a societal responsibility to render aid to the poor, and that it is the proper role of government to carry out that responsibility because other societal institutions have proven insufficient in that capacity. In contrast, conservatives not only question whether it is the proper role of government to provide aid to the poor, they also tend to support the notion that the provision of such aid will create dependence, perhaps even laziness, and thus contribute to the perpetuation of a culture of poverty (Koon, 1997, 4).

It should be noted, however, that there is a general distinction between aid to the disabled and elderly as opposed to aid to the young, "able-bodied," individuals that receive Temporary Assistance to Needy Families (TANF). Although conservatives are not completely supportive of aid to the elderly and disabled, they tend to be vehemently opposed to aid to able-bodied individuals because of the aforementioned "disincentive to work." Even Democratic President Franklin Roosevelt, whom many credit (or blame) for our current social welfare system, referred to cash relief as a "narcotic" (Koon, 1997, 4).

The Reagan revolution of the 1980s brought with it a public backlash against the American welfare system that had developed from FDR's New Deal of the 1930s and Lyndon Johnson's "Great Society" of the 1960s. The backlash continued into the 1990s and culminated with the Personal Responsibility and Work Opportunity Reconciliation Act (PRWORA) of 1996 which brought about major welfare reforms. The struggle for the passage of PRWORA encapsulates these clashes of ideology and societal values.

The Passage of PRWOR

In the late 1980s, the Democratic Party was in somewhat of a state of disarray after losing three straight Presidential elections to Republican candidates Ronald Reagan and George Bush (1980, 1984, and 1988). As if three straight losses weren't bad enough, the Democrats had lost two of the three Presidential elections previous to 1980, giving them losses in five of the last six Presidential elections (Jimmy Carter's 1976 success in the wake of Watergate the lone victory). The defeats convinced some Democratic Party leaders that the party must reformulate their platform that had been so successful for them from the New Deal of the 1930s through the Great Society of the 1960s, but had faltered in the two decades since. In response to the latest electoral losses, a new party leadership group, the Democratic Leadership Council (DLC) was created which included, among others, Paul Tsongas, Richard Gephardt, Sam Nunn, Bill Bradley, Al Gore, and Arkansas Governor Bill Clinton, who chaired the DLC just prior to his candidacy for the Presidency.

The goal of the DLC was to turn the Democratic party away from traditional New Deal "Big Government" liberalism and turn the party more toward an agenda that would retain the support of the liberals, but no longer alienate business interests and those that opposed Federal social welfare policies on ideological grounds. In 1989, the DLC released the "New Orleans Declaration: A Democratic Agenda for the 1990s" which outlined policy goals that were pro-business, yet "compassionate." To establish their credibility, the DLC sought to distance the Democratic Party from the large-scale Federal welfare programs through a promise of reform. The DLC argued for "workfare," time-limited welfare benefits, support for the traditional family, and frugal, responsible government rather than the deficit spending that had plagued the 1980s. The DLC called for replacement of cash assistance programs with investments in education, research, and job training. The DLC also supported free trade and the North American Free Trade Agreement as a means to reducing unemployment and welfare reforms, a position that was vehemently opposed by labor unions, generally thought of a major constituents of the Democratic party (Karger and Stoesz, 1998, 11-12).

During his presidential campaign of 1992, Democratic Presidential candidate Bill Clinton echoed the DLC platform when he promised to "end welfare as we know it today." Although Clinton did not immediately announce the details of his welfare reform plan, he did made references to his experience in the DLC and in Arkansas where welfare was reformed by putting people to work. This idea of "workfare" evidently struck a positive chord with the American public, despite the fact that previous efforts to eliminate welfare through employment had failed to accomplish the desired results. In 1988, Congress passed the Job Opportunity and Basic Skills Program (JOBS) that was formulated based on the same goals, as was the Work Incentive program (WIN) which passed Congress in 1967, yet problems of poverty remained. Despite this, the public perception was still that welfare recipients generally did not work. This negative public perception concerning welfare and policy proposals that arise in response to that perception are not new. In fact, Congress has amended welfare programs in some way in every session of Congress since the Social Security Act in 1935, yet the public remains largely dissatisfied with the system (Dobelstein, 1996, 5).

Although Bill Clinton was able to win the election of 1992, and his welfare reform position did play a minor role as a campaign issue, Clinton and the Democrats were unable to make progress on any major welfare reform efforts during 1993 and 1994 as welfare reform took a back seat to a National Healthcare initiative and other budget battles. Clinton and the DLC, however, were not the only ones on Capitol Hill that were concerned with reforming welfare. At the same time that Candidate Clinton was arguing for welfare reform in 1992, a group of Republican House of Representatives staff members led by then chief minority council of the House Ways and Means Committee, Dr. Ron Haskins, began to meet together and study welfare reform. The group of Congressional staff members came from numerous different committees and subcommittees, but they had the common bond that all were associated with a committee that had authority over some type of welfare program.

The staff members began to collect information on welfare with the assistance of the Congressional Research Service (CRS). From plowing through the dizzying maze of welfare information, the staff members came to the conclusion that Congressional Committees must be forced to give up their jurisdiction over some of the welfare programs. The staff members were aware that persuading Congressional Committees to relinquish control over specific welfare programs would be extremely difficult. Congressional Committees and the Members of Congress that compose those committees develop constituencies around the programs over which they exercise oversight. For example, the House Agriculture Committee has authority over the Food Stamp Program, and thus receives a tremendous amount of attention from agricultural groups and retailers that benefit financially from the program, as well as other groups that represent the recipients of the Food Stamp Program. These interest groups can supply needed contributions (both monetary and otherwise) to the campaigns of Congressional House Members and thus play a role in determining whether those Members remain in Congress or not. To reduce the control of Congressional Committees over specific welfare programs would result in reduced support for these Congressional members from their constituent interest groups, and thus jeopardize their campaign contributions and, ultimately, even their positions in Congress.

A second conclusion reached by the Republican Congressional Staff Members was that the Federal government should have to return some of the authority over welfare to the States. This conclusion is obviously somewhat partisan and ideological in character, consistent with the "return authority to the States" position of the Republican Party and the conservative elements of the voting public. The downside of such an action is that if the States bungled the welfare programs on their level, politically it is still Congress that takes most of the heat for the failures; consequently, relinquishment of Federal authority to the States could be dangerous for members of Congress who would lack control over the welfare programs, but still be likely to absorb the blame for welfare's problems. Due to these problems, "return authority to the States" measures could be expected to be met with stiff resistance on the floor of Congress.

The Republican staff members were also faced with a conflict between conservative "return authority to the States" rhetoric and attempts to use the

Federal government, of which they are a part, to solve societal problems. At the same time that conservative reformers were attempting to find ways to return welfare authority to the States, Republicans in the House were busy proposing legislation that would prevent the use of government funds to aid illegitimate children of teenagers or illegal immigrants. Obviously, it is a contradiction to on the one hand claim to return authority to the States, yet on the other hand tell the States exactly which individuals would, or would not, be receiving government aid. This contradiction was a major stumbling block to "devolution" (the return of authority from the Federal government to the States) and is exemplified by the statements of Republican House Member and chair of the Economic and Educational Opportunities Committee William F. Goodling, who argued that:

As an authorizing committee, we will have a major responsibility in making sure that those who haven't dealt with these programs day in and day out don't make any mistakes that would come back to embarrass us. We should not have the right to send Federal taxpayers' money anywhere unless they know what it is we expect to accomplish. I'm not just for block-granting money back and saying, 'Here, do your thing.' There has to be a purpose and goals…and oversight to see that's what's happening" (Stanfield, 1995, 228).

Republican staff members were faced with this contradiction continually in attempting to formulate consistent policies that would eventually become part of their "Contract with America" campaign of 1994. Consider the statements of Republican Presidential Candidate Bob Dole on crime: "Republicans…believe that our country's increasingly desperate fight against crime is an area where more freedom is needed at the State level." Dole followed this statement with: "Our crime bill will impose mandatory minimum sentences on those who use guns in the commission of a crime, and make sure the jails are there to lock them up" (Stanfield, 1995, 230). Obviously, if the Federal government imposes a mandate on the States forcing them to adopt new Federal standards regarding sentencing, "more freedom and authority at the State level" will not be the end result. What this illustrates is that "devolution" of authority to the States has proven to be fraught with problems, not the least of which are contradictory positions taken by Republican lawmakers in Congress that propose laws that limit State authority while theoretically favoring "devolution."

Contract with America

In order to gain control of Congress, the Republicans in 1994, led by Speaker-to-be Newt Gingrich of Georgia, unveiled their "Contract with America" platform. The "Contract with America" contained, among other things, proposals for welfare reform that had originated with the Republican staff members. The "Contract" called for several reforms, including: repealing a means tax that had been placed on affluent Social Security recipients; cutting Medicaid and transforming it into a block grant program with greater State control; cutting $137 million from the Head Start program (which offered preschool education and healthcare to impoverished children); eliminating the Americorps program, through which people could earn money for college in exchange for performance of community service; cutting Medicare by over $200 billion; and the cornerstone of reform, the replacement of Aid for Families with Dependent Children (AFDC) with a new program (which eventually became Temporary Assistance for Needy Families or TANF). TANF was expected to return welfare authority to the States, force welfare recipients to work, and limit the time that individuals could receive aid over their life span. The reformers also sought to deny welfare benefits to unmarried teenagers and children born out of wedlock to mothers who were receiving welfare (Franklin, 1995, 29-32).

Despite roadblocks and setbacks, on Wednesday afternoon, March 22, 1995, a roll call vote was announced in the U.S. House of Representatives concerning House Resolution 119 on Welfare. Andrew Dobelstein records the following conversation between two Republican House Members in the hall on the way to the House floor: "What is it?" asked one member, meaning what is it that we are voting on? "House Resolution 119 on Welfare" replied the other member. "What's Dick Armey (Republican House Majority leader) say," says one Republican Congressman to the other. "Yes," replies his colleague, meaning that the Majority Leader wants all Republicans to vote for the bill. "What about the Christian Coalition?" the first Member asked his colleague. "Leadership says we just eat it Frank. That's it. Period!" Both legislators then made their way to their places on the floor of the House (Dobelstein, 1996, 3).

House Resolution 119 passed the House, 217-211, largely along party lines. Three Democrats voted for the bill, but fifteen Republicans broke with their party and voted against the bill. Most of the Republicans who voted against the bill did so because of pressure brought upon them by anti-abortion groups. The welfare reform legislation would deny cash assistance to teenage mothers and reward States for reducing out of wedlock births. Some Anti-abortion groups, such as the National Right to Life Committee and the U.S. Catholic Conference, feared that these provisions could induce some women into having abortions when they otherwise would not. Once again, conservative ideologies were in conflict with each other. The Classic Liberal and Libertarian wings of the Republican Party favored the measure because it reduced welfare payments, and welfare represents a socialistic violation of free market principles as well as the Libertarians' "less government" principles. Traditional Conservatives, on the other hand, in this case would use government to correct a societal weakness (abortions) and approve "welfare" in this case if it helped prevent abortions even if it meant support for a socialistic welfare program.

In contrast, however, some other anti-abortion groups, such as the Family Research Council and the Christian Coalition, supported the provisions of the bill as a means of taking a stand against teen pregnancies and births out of wedlock. Consequently, Republicans had been deeply divided over the "abortion" provision of the welfare reform bill and conflicts within their ideologies produced intra-party bickering over the wording of the bill and delayed its passage for weeks. In fact, the divisions over abortion within the Republican delegation had been so severe that some observers believed that welfare reform would not pass during that session of Congress (Dobelstein, 1996, 3-4).

Welfare reform did subsequently pass both Houses, but President Clinton vetoed the proposal in January 1996, the second welfare reform veto of his Presidency. Both Houses went back to work and hammered out a new resolution, which became eventually the Personal Responsibility and Work Opportunity Act of 1996. Democrats opposed the bill's provisions, which again included the denial of welfare benefits to aliens and unwed mothers. Consequently, liberal Democrats urged the President to again veto the bill. President Clinton feared that if he vetoed the welfare reform bill this time, so close to the election in November, he could lose important "middle" voters who were not necessarily in favor of welfare. Indeed, Republican campaign commercials attacked Clinton for "giving welfare benefits to illegal immigrants." Consequently, Clinton reluctantly signed the bill into law amid protests from liberal Democrats in August of 1996 (Koon, 1997, 156-157).

The story of the passage of the PRWORA of 1996 illustrates that the politics surrounding social welfare policy in the U.S. are complex, and driven by partisanship, and vested interest groups, but also ideology.

Contemporary Liberal Views

Since the 1930s, liberals in the U.S. have typically viewed government intervention into the free market as the remedy for harsh dislocations that occur in the democratic free marketplace. Liberals reject the notion that democracy and the free market always produce the greatest good for the greatest number and instead argue that the free market may produce harsh dislocations, income inequality, impediments to equal opportunity, and a permanent underclass. Liberals also tend to reject the notion that poverty is an individual choice. Instead, liberals argue that poverty has societal causes outside of the control of the individual. In order to correct for these problems, government must intervene into the economy to provide both temporary and permanent assistance to those whom have been left wanting by the free market's harshness. Furthermore, the majority may democratically approve of impediments to equal opportunity (for example, segregation for much of the twentieth century); hence, government must intervene on the behalf of the oppressed minority to restore equality of opportunity. For example, liberals argue that equal opportunity was/is often denied to minorities and women under the democratic free market; hence, Affirmative Action is necessary to correct for the societally created inequality of opportunity.

Liberals also tend to favor Federally mandated social welfare policy as opposed to State and local efforts. There are a number of reasons for this preference for Federally driven policy at the expense of State autonomy. First, liberals argue that if social welfare policy is left to the States, it tends to exert downward pressure on welfare benefits since each State has an interest in having lower benefits than other States in order to avoid becoming a "welfare magnet" and "attracting" welfare recipients. Secondly, it is State, rather than Federal laws, that liberals have historically viewed as impediments to equal opportunity; and efforts to correct problems of equal opportunity in the States generally have been remedied through Federally mandated programs such as Affirmative Action.

In order to accomplish their goals, liberals generally favor heavier taxation on the wealthy and redistribution of the income produced from that taxation to the poor. Liberals argue that such policies are not a significant drain on the economy since the poor will then consume with the redistributed income and thus boost the economy. Liberals also favor policies that provide services to the poor that are designed to help the poor overcome barriers to poverty. Thus, Affirmative Action along with educational and job-training programs tend have broad-based support among liberals.

Conflict over Scarce Resources

Although the U.S. should be considered a "land of plenty," the resources that are available to the government and social welfare policy are far from unlimited. This problem has been exacerbated by the current budgetary situation where an increasing percentage of the Federal budget is allocated to entitlements and interest on the debt that are outside of Congressional discretionary spending. In other words, in an annual budget cycle, funding for Social Security, Medicare, Veteran's benefits, and a host of other programs are not controlled by Congress, but by how many Americans meet the criteria (age, disability, veterans' status, etc.) that qualify them for various assistance programs. Currently, nondiscretionary spending accounts for the majority of all Federal outlays, meaning means-tested social programs are competing for an ever-shrinking piece of the discretionary spending pie.

Social Security and other entitlement programs have experienced rapid growth since the 1960s and have thus become an important political issue at the end of the twentieth century. Social Security alone grew 1,859% between 1965 and 1995, from a $17 billion program to a $333 billion program. The growth in social security was accompanied by similar rapid growth in virtually all entitlement programs; consequently, there are considerable questions as to its continued viability in its present form. All major entitlement programs combined grew 2,579% between 1965-1995, from a total expenditure of $29 billion in 1965, to $777 billion in 1995. This rapid growth is not expected to level off any time soon due to rapid inflation of healthcare costs along with the aging of the American population (and it is the elderly population that garners the lion's share of this nondiscretionary spending through Social Security and Medicare); consequently, the continued rapid growth may render the entitlement system untenable in the near future.

The Congressional Budget Office projects that after the baby boom generation starts to become eligible for Social Security and Medicare in 2010, America's ability to fund the programs will be quickly overwhelmed. By 2020, there will be only two Americans working for every one person who is drawing full social security benefits. By 2030, entitlement spending is expected to exceed all Federal tax revenues. Cutting in-kind aid programs will do nothing to solve the entitlement spending problems. In the words of John Attarian:

Whatever welfare's flaws, budget busting is not one of them. The conclusion is inescapable: America's fiscal crisis cannot be resolved without radical reform of Social Security and Medicare (Attarian, 1996, 52).

Despite this fact, reforms of 1996 focused on aid to the poor, the much smaller portion of the Federal budget, rather than on entitlement spending.

Constituent Interest Groups

Social welfare policy, like any other policy area, has its beneficiaries as well as those who contribute more to the system than they receive. Among the beneficiaries of social welfare policy are clearly the disabled, the aged, and the impoverished. It should be reiterated, however, that the impoverished are not necessarily the primary beneficiaries of social welfare policies since over five times as much is expended on non-means-tested programs, such as Medicare, as is spent on means-tested programs, such as Food Stamps or TANF. Consequently, one can expect some powerful constituent interest groups such as the American Association of Retired Persons (AARP) to favor continuation of some aspects of the social welfare system. The AARP routinely opposes reductions in Social Security and Medicare, but the group is generally much less supportive of means tested programs. These recipients of benefits, however, are not the only groups with a vested interest in the system that is already in place.

Professional service providers, whether they are doctors working with Medicare patients, social workers, or psychologists, also clearly may benefit from government social welfare spending. Consequently, professional groups and other potential vendors lobby for vendorship privileges that provide them income through socially insured clientele. Among these professional service providers are also thousands of government bureaucrats who pressure Congress to ensure that their program is viewed as viable and beneficial.

Manufacturers of countless products also benefit from the social welfare system. From the makers of high-tech medical equipment that is used by Medicare patients, to the growers and processors of food products that are consumed by Food Stamp recipients, to the housing and construction businesses that benefit from government spending on public housing, business entrepreneurs throughout the American economy pressure Congress to retain the programs from which they benefit, and compete with one another for their share of the social welfare spending.

Value Oriented Groups

Social Welfare policy, as illustrated by the debates surrounding the passage of the PRWORA of 1996, often becomes subject to posturing from value-oriented or ideologically-based interest groups. Social conservative groups seek to structure social welfare policy in a manner that is supportive of traditional families and religious values; hence the opposition to social welfare policies that may lead to more abortions or discourage marriage. Conversely, civil libertarians support social welfare policies that tend to expand individual rights, such as the rights to privacy and reproductive choice.

Formulating Welfare Policy Alternatives

The formulation of alternatives to social welfare policy is now impacted greatly by political/intellectual institutions called "policy institutes" or "think tanks" that contain staffs of prominent scholars and researchers. Policy institutes often have multimillion-dollar budgets funded individuals and other entities that support the political positions of the institutes. Prior to the Reagan revolution, policy institutes traditionally provided technical support to governmental agencies when called upon. Since the late 1970s, however, policy institutes have taken a more active role in providing unsolicited information to policymakers in an effort to impact and shape the political agenda. Policy institutes are far from apolitical, and on the contrary tend to produce research that supports a particular partisan policy position. Policy institute associates prepare position papers and other sources of information on the differing facets of social welfare policy and offer them to policymakers both in Washington and in State capitols in efforts to shape policies consistent with the views of the institutes' benefactors.

These policy institutes, such as the conservative Heritage Foundation and the liberal Institute for Policy Studies are closely tied to political parties and it is common for their associates to move in and out of government positions with the change of Presidential administrations. For example, Anna Kondratas, a conservative policy scholar with the Heritage Foundation in the 1980s, was appointed by then HUD Secretary Jack Kemp to manage programs for the homeless during the Bush Administration. Upon the inauguration of Bill Clinton in 1993, Kondratas accepted a position with another conservative think tank, the Hudson Institute. Similarly, conservative think tanks such as the Heritage Foundation were credited with helping shape social welfare policy during the Reagan/Bush Administrations and in the Republican Congress during the Clinton Presidency since 1995. Conversely, liberal policy institutes such as the Children's Defense Fund and Progressive Policy Institute have become important policy think tanks surrounding the Clinton Administration (Karger and Stoesz, 1998, 235).

In addition to the input from these intellectual think tanks, the shift in public sentiment against welfare that has occurred since 1970 has also had a major impact on policymakers and resulted in a reduction of real welfare benefits since that time. Between 1970 and 1990, benefits for AFDC decreased 40% in constant dollars. The attacks on welfare continued into the 1990s with nine States reducing AFDC in 1991 and 22 States reducing General Assistance (GA) benefits in 1991-1992 and two States eliminating GA completely (Lav, et al., 1993).

It should be noted, however, that public sentiment is not necessarily opposed to all forms of public assistance. Government assistance programs for the elderly, veterans, and the disabled tend to have broad-based support. Interestingly, these programs, including Social Security and Supplemental Security Income, are indexed to adjust for inflation and are overwhelmingly more costly than means-tested programs (Henly and Danziger, 1996, 219).

Eliminating Welfare

The first policy choice of many conservatives has been largely the choice of eliminating welfare benefits altogether, or at the very least reducing present benefits. This policy choice is reminiscent of the famous words of Voltaire concerning the Catholic Church in pre-Revolutionary France: "Crush the infamous thing." Advocates of eliminating welfare found a voice in the works of Charles Murray (1986). Murray argues that government welfare benefits should be abolished because government antipoverty programs have actually made the situation worse by creating dependency and a culture of poverty. Murray argues that welfare is an incentive for poor women to have children in order to receive welfare, and that the deterioration of the poor communities is exacerbated by government support of women who have children out of wedlock, thus contributing to the erosion of the moral fabric of American society. Murray argues that the problem of hungry children could be remedied by forcing poor women who cannot feed their children to give them up for adoption. Hence, Murray contends that the unavailability of aid would reduce the fertility rate among the impoverished, and therefore reduce poverty (Murray, 1986). A major problem with Murray's thesis is that poverty existed for thousands of years of human history in societies without social welfare systems; thus, it is unlikely that welfare is the primary cause of poverty and therefore just as unlikely that poverty can be solved through its elimination.

Workfare: The Clinton Plan

Murray's plan of eliminating welfare altogether is an unlikely and politically infeasible alternative; however, the attractiveness of his proposals to ideological conservatives forced opponents on the political left to develop alternatives of their own.

For example, in 1994, President Clinton proposed a plan of welfare reform that called for programs designed to foster employment among unemployed welfare recipients. Under the Clinton plan, single mothers would receive job training along with childcare and assistance while they were in training. After the completion of a government-funded job training program, the beneficiaries of the program would have two years to secure gainful employment before losing all of their cash subsidies. Those who were unable to find employment would be given temporary, tax-subsidized work provided by the Federal government. The Clinton plan would also address the "morality" problem of unwed motherhood and teen pregnancies by eliminating benefits for unwed minors living apart from parents or another responsible adult. Furthermore, the Clinton plan called for a nationwide propaganda campaign against teen pregnancies. The Clinton plan also called for more responsibility from fathers by requiring all unwed mothers to identify fathers of their children prior to receiving welfare benefits. The Federal government would then intensify its assistance to States in helping locate delinquent fathers and in enforcing child support collections. Wages, professional and occupational licenses, and drivers' licenses would be withheld from fathers who failed to pay their child support (Zastrow, 1996, 95-96).

The Clinton plan quickly came under attack from conservatives as another "big government program." Although the major goals of the plan, to stimulate both employment and parental responsibility among welfare recipients, are consistent with conservative ideology, it is estimated that the Clinton plan would have increased welfare costs almost $2 billion per year (Rankin and Hess, 1994, 1A-2A). Any increase in welfare costs would be unacceptable to conservatives, who tend to make reduction of costs a top priority. That being the case, Clinton was unable to achieve passage of his plan prior to the Republican electoral victories in the elections of 1994 that installed his Republican opposition into the majority in both Houses of Congress.

The adoption of the PRWORA of 1996 as social welfare policy should therefore be viewed as a triumph of the interests against welfare, as represented by conservative interest groups, PACs, and think tanks, over the ill-equipped social welfare advocate groups, and a triumph of conservative ideology. The PRWORA reflects the conservative ideology that is supportive of stimulating the work ethic among the poor by requiring welfare mothers to work after two years of assistance. The PRWORA is also reflective of the conservative "traditional family" values, that are opposed to the bearing of children out of wedlock, through the denial of assistance to unwed mothers under age eighteen unless they live with their parents or another responsible adult. The Act also reflects the conservative ideological position of eliminating welfare altogether by setting a limit of five years of aid during one's lifetime.

Evaluation of Welfare Policy

The poverty rate in 1960 prior to the implementation of the "Great Society" programs was approximately 23%. After the passage and implementation of the "Great Society" in the mid-1960s, the poverty rate declined to approximately 12% in 1974. Although the "war on poverty" was not won, significant progress had been achieved. The election of Ronald Reagan in 1980 brought an anti-welfare backlash and more free market economics. Simultaneously, the poverty rate increased again, eclipsing 15% in the early 1980s and during the recession of the early 1990s prior to returning to 13.6% in 1996, the year of welfare reform (U.S. Census Bureau, 1998). These figures support the position that the greatest inroads against poverty were made when more was spent on welfare, rather than less.

Consequently, it is reasonable to expect the poverty rate to rise again in the near future as both the States and the Federal government reduce their welfare rolls.

Without question, the welfare reforms of 1996 accomplished the Republicans' goals. Between 1996 and 1999, welfare caseloads were cut nearly in half, from 12.2 million people to 6.6 million and 55 to 80% (depending on the State) of those leaving welfare entered the work force (Serafini, 2000, 1978).

Unfortunately, however, multiple problems remain. As of 2002, many welfare recipients faced the five-year maximum time limit for receiving Federal cash assistance, and it is unclear how they will survive the elimination of aid. Furthermore, the jobs that welfare recipients were able to secure after being bumped from TANF tended to be minimum wage jobs or other low wage positions under $8.00 per hour that would not lift a family of four to a level above the poverty line. As a consequence, some 20%-40% of recipients that left TANF for employment have had since to be reinstated (Tweedie, 1998, 31).

It appears at present that these goals of social welfare policy makers in the U.S. are multidirectional, and in some cases in conflict with themselves. On the one hand, the goals of eliminating poverty and providing the elderly, disabled, and children with a minimum standard of living and care remain. On the other hand, there are the goals of reducing public welfare expenditures and reducing the number of welfare recipients. It is possible that these two groupings of goals are incongruent. In other words, reducing welfare rolls may not result in an elimination of poverty, but could possibly have the opposite effect. At any rate, the differing goals were not prioritized and the reforms aimed at achieving them are therefore hindered from the beginning.

Moral-Ethical Analysis

The goals of social welfare policy are confounded by ideological wrestling over revitalizing morals and the work ethic among the poor. The prevalent perception in the U.S. in 1996 was that taxes were too high and that welfare was in need of reform. Furthermore, the public perception was that the two problems were inextricably linked. Since all assistance to the poor in the U.S. accounts for less than 5% of GDP, the contribution of assistance to the poor to high taxes is perhaps more myth and misperception than reality. If the goal of welfare reform was to significantly reduce taxes, then the results were predestined to failure, since assistance to the poor is not the primary cause of high taxes.

Clearly, however, the impetus to welfare reform was not purely financial, but based on the ideological perception that welfare recipients were averse to work and that the system under AFDC "rewarded" young women without education or skills for bearing children out of wedlock. Furthermore, some even argued that the system under AFDC supported nonworking, substance-abusing women and contributed to the spawning of a "criminal class" (Koon, 1997, 169). Consequently, the alterations to the welfare system under PWORA were largely aimed at ending the life-permanent welfare dependence and force welfare recipients into the workplace. These policies were pursued in spite of the fact that the majority of AFDC adult recipients were employed, and 75% of AFDC recipients exited the AFDC program within two years (Koon, 1997, 169).

Reforms also ignore the fact that the Federally imposed poverty line of $16,400 for a family of four in 1998, is significantly over the $10,920 per year that one would earn working full time (40 hours per week) to support a family on minimum wage. Thus, merely finding employment does not necessarily eliminate poverty. The current situation where so many recipients that left TANF for employment since 1995 have returned to the program is a testimony to this fact. Hence, the welfare reforms themselves were perhaps based on some misguided assumptions about welfare recipients and therefore may be unlikely to achieve their goals. As such, the recent reform of welfare should be viewed as more of a moral/ideological backlash than an effort to achieve fiscal responsibility. Clearly, in the recent reform of welfare, facts were superseded by rhetoric, and ideology, rather than rationality, was the driving force behind policy.

It should also be reiterated that perhaps the biggest problem of the American social welfare system (uncontrollable and untenable entitlement growth) has yet to be addressed amid all of the political squabbling over reform of assistance to the poor. Although both parties are currently giving lip-service to either "saving" or "reforming" Social Security, no serious measures have been passed recently in Congress that provide even partial remedies to the impending fiscal disaster, thus, we drift toward inevitable crisis. In this sense, the American pluralist system based on entrenched interests is clearly thus far a failure.

On the positive side, when evaluating social welfare policy one should consider what are the most important goals of social welfare policy. Clearly, providing sustenance to the needy children so they do not starve to death is a top priority (unless one wants to adopt the position of Jonathan Swift, who once satirically argued that we could simply eat the poor children). If this is most important, then the American social welfare system should be considered a smashing success since instances of children starving to death in America (except for cases of abuse or neglect) are rare indeed. Similarly, though malnutrition is often present among the poor, adult starvation to the point of death is equally rare, even among the elderly and disabled. Unfortunately, these noteworthy successes are generally obscured by the problems endemic to the system that are the focus of those ideologically opposed to public assistance. Whether or not these situations are seriously altered under the recent welfare reforms remains to be seen.

Concluding Remarks

Clearly, a shift has occurred in the American political consensus from the 1960s when government was viewed as the solution to the problems of social welfare, to the 1990s where government is often viewed as "the problem." Much of the impetus to change comes from American moralist and individualistic ideologies that are often contradictory. For example, a consistent theme in American history is a link between wealth, power, and virtue (Katz, 1989). This link has allowed Americans to draw a distinction between those deserving government benefits (the elderly middle class) and those that are undeserving of benefits (the able-bodied poor). Consequently, the result is a lack of empathy toward those who have been unable to support themselves. Poverty is therefore viewed as individually, rather than socially caused, and society is released of its responsibilities. To compound matters further, "rehabilitation" programs of the 1960s have become discredited since the impoverished have remained a large segment of society in the decades since their implementation.

The recent welfare reforms in the U.S. have been designed to both reduce welfare rolls and force welfare recipients to find employment. Although the early indications are that the reforms will be somewhat successful at accomplishing both, it must be reiterated that employment in the U.S. does not guarantee an escape from poverty. As long as the situation remains that the lowest paying jobs remain below the poverty line, the problem of poverty will remain (with or without employment) and a strong "work ethic" will not alleviate the problem. A foolproof plan to alter this situation has yet to be developed. At present it is not clear that an economic model can be developed that will ensure prosperity for all without government intervention. None have done so to date; hence, a need for some type of collective income redistribution system to the poor can be expected to continue. Future welfare debates should therefore focus on what objectives can and cannot be accomplished within these constraints, but conservative ideology is likely to continue to cloud sound analysis.

Chapter 11
Conservatism and Crime Policy

Crime policy is among the most decentralized public policies, yet intensely political of any policy area due to the high place that crime occupies in the hierarchy of public opinion. The general public are generally outraged about the some 35 million crimes that occur annually in the U.S., and driven by the conservative ideological approach to crime, almost constantly apply pressure to public officials to "get tough on crime" (U.S. Department of Justice, 2003). Concurrently, the most important actors in the crime policy process tend to be those that are involved in the process of administering criminal justice on local levels. Some of the most important actors within the crime policy arena are also are provided with a great deal of discretion under existing structures (local prosecutors and judges, for example). Judges have traditionally had wide latitude in sentencing, and prosecutors have traditionally also had wide latitude in determining which cases will, or will not, be prosecuted. Since many of these individuals are elected, the pressure on them to take a hard-line retributive approach toward management of offenders is immense. Similarly, public pressure on legislators to "do something about crime" has led to the passage of harsher, often rigid, mandatory sentencing that has had the impact of reducing the discretion of judges and juries. As a consequence, the area of greatest discretion concerning crime policy (that once rested within the courts) has perhaps shifted from the courtrooms to prosecutor's offices across the U.S.

Since prosecutors are also elected officials who occupy a high profile position in their local communities, there is intense public pressure on them to make sure that offenders are "convicted and brought to justice." Reflecting conservative ideology, public scrutiny is often more directed at "soft" or "bleeding heart" judges that award more lenient sentences or alternative forms of punishment. Some of the public pressure on "bleeding heart" judges may be misdirected, however, since it is often the prosecutors, rather than the judges, that may be in reality more important since, on the average, police will bring to prosecutors thirteen felony cases for every one case that goes to trial before a judge. In other words, twelve of thirteen cases that are delivered to the prosecution by law enforcement are closed by prosecutors through plea bargaining or decisions not to prosecute (Forst, 1995, 364).

Prosecutors have a vested interest in developing a "tough on crime" image in order to enhance their standing with the voting public. To facilitate the development of this image, prosecutors tend to give significant attention to cases that receive greater media attention and make public appearances concerning those cases to clarify their "tough on crime" stance. In the words of Brian Forst:

If a prosecutor says he is tough on criminals and appears to put up a good fight in the exceptional cases that make the news, any failures in managing his office efficiently or in dealing effectively with the larger pool of cases involving predictably dangerous offenders—cases that rarely make the news—will not jeopardize his prospects for reelection or advancement to higher political office (Forst, 1995, 372).

Empirical research suggests that the outcomes of the few exceptional criminal cases that receive intense media scrutiny may have a significant impact on public opinion concerning a prosecutor (Forst, and Brosi, 1977). As a result, some prosecutors may be tempted to overstep the ethical and or legal limits of their discretion in order to get convictions in high profile cases and satisfy the retributive-minded electorate.

Additionally, since crime rates are higher among minorities with low levels of income and education who are less likely to vote (for example, blacks are eight times more likely than whites to commit homicide), there may be pressure on prosecutors to avoid any leniency toward such individuals (U.S. Department of Justice, 2003, 2). When the fact that many individuals that fit this "profile" cannot afford the best legal counsel is added into this situation, the result is an overflowing prison system in which ethnic minorities account for approximately two thirds of the incarcerated population. Consequently, the system is frequently criticized by liberals for bias against minorities and poor and in favor of punitive retribution against them.

Prior to the 1960s, crime was not a major component of the Federal agenda. There are a number of reasons for this, but among the most important is the fact that crime and police powers are traditionally areas that are reserved for the States under the Tenth Amendment and therefore Constitutionally removed from Federal responsibility. Concurrently, Americans have traditionally viewed crime as a State and local, rather than Federal, concern, consistent with conservative ideology (Wilson and Dilulio, 1995, 705). As such, Federal efforts to limit criminal activity through a restructuring of criminal codes is seriously hindered since most crimes fall under exclusive State jurisdiction where the Federal government does not share authority. Furthermore, in areas such as crime policy, where the Federal government has become involved in a policy area that has been traditionally the exclusive jurisdiction of State and local governments, problems of intergovernmental relations are exacerbated.

State and local dominance of crime policy is reflected in aggregate data for investigations, arrests, and convictions. Currently, there are nine times as many inmates incarcerated by State and local governments as there are by the Federal government, and State and local governments report approximately 15 times as many arrests (Gilliard, 2003). Similarly, State and local spending on crime far exceeds that of the Federal government.

Liberal and Conservative Perspectives

As in other policy issues, what policy tools that one chooses may be restricted by a liberal or conservative ideological perspective. Also like other policy issues, liberals and conservatives are somewhat divided over what are the appropriate policy tools.

Since conservatives generally espouse the "realist" view of human nature that holds that people are "naturally bad," the crime policies of Conservatives then tend to focus on the erection of societal constraints that coerce individuals to deter or prevent criminal behavior. Conservatives tend to favor incarceration over counseling, rehabilitation, job training, or any other kind of treatment program. Conservatives argue that treatment does not work, and that the only thing the criminal understands in punishment (Martinson, 1974,

22). Consequently, conservative prescriptions tend to favor longer prison sentences, mandatory sentences, corporal punishment, and the death penalty. Conservatives also tend to favor greater expenditures on law enforcement agencies as opposed to social programs aimed at preventing crime. In the words of President Ronald Reagan, "right and wrong matter; individuals are responsible for their actions; retribution should be swift and sure for those who prey on the innocent" (*Justice Assistance News*, 1981, 1).

In contrast, the liberal "idealist" view of human nature that people are naturally good, and cooperative, but corrupted by society and their own socialization experiences, leads to prescriptions that are much less retributive in character and geared toward treatment or rehabilitation. Liberals focus on eliminating the social conditions, such as poverty, low education levels, handguns, racial injustice, and substance abuse, that contribute to criminal behavior.

The liberal view of crime became the policy guide in the late 1960's until the mid-1970s. The liberal position is reflected in the 1967 report of the Presidential Commission on Crime. The commission concluded that crime was the result of disorganization in American society and a lack of resources dedicated to law enforcement, adjudication, and corrections. The Commission also concluded that rehabilitation had been insufficiently emphasized in the treatment of offenders, and therefore corrections should be reoriented away from retribution and toward rehabilitation. Consequently, the Commission recommended focusing on the elimination of social conditions that contribute to crime and focusing on the elimination of racial injustices (Clear and Cole, 1990, 33).

Congress and Crime Policy

Instead of following the Commission's recommendations, the largest role of Congress in crime policy since the 1967 Presidential Commission's report has followed the conservative ideological preferences and oriented toward retribution in the form of support of State and local government anti-crime efforts. Congress has supplied funding, technical assistance, fingerprint records, and aggregate data to State and local law enforcement. A prime example of this type of effort was the passage of the Law Enforcement Assistance Act of 1965. Under this Act, administered by the Office of Law Enforcement Assistance (OLEA) within the U.S. Department of Justice, Congress funneled over

$20 million to State and local law enforcement agencies between 1966 and 1968.

Despite the efforts of the OLEA, crime rates continued to rise. In 1967, President Lyndon Johnson commissioned a Special Presidential Commission on Law Enforcement and the Administration of Justice to further study the issue. The Special Presidential Commission concluded that the Federal government should vastly expand its role in technical support of State and local anti-crime efforts in spite of the fact that similar efforts under OLEA had not proven effective. The conclusion of the Special Presidential Commission therefore appears to be ideologically driven toward retribution since the facts suggested retributive policies carried out on the State and local level were not working.

In 1968, Congress superseded the Law Enforcement Assistance Act with the passage of the Omnibus Crime Control and Safe Streets Act, a product of President Lyndon Johnson's Commission on Law Enforcement and the Administration of Justice. The primary goal of the Act was to combat organized crime and urban riots (Dilulio, 1995). In order to accomplish these goals, the Act expanded Federal wiretapping and electronic surveillance authority and prohibited possession of firearms by felons. In other words, the ideological trend toward coercion and retribution administered on the State and local level continued in spite of more data suggesting that crime was only increasing. Importantly, however, Title I of the Omnibus Crime Control and Safe Streets Act created the Law Enforcement Assistance Administration (LEAA) within the U.S. Dept. of Justice.

The LEAA, like its predecessor, the Office of Law Enforcement Assistance, the LEAA was not a crime policymaking body, nor was it an instrument for administering Federal crime policy. Instead, the LEAA was a funding agency that funneled Federal money to State and local authorities to help them fight crime. In furtherance of their objectives, the LEAA sponsored law enforcement training institutes for State and local governments and developed national criminal justice data-gathering and information-sharing networks; however, the LEAA was prohibited from involvement with administration of State and local law enforcement operations. Congress expanded the LEAA with the Omnibus Crime Control Act in 1970 to include funding for State and local correctional programs and facilities as well (Dilulio, 1995, 454). In its first decade of existence, from 1969 to 1979, the LEAA funneled over $8 billion in Federal funds to State and local crime fighting efforts, thus building on the failed policies of the past.

Despite the LEAA assistance, (and perhaps predictably) the crime rate in the U.S. increased during the decade of the 1970s, and the LEAA was therefore perceived to be a failure and abolished by the Reagan administration in 1982 (Dilulio, 1995, 455). In his 1983 budget message to Congress, President Reagan stated that "Public safety is primarily a State and local responsibility. This administration does not believe that providing criminal justice assistance in the form of grants or contracts is an appropriate use of Federal funds" (Congressional Quarterly Weekly Report, 1983, 275). Is one then to conclude from Reagan's statement that he believed that the failure of the LEAA to reduce crime was due to Federal involvement in State affairs?

This position would not last for long, however. In 1984, Congress passed the Comprehensive Crime Control Act that included $2 billion in aid for States for Federal prisons and provided for harsher sentences on the Federal level, once again reflective of conservative ideology that focuses on retribution. The Act also allowed the Federal authorities to incarcerate dangerous offenders without bail while they are awaiting trial, abolished parole release in the Federal prisons, and placed limitations on the insanity defense in Federal courts (Clear and Cole, 1990, 33).

In 1986, Congress passed the Anti-Drug Abuse Act that quadrupled the amount of funds that the Federal government supplied to the States earmarked for combating drug abuse (Wilson and Dilulio, 1995). Administratively, a new grant-making agency, the Bureau of Justice Assistance (BJA), assumed the responsibilities once held by the LEAA despite President Reagan's statements that transfers of funds from the Federal government to the States were not to be part of the overall Federal crime policy. Obviously, this conflicts with conservative "States' rights" ideology since Federal money comes with strings attached, but once again, the policy of the conservative Republican (Ronald Reagan) very much resembled that of the Nationalist, "big government" liberal Democrat, (Lyndon Johnson).

In order to receive the funds dispersed by the BJA, States must designate a State planning agency which submits a strategy for drug and violent crime control to the BJA. If the BJA approves of the State strategy, it awards the funding to the States based primarily on population. Although the BJA makes no crime policy itself, its power over Federal funding clearly creates a situation where the Federal government could exert influence over State crime policies through Federal grant conditions. In other words, once again, conservative "States' rights" ideology is violated.

In 1988, Congress passed, and Republican President Ronald Reagan signed, the Second Anti-Drug Abuse Act which authorized the death penalty for drug dealers who commit murders, required that contractors doing work for the Federal government certify that they have a drug-free workplace, and denied Federal benefits, including the right to live in public housing, to drug dealers. Once again, the crime policies of the Reagan administration were retributive in character, consistent with conservative ideology.

During the Presidency of George H.W. Bush, however, Congress passed and Bush signed a pair of statutes that completely violate the "States' rights" rhetoric of the conservatives. In 1990, the Crime Control Act declared schools as drug-free zones, and prohibited the sale of drug paraphernalia on school grounds. In 1992, the Anti-Car Theft Act made stealing a car from its driver with a weapon a Federal crime, thus taking another small area that was traditionally a State concern and placing it under Federal jurisdiction and once again, States' rights ideology was sacrificed.

The Nationalization of crime policy and focus on retributive policies continued under the Clinton Administration with the Crime Act of 1994 that mandated life imprisonment for Federal criminals convicted of three violent or drug offenses, banned certain assault weapons, and authorized $8 billion for State and local governments to hire 100,000 more police officers, $8 billion to the States to build more prisons, and $7 billion to the States for crime prevention programs (Wilson, 1995, 706-709).

As a result of these new Federal efforts, the National drug control budget increased from $1.5 billion in 1981 to $12.7 billion in 1993, with 28% of that budget targeted as direct assistance to State and local governments in their anti-drug efforts. The over 800% increase is obviously inconsistent with conservative "less government" ideology. Concurrently, the number of drug traffickers sentenced to prison in the U.S. quadrupled between 1980 and 1992 and the number of drug offenders in Federal prisons increased more than five-fold, from 5,000 in 1980, to 27,000 in 1990 (Diliulio, 1995, 457). By 1994, 60% of persons incarcerated in Federal prisons and 25% of those in State prisons were there on drug charges, a growth rate of over 300% from 1986 (Beck, 1995, 4).

Cross-National Comparisons

The conventional wisdom in the U.S. is that the U.S. is the most crime-ridden of any industrialized nation. This conception, however, is only partially true since the U.S. does lead other industrialized nations in homicides, but trails some other leading industrialized nations in crimes against property such as burglary. Police statistics for international comparison are compiled internationally by Interpol and the United Nations. Victim survey data are collected by the International Crime Survey in thirty-three different countries (Lynch, 1995, 15).

There are numerous theories as to why the U.S. has become a world leader in violent crime, but among the more plausible is the notion that the violence is related to lax handgun control in the U.S. Homicides in the U.S. are most often committed with guns, especially handguns. In 1993, for example, there were over 13,000 homicides committed in the U.S. by handguns, but less than 3,000 homicides involving other types of guns, knives, blunt objects, or any other methods (U.S. Department of Justice, 1998, 1). Furthermore, the sharp increase in homicides in the late 1980s is largely attributable to gun violence by juveniles and young adults (U.S. Department of Justice, 2003, 1). The percentage of homicides committed with firearms in the U.S. typically are higher than in any other industrialized democracy (Fingerhut and Kleinman, 1990). The rate of homicide with handguns in the U.S. in the 1990s was 14.6 times that of Canada, its neighbor to the north on the same continent that has greater restrictions on handguns (Sloan et al., 1998). Furthermore, in a sister-cities study of Seattle and Vancouver, Sloan et al. (1998), found that the much higher rate of homicide in Seattle as opposed to Vancouver could be accounted for almost completely by a higher rate of homicide by firearm in Seattle. The rates of homicide by knives and other methods for the two cities were almost the same, suggesting that those who might commit a homicide by firearm do not necessarily switch to another method if firearms are unavailable. Similarly, overall homicide rates in the U.S. were 5.6 times that of England in 1993, but only 2.4 times that of England if homicides by firearms are excluded (Lynch, 1995, 23). In 1999, the murder rate in the U.S. was 8.2 per million compared to the following numbers in selected countries with more restrictive handgun laws: 1.02 in Japan, 1 in the U.K., 5.13 in Canada, 1.13 in Denmark, in 4.42 in France, 4.86 in Germany, 2.29 in Switzerland, 4.9 in Italy, and 3.45 in Australia (OECD, 2002). Taken collectively, the evidence is strong that the lack of restrictions on firearms, and especially handguns, in the U.S. has become a major contributor to higher rates of violent crime as compared to other industrialized democracies that otherwise have similar levels of property crimes.

Except for homicide, the crime rates in the United States generally have been on the decline since 1980. For example, robbery rates declined 15% between 1980 and 1995 (Wilson, 1995, 490). The decline in crime rates in the U.S. (other than homicide) has been linked to several factors, none the least of which is the aging of the population. In the decade of the 1980s, the number of males between the ages of fifteen and nineteen in the U.S. declined from 9.3% of the population to 7.2%. Similarly the absolute number of males between the ages of fifteen and nineteen declined by over 1.5 million (Wilson, 1995, 490). Fewer young males typically means less crime, but despite these shifts in demographics, the homicide rate among white males between the ages of fourteen and twenty-two doubled between the years 1985 and 1992. For black males of the same age, the homicide rate tripled during the same time period. Coterminously, the use of guns by and against people in this same age bracket increased 83% between 1985 and 1992 (Blumstein, 1995, 411-413).

Given such overwhelming evidence that lax handgun control makes the U.S. a more violent and dangerous place, one would expect rational policymakers to be compelled to institute more restrictive gun laws throughout the U.S. While it is true that some lawmakers have tried to do just that, it is also true that the individualistic conservative ideology has been a major force in preventing the implementation of such laws. Conservative ideologues instead prefer to ignore the data and stick to slogans (when guns are outlawed, only outlaws will have guns) that they mistake for analysis.

Expansion of Federal Government Crime Policy

Despite the traditional and Constitutional limitations on a large national government role in crime policy, public sentiments over the last several decades appear to be shifting toward acceptance of a greater Federal role in combating crime. In the 1960s, crime rates in the U.S. doubled during a ten year period, leading to greater attention to crime from the courts, the media, the public, and politicians. Politicians may be credited with elevating crime to the forefront of the national agenda by making it a major issue of Presidential campaigns. Barry Goldwater made "crime in the streets" a major campaign issue in his unsuccessful Presidential campaign in 1964 and Richard Nixon similarly made "law and order" a central piece of his successful 1968 Presidential campaign. Crime has remained on the national agenda ever since (Dilulio, 1995).

Concurrently, the 1960s witnessed the criminal rights revolution in the U.S. Supreme Court under Chief Justice Earl Warren. The Supreme Court has the power over its own docket, and hears only a very small percentage of petitions that come before it. The criminal rights revolution of the 1960s should therefore be viewed as a choice by members of the Supreme Court rather than a role that was thrust upon them. It should also be remembered that the rulings issued during the Warren Court generally expanded criminal rights on the State level, resulting in greater impediments to law enforcement in apprehending and convicting persons suspected to be involved with criminal activity. The prospect that an accused person could now "get off on a technicality" had been enhanced, producing a conservative backlash and condemnation of the courts and again elevating crime issues on the national agenda.

The public in general also played a role in placing crime on the national agenda. Citizens are constantly polled for their opinions on multiple political issues, and crime is no exception. Polling results that give a high place crime in a hierarchy of political issues will not go unnoticed by policymakers in a democratic society. In 1987, 52% of Americans polled believed that the Federal government "was not spending enough to control crime" as opposed to 9% who responded that Federal spending levels on crime were "too large" (National Women's Caucus, 1987). The fact that Congress passed the second Anti-Drug Abuse Act the next year may not be a coincidence. Similarly, in a 1994 poll, 83% of Americans responded that they "believed that the Federal government could do much more to make the crime problem better" (*Washington Post*, 1994) and that same year, Congress responded with the Crime Act of 1994. The fact that 83% responded that the Federal government could do more to solve the crime problem exposes the conservatives for contradicting their "States' rights" ideology again. Since 30-40% of Americans self-identify as "conservative" depending on how the question is asked, it appears that at most conservatives say they want more Federal involvement in the crime problem while simultaneously claiming to espouse "States' rights."

All developed societies contain primarily two restraints on behavior. First, there are societal mores and folkways and morality that are enforced by the individual's conscience, parents, peers, and fellow citizens through informal sanctions. Secondly, behavior is restrained by civil and criminal laws, which are enforced by police, courts, and other agents of the criminal justice system. Modern industrial democracies are societies where many traditional and familial constraints on behavior have eroded, thus requiring an increased reliance on criminal laws and their agents of law enforcement. Crime policy is in some respects less complicated than other policy areas since there is little conflict over the goals of preventing and controlling crime; however, there is a lack of consensus on what policies provide the best vehicles to achieve those goals.

Perhaps for as long as humans have been on the earth, reward and punishment have been used as tools for controlling behavior. The employment of rewards and punishment as tools for controlling behavior is based on the assumption that humans seek to maximize pleasure and minimize pain, discomfort, or the unpleasant. The effects of reward and punishment, however, are by no means exact. Punishment may be completely unsuccessful in deterring any particular behavior and rewards may be similarly unsuccessful in encouraging another behavior; however, as tools for controlling behavior, reward and punishment have stood the test of time and may yet be the best known tools available (Smith and Vetter, 1982).

The use of punishment as a method for controlling criminal behavior is traditionally justified by one of three rationales: retribution, deterrence, and incapacitation (Territo, Halstead, and Bromley, 1989, 372). Retribution definitionally means "something for recompense." In other words, those who injure someone else will sustain injury themselves in return. The retributive theory of punishment is known as the "law of just desserts." Retributive theory requires that the severity of punishment, or degree of injury inflicted upon the criminal, be equal to the injury that was produced by the crime. The retributive theory of justice is reflected in the U.S. in the use of the death penalty for murderers. The prevalence of the retributive theory was also reflected during the Iranian Hostage Crisis of 1980, when American newspapers around the country received letters from constituents suggesting that the U.S. round up an equal number of Iranian hostages and hold them in the same conditions as the U.S. personnel in Teheran (Territo, Halsted, and Bromley, 1989, 372). The retributive theory is the theory that is most staunchly supported by conservatives and reflects their negative ideological view of human nature.

Deterrence

Justification for the punishment of offenders may be found not only through "just desserts," but also through the aggregate impact of punishment on reducing the crime rate. Deterrence advocates argue that swift, severe punishment for offenders will not only make them think twice about offending again, but also deter other potential offenders through the threat of arrest, conviction, and severe punishment. Scholars and policymakers are generally in disagreement over the deterrent effect of severe punishment, however, the conventional wisdom is that punishment only has a deterrent effect if it is severe, swift, and certain. Obviously, the death penalty in its present form in the U.S. is neither swift, nor certain, and therefore does not appear to be a strong deterrent (Grunhut, 1948, 3).

Incapacitation

A further justification for the punishment of criminals is found through the fact that incarcerated criminals cannot commit any more crimes outside of the prison while they are incarcerated. Those who favor incapacitation (predominantly conservatives) point to high rates of repeat offenders for the same crimes and therefore argue that incapacitation will reduce crime rates simply by getting the criminals off the street and in jail. Incapacitation as a strategy receives further justification from the fact that the vast majority of violent crimes are committed by a very small percentage of the population. As such, the contention (favored by conservatives) that building more prisons and keeping more offenders incapacitated for longer periods will reduce the crime rate is at least plausible (Packer, 1968, 50).

Rehabilitation

The liberals' alternative to retribution, deterrence, and incapacitation is rehabilitation. Rehabilitation is based on the liberal's idealist assumption that criminals can and do learn to reform from their criminal behavior. Those who favor rehabilitation are quick to point out that incapacitation often has the effect of increasing, rather than decreasing, the offender's commitment to criminal behavior (Vachss and Bakal, 1979). Though the liberals' support for rehabilitation is undoubtedly in some part ideologically based, at least it is also supported by data analysis whereas the death penalty as a deterrent, for instance, is not. The rehabilitative prescription is widely endorsed by psychotherapists, who view the problem of crime as personality-based; hence, the goal becomes to change the personality of the offender to produce more socially acceptable behavior (Territo, Halstead, and Bromley, 1989, 374). Rehabilitative programs do not stop with personality, however, and may include education and job training to provide the convict with the skills necessary to survive in society outside of the prison walls.

Liberal "rehabilitation" strategies were implemented in the 1960s and 1970s along with the conservative retribution, deterrence, and incapacitation. As of the late 1970's, and certainly by the election of Ronald Reagan in 1980, there was widespread sentiment in the U.S. that the "liberal" policy prescriptions were not working, although they existed alongside the conservative prescriptions that evidently were not working either (Wilson, 1983, 3). As a result, public sentiments favored a more conservative approach and Federal crime policy shifted away from rehabilitation (although it remains as a component) and back toward retribution, deterrence, and incapacitation. The policy of addressing the crime problem through Federal support for the States that had begun during the 1960s was to continue. Additionally, the Federal government would be more active in expanding the scope of Federal authority over crime and limiting criminal rights where possible to aid criminal justice officials in apprehending and convicting criminals. The expansion of the Federal role, once again, conflicted with conservative "States' rights" rhetoric and the limitations on criminal rights violated the "less government and more individual freedom" ideological positions of Classic Liberal and Libertarian conservatives.

In 1981, a Reagan Administration Task Force on Violent Crime recommended that $2 billion in Federal aid should be granted to the States for the construction of prisons. Furthermore, the Task Force recommended that Federal statutes be amended to allow authorities to hold dangerous or repeat offenders without bail and also called for the loosening of the rules of evidence that had been constructed by the Warren Court in the 1960s. The Task Force's recommendations would eventually become central components of the Comprehensive Crime Control Act of 1984 (Clear and Cole, 1990, 33). Obviously, Reagan's Task Force produced recommendations that are inconsistent with the ideologies of Libertarian and Classic Liberal conservatives since the Task Force called for an increase in governmental power and erosion of individual rights. Furthermore, the call for an additional $2 billion in spending certainly was not consistent with the idea of "less government."

Conservatism and the Prison System

Since the 1970s, there has been a political shift concerning basic views about the roles of the nation's prisons. For the first half of the twentieth century, the dominant view of prisons was that they were a vehicle for correction or rehabilitation. Consequently, prison administrators were charged with recommending release of prisoners when they could show that they had been rehabilitated. Empirical research into rehabilitation in the late 1970s suggested that rehabilitation strategies were not having an impact on correcting former inmate behavior once they leave prison (Martinson, 1974). A loss of confidence in rehabilitation has meant a swing in the political mood toward retribution and longer prison sentences, thus contributing to the growth in prison populations. Greater prison populations can only result in "more government" rather than less, since more prisons, guards, food, supplies, etc. will have to be funded. Once more, the conservative ideological positions (retribution and incapacitation) conflict with another conservative ideological position (less government). Conservatives in State Legislatures have also passed numerous determinate-sentencing laws that tend to reduce judicial discretion and mandate longer, more rigid, sentences for inmates; hence, the prison population (and government) may grow even larger as more and more mandatory sentencing laws are passed.

Conservative Ideology and Crime Policy Evaluation

Crime policy evaluation is very much impacted by the political arena since problems of crime have been and always will be significant social problems. Safety from societal predators is one of the primary reasons for the formation of government in the first place. Fear of crime not only leads people to form governments, but continually take measures to prevent crime both individually and collectively. The recent decline in crime rates has thus far not reduced the public fear of crime or the importance of crime on the national agenda. Furthermore, high-profile tragedies such as the 1999 shootings at Columbine High School in Littleton, Colorado are likely to serve as precipitants that mobilize public efforts behind new policies aimed at combating crime. Consequently, ideological factors, rather than policy based on empirical analysis, are more likely to influence criminal justice policy in the end. For example, despite the fact that the deterrent effect of the death penalty is unclear, approximately three fourths of Americans favor its use (Palumbo, 1994, 300).

Probation is often heralded as a more cost-effective alternative than incarceration, and the repeat offender rates for inmates who receive probation are somewhat better than the repeat offender rates for inmates who receive incarceration; however, the effectiveness of probation also has been widely criticized. Studies have revealed that approximately two thirds of persons receiving probation can be expected to be re-arrested for another law violation, and that three fourths of the new arrests would be for serious crimes (Petersilia, et al., 1985). Similarly, Parole has come under criticism in recent years due to studies that found that almost two-thirds of parolees were re-arrested within six years after their release. As a consequence, some States do not use parole boards and instead allow inmates to reduce their sentences through proper behavior in prison. Inmates accumulate this "good time," which is deducted from their mandatory sentence and their release is determined mathematically, rather than through the subjectivity of a parole board (Hoffman and Stone-Meierhoefer, 1979, 215). The trend toward the abolition of parole will shift discretion away from prisons and parole boards and back to prosecutors and judges. Prison administrators also argue that the abolition of parole will hinder prison discipline since it will remove a major incentive for prisoners to behave properly.

Concluding Remarks

Attempts to control crime have resulted not only in concerted attempts at all levels of government to both punish and rehabilitate offenders, but have also resulted in programs aimed at attacking the societal factors that have been linked to crime such as substance abuse, unemployment, racism, low education levels, and guns. Thus far, neither retribution, rehabilitation, nor attempts to eradicate the "causes" of crime have been overwhelmingly successful. Part of the problem is that there is no consensus on what factors tend to cause crime or other deviant behaviors to begin with. One may argue that poverty, low education levels, racism, and a "culture of violence" produce criminal behavior; however, one cannot explain why all children raised under these conditions do not become criminals, and all children with greater "societal advantages" do not avoid later criminal activity. Consequently, any programs directed at these "root causes" of crime cannot be expected to produce foolproof success any more than these "root causes" are foolproof predictors of failure.

Retributionists argue that justice could be made more swift, and more certain, and point to other countries such as Singapore where this is indeed the case, and the crime rate is accordingly lower; however, punishment can neither be made more swift, or more certain, unless Americans want to forfeit some of their individual rights. Thus far, conservatives have tended to lean toward greater forfeiture of individual criminal rights in spite of their ideologies that typically oppose greater governmental power. Furthermore, more certain, swift punishment would almost certainly mean a much greater police presence, more prisons, and a greater court capacity, all of which would mean more government and higher taxes, both anathema to conservative ideology.

Finally, perhaps the most foolproof predictors of criminal activity are the age and gender factors. Criminal activity rises sharply for young males during the early teens and remains quite high until it declines after age twenty-five. Due to the "echo effect" of the baby boom, this segment of the population is larger by more than a million persons than it was in the late 1980s when the crime rate began to decline somewhat. With this greater percentage of people at present in the "criminally prone years," it is perhaps not surprising that there has been a recent series of shootings in public schools and other youth-related violence. If there becomes another major precipitant, such as a major economic downturn or a disastrous foreign war, then the situation is perhaps ripe for crime rates to once again swing upward. The modest gains of the late 1990s would then be quickly and easily forgotten.

Chapter 12
Conservatism and George W. Bush

In an appearance at Crawford Elementary School in Crawford, Texas, two weeks before the 9/11 terrorist attacks, a student asked President Bush if it was hard to make decisions as President. Bush's response was, "Not really. If you know what you believe, decisions come pretty easy" (Quoted in Miller, 2002, 298). Furthermore, in Genoa, Italy in July the previous month, the President stated, "I know what I believe. I will continue to articulate what I believe and what I believe—I believe what I believe is right" (Quoted in Miller, 2002, 298). These statements are essentially a summation of the Presidency of George W. Bush, which as will be demonstrated below, has proven to be one of the most ideologically driven administrations in American history, with ideological concerns, rather than sound analysis based on factual evidence, taking precedent (Clarke, 2004, Suskind, 2004, Corn, 2003, Miller, 2002, Ivins and Dubose, 2002).

Although it is certainly a good thing to have principles, depending on what they might be, it is not so good to have a mind that is closed to all contradictory ideas. After all, Hitler had his anti-Semitic principles, Osama Bin Laden has his anti-infidel principles, Saddam Hussein had his "I will not step aside" principles, and so on. Bush, however, put it thusly, "I'm the kind of person that when I make up my mind, I'm not going to change it" (Quoted in Miller, 2002, 299). Unfortunately, this means at times that Bush will stay the course after he has made a decision regardless of any and all evidence that might suggest that his decision was the wrong one. This is quite a contrast with Franklin Roosevelt's "Try Something" approach in the 1930s. In attempting to combat the Great Depression, FDR admitted that he did not have all the answers, but instead argued, "The country needs bold, persistent, experimentation. It is common sense to take a method and try it. If it fails, admit it frankly and try another, but above all, try something" (Quoted in Goodwin, 1995). The difference in the approaches of Bush and Roosevelt reflect differences in the way the two men thought about policy, namely, Bush's ideologically driven character as opposed to the pragmatism of Roosevelt.

The fact that Bush is so obviously driven by ideology rather than pragmatism will be demonstrated in greater detail in the pages that follow, but it should also be understood that there are some important factors that have perhaps predisposed Bush towards ideological thinking instead of pragmatism. First of all, since Bush's father, George H.W. Bush, once stated, "I will never apologize for the United States of America—I don't care what the facts are" (Quoted in Miller, 2002, 81), one possibility is that Bush's "don't confuse me with the facts, my mind's made up" ideological thought processes were to him transferred from his father through the socialization process. After all, the two President Bush's also appeared to have the same modest study habits. In the words of the elder Bush,

I had to read *War and Peace* when I was like sixteen or seventeen. Don't give me a quiz on the thousands of characters in it, but I guess it had an influence because it was a discipline. It was more that than remembering anything in it. And of course, we had to read Shakespeare in school. It was required (*New York Times*, 1988).

Lack of study (and therefore knowledge) and socialization aside, another part of the reason for Bush's reliance on ideology may stem from the fact that Bush lacked experience in Washington and foreign affairs prior to becoming President. It must be noted, however, that Bush's lack of experience before his election is hardly a novelty since his predecessor, Bill Clinton, like Bush had ascended to the Presidency from his position as a State Governor with no prior experience in the Federal government. Similarly, former Presidents Jimmy Carter and Ronald Reagan had become President in the 1970s and 1980s with resumes that included State governorships, but no Federal governmental experience. Clinton and Carter attempted to compensate for their lack of experience through intense study and rigorous work schedules (Brinkley, 2003). Reagan compensated for his lack of experience through delegation of authority, but his administration, like Bush's, was also widely criticized for being ideologically motivated rather than driven by sound analysis of facts (Skidmore, 1994, Stockman, 1987).

Bush, unlike Reagan, however, appears to assume control of policy on a grand scale, often guided only by his "instincts," or, in the words of Molly Ivins, "his gut" (Ivins and Dubose, 2002). In the words of Ivins and Dubose (2002, xxxix):

When Bush feels he is right "in my gut," no amount of evidence will sway him. His thinking process is very much swayed by what he sees as higher moral claims, so he is not prone to rethink his stands on anything other than limited straight political issues. On larger ideological issues, evidence is irrelevant, for example, his repeated pushes for even more tax cuts in the face of increasing deficits.

Ivins and Dubose, however, are merely political observers and not insiders to Bush's White House. Their analysis could be discounted if it were inconsistent with the views of those who have been close to the President. Instead, however, more and more individuals that have worked closely in the White House with Bush are providing similar observations. For example, John J. Dilulio, who was in charge of Bush's Faith-based Initiative, described Bush and his policy apparatus thusly:

Every modern Presidency moves on the fly, but on social policy and related issues, the lack of even basic policy knowledge, and the only casual interest in knowing more, was somewhat breathtaking: discussions by fairly senior people who meant Medicaid but were talking Medicare; near-instant shifts from discussing any actual policy pros and cons to discussing political communications, media strategy, et cetera. Even quite junior staff would sometimes hear quite senior staff pooh-pooh any need to dig deeper for pertinent information on a given issue (Quoted in Suskind, 2004, 172).

Once again, if Dilulio were unique, then perhaps his comments should be disregarded; however, Dilulio is not the only Bush administration insider with a view of Bush and the administration in general as ideologically driven.

Richard Perle, a fellow at the American Enterprise Institute and former Assistant Secretary of Defense under Ronald Reagan sized up Bush thusly:

The first time I met Bush, I knew he was different. Two things became clear. One, he didn't know very much. The other was he had the confidence to ask questions that revealed he didn't know very much. Most people are reluctant to say when they don't know something, a word or a term they haven't heard before. Not him. You'd raise a point, and he'd say, 'I didn't realize that. Can you explain that? (Quoted in Suskind, 2004, 80).

Perle's observation that Bush's knowledge is lacking is shared by many, including even many of Bush's own supporters (Brinkley, 2003). Unfortunately, when knowledge is lacking, there is little left to guide one besides ideology.

Similar to the observations of Perle, Bush's first Treasury Secretary Paul O'Neill also describes both Bush and his administration as ignorant and ideologically driven individuals that ignore facts and analysis in favor of predetermined ideological answers. O'Neill presents a picture of a President that has read little, and is greatly ignorant of the issues, but has the confidence to make decisions on any issue due to his internal ideological guide. O'Neill states that he kept his memos to the President to three pages "designed for the President's study habits" (quoted in Suskind, 2004, 231), suggesting the President is not only ignorant, but stays that way. O'Neill also questioned the President's intellectual capacity. According to O'Neill's wife, Nancy, the Treasury Secretary would often "leave meetings with the President and shake his head. It was like, I'm not sure if this guy's got what it takes to pull this off" (Quoted in Suskind, 2004, 188). Similarly, O'Neill brings into questions the President's critical thinking ability, adding that he personally, had never "heard the President analyze a complex issue, parse opposing positions, and settle on a judicious path. In fact, no one—inside or outside the government, here or across the globe—had heard him do that to any significant degree" (Quoted in Suskind, 2004, 114).

Finally, O'Neill essentially argues that Bush does not have to think because his guiding ideology provides all of his predetermined answers for him. In the words of O'Neill, "Ideology is a lot easier, because you don't have to know anything or search for anything. You already know the answer to everything. It's not penetrable by facts" (Quoted in Suskind, 2004, 292).

Critics might argue that O'Neill is merely an opportunist, profiting off of his time in the Bush administration through book sales and merely sounding off against his former boss as a disgruntled employee who was asked to resign. The policies of the George W. Bush administration, however, reflect that there may be more to O'Neill's comments than merely sour grapes. Bush himself essentially admitted in an interview with Tucker Carlson in *Talk* magazine in September 1999 that he has little knowledge of policy. When Carlson asked Bush to name something he isn't good at, Bush replied, "Sitting down and reading a 500-page book on public policy or philosophy or something" (*Talk*, 1999). A discussion of some of those policies that Bush has not read "500 page books" about is presented below.

George W. Bush and Environmental Policy

From the opening weeks of his Presidency, George W. Bush and his administration have exemplified the Classic Liberal and Libertarian attitudes concerning environmental regulation of business. Though he campaigned as a moderate, and in his campaign debates with Al Gore even argued for reductions in greenhouse gases (Begala, 2002, Miller, 2002, Corn, 2003), perhaps no Presidential administration in history has proven to be more ideologically opposed to governmental environmental regulations than that of George W. Bush, and that ideology has been transposed into policy action. In the words of former EPA Directory of Regulatory Enforcement Erick Schaeffer,

In a matter of weeks, the Bush administration was able to undo the environmental progress we had worked years to secure. Millions of tons of unnecessary pollution continue to pour from these power plants each year as a result. Adding insult to injury, the White House sought to slash the EPA's enforcement budget, making it harder for us to pursue cases we'd already launched against other polluters that had run afoul of the law, from auto manufacturers to refineries, large industrial hog feedlots, and paper companies. It became clear that Bush had little regard for the environment— and even less for enforcing laws to protect it (Schaeffer, 2002).

In furtherance of Bush's ideological goal of freeing business from costly environmental restrictions, the Environmental Protection Agency's budget was sliced by $500 million (Moore, 2001, 33). As a result, the pace of the cleanup of Superfund sites under the Bush administration has been cut approximately in half from what it was in the Clinton years. Eighty Superfund sights were cleaned up in each year of the Clinton administration, but only 47 were cleaned up in Bush's first year and 40 in each of the next two years (*New York Times*, 2002).

In March 2001, just Bush's second full month in office, the Bush administration began their full fledged assault on environmental rules that had been issued under the Clinton administration. Funding for research into renewable energy sources was cut by 50% and funding for research into cleaner, more efficient motor vehicles was cut by 28%. Also in March 2001, the Bush administration announced that several Clinton administration initiatives that imposed environmental restrictions on the mining industry would be suspended. Included among those was a rule that allowed the Federal government to prohibit mining projects that caused "substantial, irreparable harm" to the environment (*New York Times*, 2/4/02). These relaxations of Federal regulations are representative of the Classic Liberal and Libertarian positions against greater government spending and regulation, but they also, suspiciously, are friendly to the petroleum and mineral extraction industries where both President George W. Bush and Vice President Dick Cheney have strong ties. In these cases, critics have argued that the policies could be driven by interest group connections as much as ideology.

Bush and Clean Water Regulations

On the day of Bush's inauguration, Bush's Chief of Staff Andrew Card issued a memo to all Federal agencies ordering a 60-day freeze on new rules that had been finalized by the Clinton administration at the end of Clinton's term. This freeze covered a number of environmental standards including rules issued under the Clinton administration that were designed to limit the discharge of raw sewage into the surface water, and requiring public notice when sewage does overflow (*Natural Resource Defense Council*, 2002). Simultaneously, a rule that strengthened the power of the Federal government to deny contracts to companies that violate Federal environmental laws was also revoked (Moore, 2001, 32). This is obviously the type of policy that one can expect to produce a political backlash from environmentalists and unfavorable press, but the Bush administration pursued the policy anyway, consistent with the President's ideological leanings against Federal government regulations of business.

As if raw sewage in the water were not controversial enough, also in March, 2001, Bush's EPA director, Christine Todd Whitman, announced that the EPA was overturning a rule issued during the Clinton administration that lowered the allowable level of arsenic in drinking water from 50 parts per billion (ppb) to ten (*Boston Globe*, 2001). Whitman conceded that most scientists agreed that the 50 ppb standard was not safe, but Bush argued that the 10ppb standard had been rushed through by the Clinton administration and required further study (Corn, 2003, 74). In fact, however, Congress had directed the EPA to establish a new standard and appropriated $2.5 million for the study of the problem between 1997 and 2000. The EPA concluded from its study that a 3 ppb standard was justified by scientific evidence, but they recommended the 10ppb standard due to exorbitant costs of implementing a 3ppb standard. Furthermore, a separate study by the National Academy of Sciences (NAS) concluded that a 50ppb standard could easily result in a one per hundred-person cancer risk. The NAS then recommended the lowering of acceptable levels of arsenic in drinking water as quickly as possible (Corn, 2003, 75). As could be expected, a plan to increase the allowable levels of arsenic in drinking water was met with opposition from environmental groups, but it was only after enormous public outcry when the results of the NAS study were leaked to the press that the Bush EPA determined that it was best to keep the more stringent 10 ppb arsenic standard.

The Bush administration continued to push, however, for a loosening of Federal standards on water pollution consistent with their Classic Liberal and Libertarian ideological positions against Government regulations. August 7, 2002, the EPA eroded the Clean Water Act with a new rule to discard the Act's primary program for cleaning up 20,000 polluted lakes in the United States. Three days later, Bush's White House moved to lift environmental review provisions that applied to oceanic waters and regulated waste dumping by the oil and gas construction industry. The next week on August 19, 2002, Congress forced the EPA to withdraw a new penalty calculation scheme for fines levied against clean water, air, pesticide, and waste management violations, after Congress determined that the new scheme would result in a smaller increase in penalties than is provided by law (Ivins and Dubose, 2002, xxxii).

Bush and Clean Air Regulations

Bush's record on clean air has proven to be ideologically opposed to government regulations of business in a manner similar to his record on clean water. Before the end of March 2001, President Bush had written a letter to Republican Senator Chuck Hagel, where he informed Hagel that he had decided to renege on his 2000 campaign promise to regulate carbon dioxide emissions (a leading global warming gas) from power plants after encountering strong resistance from the coal and oil industries (*Washington Post*, 2001). Bush also declared that he was opposed to the Kyoto Protocol, the 1997 international accord on global warming. The Treaty called for the reduction of greenhouse gases to 1990 levels by 2012. This Treaty, was signed by President Clinton, but never ratified by the U.S. Senate.

Bush's abandonment of the Kyoto Protocol is in spite of the fact that in February 2001, Bush's own EPA director Christine Todd Whitman stated, "There's no question but that global warming is a real phenomenon that is occurring." Furthermore, Whitman added, "while scientists can't predict where the droughts will occur, where the flooding will occur precisely, or when, we know those things will occur" (Quoted in Suskind, 2004, 98-99). Obviously, these statements indicate that Bush's own EPA director viewed global warming as real, and her perspective reflects that of the scientific consensus.

Bush, however, was unpersuaded by scientific consensus and strictly adhered to the Classic Liberal/Libertarian ideological position against government regulation of business. Bush claimed that the Kyoto Treaty would be too costly for the U.S. and argued that the Kyoto Treaty was unfair to the U.S. because it called for developed nations to reduce their emissions prior to the implementation of reductions by lesser-developed countries. Bush suggested that the Treaty should be altered so that lesser developed countries would instead be forced to reduce their emissions first (in spite of the fact that 25% of greenhouse gases worldwide are released by the U.S.). Bush also claimed that the science behind Global warming was uncertain, thus contradicting the opinion of his own expert, EPA director Christine Todd Whitman; consequently, Bush called for more study, including a report from the National Academy of Sciences (Corn, 2003).

In June 2001, the National Academy of Sciences released their report on global warming as Bush had requested. The opening lines of the report stated:

Greenhouse gases are accumulating in Earth's atmosphere as a result of human activities, causing surface air temperatures and subsurface ocean temperatures to rise. Temperatures are, in fact, rising. The changes observed over the last several decades are likely mostly due to human activities, but we cannot rule out that some significant part of these changes are also a reflection of natural variability. Human-induced warming and associated sea level rises are expected to continue through the 21st Century (Quoted in Corn, 2003, 110-111).

The last paragraph of the first page of this same NAS document states that the NAS agrees with the conclusions of the International Panel on Climate Change (an international body of scientists that issued a report stating that the increase in global temperatures is at least in part due to human activities) (Corn, 2003). After receiving the study from the NAS, Bush's Press Secretary at the time, Arie Fleischer, stated that the report "concludes that the earth is warming, but it is inconclusive on why—whether it's man-made causes or whether it's natural causes" (Quoted in Corn, 2003, 111). Obviously, since the report from the NAS attributes global warming to human causes no less than three times on the very first page, Fleischer and the Bush administration had decided to again ignore the consensus of their own experts in favor of their pre-determined anti-regulatory ideology rather than base policy on science or sound analysis. It is also possible, however, that the decision was influenced by energy industry lobbyists since, according to former Treasury Secretary Paul O'Neill, compliance with the Treaty would have also meant a decline in U.S. energy consumption by over 30% by 2012 (Suskind, 2004, 104). The fact that President Bush and Vice President Dick Cheney were heavily involved in the energy industry as private citizens before their tenure in the Executive branch has caused their critics to suspect that they were unduly influenced by the energy industry in their Kyoto decision-making.

Bush and the Electric Power Shortage

Later in the summer of 2001, Dick Cheney provided more fuel to the environmental critics when he suggested that California's electric power shortage, a hotly debated issue that summer, was caused by too many government environmental regulations that had slowed the building of new electrical power facilities. Cheney then called for the reduction of those governmental regulations (Suskind, 2004). Cheney's position on the issue, whether correct or incorrect, was again consistent with the Classic Liberal and Libertarian ideological positions against governmental regulations of business. Given that Cheney offered no facts to support his claims, however, the appearance is that Cheney's position was again based on ideology rather than sound analysis.

Liberals such as Michael Moore (2001) countered Cheney's statement with the argument that the California electrical power problem was caused by deregulation policies favored by conservatives that went into effect in 1996. Moore (2001, 139) illuminated the fact that Los Angeles and other areas where the public still owns the energy did not experience electrical power shortages. Furthermore, Moore states that under the new electrical power "deregulation," electricity prices were frozen for four years at above-market prices. Additionally, competition under the new "deregulation" was limited. In effect, Moore argues that "deregulation" created a prohibition against the building of new power plants, so California had to grow more dependent on out-of-State power that was sold to them at daily spot market prices that tended to be higher (Moore, 2001, 139). Furthermore, Moore argues that the California energy crisis was not due to a lack of electrical power. Moore states that California has access to enough power for summertime peak demand, but that power companies held back as much as 13,000 megawatts of power. Furthermore, according to the *Wall Street Journal* (Quoted in Moore, 2001), in August of 2000, 461% more electrical capacity was being held back "off-line" in 2000 than in the previous year, thus increasing electrical power prices. It appears then that Dick Cheney's ideological assertion that that the California electrical power crisis was created by too much government regulation does not hold up to sound analysis, but it is not apparent that Cheney studied any facts on the matter. Ideology does not require study since it provides the answers without any.

Bush and Protected Lands

Finally, perhaps the most controversial Bush administration environmental policy was Bush's proposal for drilling for oil in National Monuments and Wildlife refuges. In his first year in office, Bush approved plans to auction off areas close to Florida's eastern shore for oil and gas development and announced plans to allow oil drilling in Montana's Lewis and Clark National Forest (Moore, 2001, 34). The policy making the most headlines and stirring the greatest controversy, however, was Bush's proposal to drill for oil in the Alaskan Arctic National Wildlife Refuge (ANWR) (Denver Post, 2001). Vice President Dick Cheney pushed the plan to the public for the Bush administration, arguing that the ANWR covered 19 million acres, but the amount of land affected by oil production would only be 2,000 of those acres. In coming up with this 2,000 acre estimate, Cheney only counted the space of the oilfield and pipeline equipment actually touching the ground. Even road widths were left out of Cheney's estimate. According to the U.S. Geological Survey, however, the main collections of oil in the ANWR lay in over thirty deposits spread over 1.5 million acres (Corn, 2003). In the final analysis, Bush's plan to drill for oil in the ANWR was inconsistent with his campaign pledges to protect the environment, but his policy in the ANWR was consistent with the Classic Liberal and Libertarian positions against Federal government regulation of business. Bush's goal of developing the oil potential of the ANWR failed, but his ideology has otherwise resulted in perhaps the greatest reversal in environmental policies in the last forty years. Whether or not the policies that have been pursued are in the best interest of the country (and the world) remains a matter of intense debate.

Bush and Civil Rights

In 1917, Woodrow Wilson asked Congress for a Declaration of War against Germany to "Make the world safe for Democracy." Similarly, in 1941, Franklin Roosevelt called for war against the Axis for the purpose of creating a world of four fundamental freedoms: freedom of speech, religion, freedom from want, and freedom from fear (*Economist*, November 1, 2003). George W. Bush also has launched war for the purpose of "making the world safe for Democracy" and securing "freedom from fear." In the process, however, buoyed by the terrorist attacks of 9/11/01, freedom of speech, religion, and freedom from want, as well as American Criminal Rights, have taken significant hits. The narrowing of individual rights under the Bush Administration is consistent with the Traditional Conservative ideological preference for order over freedom, but certainly inconsistent with most scholarly conceptions of the Democracy and Freedom that Bush's administration is supposedly fighting for.

Most notorious among Bush's Civil Rights innovations is a controversial piece of Congressional legislation known as the Patriot Act. Under this Act, the Federal government was granted the authority to develop a project to promote "total information awareness." Under this program, the Federal government gained the authority to obtain all sorts of information on American citizens without probable cause. This includes the authority of the Federal government to monitor religious and political institutions and organizations without probable cause, perhaps violating First Amendment Free Exercise and Assembly Rights as well as criminal due process protections (Ivins and Dubose, 2002, xxxi). Evidently, the purpose behind the Act is to allow the Federal government the authority to eavesdrop on Mosques and other Islamic organizations in order to snoop for terrorist activity. The result, however, obviously violates long-standing legal traditions protecting Americans against government infringement on their personal lives without probable cause. Numerous violations of the rights of ordinary Americans with no connections to terrorism, however, have already occurred. In one instance, 20 peace activists, including nuns and high school students, were detained as security risks for saying that they were traveling to a rally to protest against U.S. military aid to Colombia. Furthermore, the entire High School wrestling team from Juneau, Alaska was, held up at airports seven times because one member was the son of a retired Coast Guard officer on the FBI watch list (Koh, 2003, 25).

The Patriot Act also made life difficult for immigrants to the U.S. and political refugees. The number of political refugees coming to the United States declined 70% between 2001 and 2003 due to tighter immigration restrictions. To make matters worse, at this juncture, over 600 persons from 42 countries are still being held in prison at the U.S. naval base at Guantanamo Bay, Cuba, without being formally charged of anything. Of those detained, three are children, the youngest age 13, several are over 70, and one claims to be over 100. The detainees have been denied the rights of Habeas Corpus, the Rights to Speedy and Public Trials, the Rights to Counsel, and perhaps, protections against cruel and unusual punishment. Evidently, the same types of tortures that were endured by Iraqi POWs in Abu Graib prison in Iraq were have also been applied in Guantanamo Bay (Koh, 2003, 25).

The Bush administration has declared that the detainees are not POWs, and therefore do not receive the protections of the Geneva Convention under International Law, but the Bush administration also claims that the detainees are also outside of the jurisdiction of any American civil or criminal court, being in Guantanamo Bay, Cuba. Essentially, the Bush Administration has created a new designation outside of the protections of any law, and those designated as "detainees" are at the complete mercy of the Bush Administration. As a consequence, legal scholars, such as Yale International Law Professor Harold Hongju Koh, have condemned the Bush administration for creating an international law double standard where there is one set of rules for the U.S. and another separate set of rules for the rest of the world (Koh, 2003, 25). In the words of Koh (2003, 25),

The emerging doctrine has placed startling pressure upon the structure of human rights and international law that the U.S. itself designed and supported since 1948. In a remarkably short time, the United States moved from being the principal supporter of that system to its most visible outlier.

This is perhaps most important to note since the Bush administration cited Iraq's violations of International Law as reason enough for invasion, yet the same administration has tossed International Law aside like yesterday's bedpan. Koh (2003, 25) further argues that shift in American policy toward International Law and human rights is not due to a shift in American National culture, but instead is a result of "short-sided decisions made by a particularly extreme American administration." In other words, Bush's assault on liberties reflects the Traditional Conservative ideological preference for order over freedom.

Bush's disregard for Civil Rights has, predictably, encouraged similar behavior by foreign governments abroad. In Indonesia, for example, the army cited America's Guantanamo detention center as a model for a proposal to build an offshore prison camp on Nasi Island where "detainees" can be held without charges indefinitely. In China, the founder of a pro-democracy magazine was imprisoned for life on the charge of "terrorism." In Egypt, the government extended for three years its Emergency Law that allows it to detain suspected terrorists indefinitely (Koh, 2003, 25). Obviously, the message that others have received from Bush's action is that if International Law is irrelevant to the U.S., it is irrelevant to others as well.

Bush's assault on Civil Liberties does not stop with International Law, however. The Patriot Act also erodes American Fourth Amendment protections against unreasonable searches and seizures by giving the Federal government the authority to seize citizen's papers and effects without probable cause if it is in conjunction with a terror investigation. The Federal government even has the authority to review which books one checks out at the library and librarians are prohibited from informing individuals of

Federal inquiries under threat of incarceration (Ivins and Dubose, 2002, xxxi).

The Patriot Act also infringes on the Right to Counsel by granting the Federal government the authority to monitor Federal prison conversations between attorneys and clients and deny the Right to Counsel completely to those accused of terrorism activities. Finally, the Patriot Act denies the right to Habeas Corpus, the right to confront witnesses, the right to a speedy and public trial, and allows the Federal government to incarcerate suspected terrorists indefinitely without a trial (Ivins and Dubose, 2002, xxxi).

The Bush administration argues that these invasions of liberty are necessary in order to ensure safety from terrorism. Adolph Hitler, of course, made similar arguments when he ordered detainment of the Jews. The dangers of such thinking should be obvious to all, but are perhaps best summed up by Benjamin Franklin in 1759, who argued, "They that can give up essential liberty to obtain a little temporary safety deserve neither."

Gay Rights

The twenty-first century brought America a continuation of the gay rights debate and gay marriage became a central focus of the Presidential campaign on February 24, 2004, when Republican George W. Bush asked Americans: Do you want a Constitutional ban on gay marriage? Bush asked this question despite the fact that at a speech to the Republican Governor's Association just twelve hours earlier he had argued that "voters face a stark choice between two visions of government: one (Bush's) that encourages individual freedom, the other (the Democrats') that takes your money and makes your choices" (*Economist*, 2004). Obviously, by any measure, Bush's Constitutional ban on gay marriage would take away choice from gay Americans, thus not encouraging individual freedom and instead "making their choices" for them. Just as obvious, Bush's Traditional Conservative ideology that favors the use of government to "correct human weaknesses" as in his opposition to gay rights, conflicts with his own Libertarian and Classic Liberal ideologies that place premiums on personal freedoms. Of course, Bush's Constitutional ban also violates his own "States' rights" conservative ideology, and Bush himself argued that "some activist judges and local officials will permit gay marriage in one place," thus necessitating Federal intervention (*Economist*, 2004). Never mind that "permitting gay marriage in one place" would be consistent with the conservative mantra of "returning authority to the States." It is also worth noting that Bush has criticized "activist judges" on the gay marriage issue, but Bush certainly did not criticize the "activist judges" on the U.S. Supreme Court that intervened into State affairs in a Florida election and stopped the recount mandated by Florida law so that he could gain the Presidency in the first place.

Bush and Fiscal Policy

From the end of the Civil War until 1980, American conservatives consistently favored an austere fiscal policy consistent with their laissez-faire "less government" ideology. As such, conservatives criticized the New Deal for its deficit spending, and Keynesian economics was viewed as flawed and irresponsible (Dunn and Woodard, 1991). A schism developed within conservatism in 1980, however, when Republican Presidential candidate Ronald Reagan argued for a combination of tax cuts and defense spending increases that could only be expected to produce massive deficits. In fact, Reagan's most formidable opponent for the Republican nomination, George H. W. Bush, argued that Reagan's proposals would produce record deficits and labeled Reagan's program "Voo-Doo Economics." Reagan instead argued that his tax cuts would produce sufficient economic growth so that the Federal government would be able to maintain a balanced budget with taxes set at a lower rate.

Reagan was subsequently elected and his "supply-side" economics was implemented with the predictable result that the National debt tripled from $700 billion in 1980 to over $2.1 Trillion by the end of Reagan's second term. It was explained to Reagan that his tax cuts and increases in military expenditures would combine to produce unprecedented deficits by his own budget director, David Stockman. According to Stockman, however, when he discussed the problem with Reagan, the President's response was: "well, it must just be because of the mess I inherited from Carter, and you need to make the numbers show that" (Stockman, 1987). Reagan's response clearly demonstrates Reagan's own penchant for ideology rather than analysis, but Stockman was less impressed with what he termed as the "triumph of politics" and resigned. Similarly, other Republicans were aghast at the Federal deficits incurred during Reagan's terms and Congress passed the Gramm-Rudman-Hollings Act, sponsored by Texas Republican Phil Gramm, that would have forced a balanced budget upon Congress. The Supreme Court later found the Gramm-Rudman-Hollings Act unconstitutional, but the very passage of the Act itself represents a schism in conservatism over the issue of deficit spending.

In 1995, when Democrat Bill Clinton was in the White House, conservative Republicans under the leadership of House Speaker Newt Gingrich returned to their ideological balanced budget roots and essentially shut down the government in an effort to get spending and Federal deficits under control. The very next year, however, Republican Presidential candidate and Kansas Senator Bob Dole campaigned on tax cuts, an obvious contradiction with the policies being pursued by Republicans in Congress, including those of Senator Dole (who also had originally opposed Reagan's deficit spending fifteen years earlier), directed at fiscal restraint and balancing the budget. Dole's running mate, Senator Jack Kemp of New York, explained that "The Republican Party no longer worships at the altar of the balanced budget."

Whether the Republican Party was worshipping at that altar or not, the budget was eventually balanced and when George W. Bush became President in 2001, he inherited an estimated Federal budget surplus for that year of $281 billion, the largest annual surplus in American history. Furthermore, the Congressional Budget Office estimated that the ten-year surplus would be $5.6 Trillion and the national debt would be eliminated by 2009 (Congressional Budget Office, 2001). The surplus was certainly as much a result of a robust economy and runaway stock market as it was the result of fiscal restraint by the Republican Congress or President Clinton either one, but after three decades of annual deficits, both the Republican Congress and President Clinton could boast of responsible fiscal policies.

In the election of 2000, however, a major tax cut was the centerpiece of George W. Bush's campaign strategy and he made implementing that cut his top priority (Suskind, 2004). Bush argued, consistent with Ronald Reagan's supply-side economics ideology, that his tax cuts would not produce deficits. Instead, Bush argued during a radio address in early 2001 that his budget proposal, even with his tax cuts and his promise not to dip into the Social Security Surplus, would still leave "almost a trillion dollars…for additional needs." Bush went on to say, "My plan reduces the national debt…so fast, in fact, that economists worry that we are going to run out of debt to retire (Quoted in Corn, 2003, 87).

If Bush did indeed believe that his budget, complete with its tax cuts, could possibly eliminate the national debt, it reflects that he could only be living in a world of the most extreme ideological fantasy. From the outset,

Bush was told repeatedly by his Treasury Secretary Paul O'Neill that his tax cut plan would not provide much of an economic stimulus and he was certainly not informed by his Treasury Secretary that his tax cuts would eliminate the National debt (Suskind, 2004, 57). Instead, O'Neill and Federal Reserve Chairman Alan Greenspan feared that the cuts would produce a return to deficits and O'Neill argued for the inclusion of safety measures in the tax cut bills that would eliminate the cuts if deficits returned (Suskind, 2004). Former Federal Reserve Chairman Paul Volcker also came out against the President's tax cut plan as "fiscally unsound (Suskind, 2004, 131). Treasury Secretary O'Neill stated that Bush ignored his warnings about deficits and instead adhered to an ideological position on tax cuts. In the words of O'Neill, the idea was that "tax cuts were always good, the deeper the better," furthermore, O'Neill adds that the faith in "deep tax cuts" proved to be an ideology that was "impenetrable by facts" in the Bush administration (Quoted in Suskind, 2004, 280, 307). In spite of being warned of deficits by his top economic advisors, Bush argued in a speech at Western Michigan University in March 2001, "we can proceed with tax relief without fear of budget deficits even if the economy softens" (Quoted in Begala, 2002, 21).

The facts in the matter appear to fly in the face of the Bush administration's tax-cutting confidence and vindicate the predictions of O'Neill, Greenspan, and Volcker, since Bush's first budget ended in a deficit of $165 billion, the largest one-year reversal in projected budgets since 1982, the last time a conservative President (Ronald Reagan) was able to persuade Congress to implement sweeping tax cuts while simultaneously increasing military spending (Begala, 2002, 17-18). While it is true that economic downturn and a stock market malaise were partially to blame for the deficit (though Bush had stated that a softening of the economy wouldn't matter), the Congressional Budget Office concluded that Bush's tax cuts were the largest single factor in creating the budget deficit (Begala, 2002). In fact, by 2004, Bush's tax cuts accounted for over half of the Federal deficit despite the fact that the U.S. was still funding over 130,000 occupation forces in Iraq. What's more, the deficits would only get worse in subsequent years of the Bush administration as spending on the war in Iraq combined with more tax cuts to push the annual deficit to over $500 billion and over 4.2% of GDP by 2004 (Shapiro and Friedman, 2004).

Bush's tax cuts did, however, drop Federal revenues in 2004 to the lowest level as a percentage of GNP (15.8%) since 1950 (Shapiro and Friedman, 2004). In this sense, Bush has succeeded in implementing the conservatives' ideological position in favor of less government. Unfortunately, it is estimated that the debt that will result from the tax cuts will increase interest payments on the debt by $1.1 Trillion between 2005 and 2014, thus negating the impact of the tax cuts by creating another huge Federal government obligation (Shapiro and Friedman, 2004). In the final analysis then, Bush's tax cuts betray the conservative ideological position in favor of less government by creating greater Federal government obligations in the future.

Bush's tax cuts have also failed to create the kind of economic growth that was predicted by the Bush administration. For example, the Bush administration predicted that with the passage of their tax cuts, 5.5 million jobs would be created from June 2003 to December 2004. In the first nine months of this time period, only 689,000 jobs were created, or 13% of the administration's projections (Shapiro and Friedman, 2004). Although a GDP growth rate of 3.6% occurred during the period of "economic recovery" since the implementation of the tax cuts, the growth rate lags behind the growth rate in seven of the previous eight economic recoveries since WWII. Even the Bush Administration's own Economic Report of the President in February 2004 stated that: "The performance of employment in this recovery has lagged that in the typical recovery and even that in the 'jobless recovery' of 1990-1991" (Quoted in Shapiro and Friedman, 2004, 9). In other words, there hasn't been a recovery this lousy since the last time the U.S. had a deficit-spending Bush in office. Similarly, the International Monetary Fund concluded in a January, 2004 report: "the recent emphasis on cutting taxes, boosting defense and security outlays, and spurring an economic recovery may come at the eventual cost of upward pressure on interest rates, a crowding out of private investment, and an erosion of longer-term U.S. productivity growth" (Quoted in Shapiro and Friedman, 2004, 11). In other words, money is just a commodity like everything else bought and sold. Bush's governmental borrowing increases the demand for money and thus produces a crowding out of credit. Private entities that need to borrow will have difficulty finding money to borrow in the future because the Federal government will have borrowed too much of that which is available. The likely result is higher interest rates followed by a long-term slowing down of the economy. In the words of Bush's first Treasury Secretary Paul O'Neill, "one of the most significant things Ronald Reagan had proved is that deficits do matter" (Quoted in Suskind, 2004, 292), but in Bush's ideology, evidently nothing matters as much as tax cuts.

The money from the tax cuts, of course, went disproportionately to the wealthiest Americans, much as Al Gore had said it would during the campaign of 2000. Gore argued that if Bush lopped off the top 1% that he was giving in tax relief, he could pay for the cost of every other program. When asked about Gore's statement on Larry King Live, Bush replied, "Oh, I don't—you know, I hadn't—I'm not so sure. I'm not quick in my mind at math, but I don't believe in trying to pick and choose winners when it comes to tax relief" (Quoted in Miller, 2002). For Bush, obviously, such study is not necessary because in his supply-side ideology, tax cuts for the rich will "trickle-down" to the poor and thus benefit all. Actual analysis of such things is therefore unnecessary.

Those who do study such things, however, are able to pick and choose such "winners and losers." According to the Urban-Brookings Tax Policy Center, 24.2% of Bush's cuts from 2001-2004 went to the top 1% of Americans in income. Tax cuts for millionaires, just 0.2% of American households, accounted for 15.3% of the tax cut revenue (Shapiro and Friedman, 2004). Furthermore, almost a third of the poorest households with children received no tax cuts at all (Begala, 2002, 20). This is in spite of the fact that Bush claimed in his radio address on February 3, 2001, that his plan "reduces taxes for everyone who pays taxes" (Quoted in Corn, 2003, 80). Two days later, Bush asserted at a White House event that "the bottom end of the economic ladder receives the biggest percentage cuts" from his tax package (Quoted in Corn, 2003, 80). Obviously, Bush's statements were in conflict with reality.

This is a repeat of Ronald Reagan's "trickle-down" economics of the 1980s, an ideologically-based economic policy that has not proven itself with economic performance. The theory behind "trickle-down" economics is that tax cuts for the rich will allow the rich to accumulate capital. The accumulation of capital, as every student of Adam Smith knows, will then allow the rich to consume and invest, thus creating employment and wages for the common people. The tax cuts will then "trickle down" to the poor and working classes through the investment and consumption of the rich. The operative word here in practice, unfortunately, has been "trickle." In the two decades following the implementation of Reagan's trickle down economics in the 1980s, the income gap between the rich and poor grew, the rich got richer, and the poor got poorer as measured by income adjusted for inflation. Furthermore, the greater inequality appears to correlate with slower economic growth (*Economist*, 1994).

The trends that had surfaced during the trickle-down years of Ronald

Reagan have repeated themselves in the George W. Bush years. In the first two years of Bush's Presidency, the number of poor increased by 3 million people to 34.6 million, the poverty rate rose from 11.7% to 12.1%, the median household income fell by $500 or 1.1%. Furthermore, the average amount by which the incomes of those who are poor fall below the poverty line was greater in 2002 than in any other year on record. Unemployment was 5.8% in 2002, up from 4.0% in 2000. The number of long-term unemployed, those out of work for more than six months, increased from 650,000 in 2000 to 1.55 million in 2002 and 1.89 million in 2003. Once again, it appears that the operative word in "trickle down economics" is certainly "trickle "unless, it appears, one is discussing unemployment and then the operative word should perhaps be "flood" (Center on Budget and Policy Priorities, 2003).

Given these kinds of numbers, one would think that Bush and the supply-siders would have learned from their folly, but this does not seem to be the case. Ideology is a blinder that is immune to facts and Bush therefore stayed on his tax-cutting course in spite of all of the bad news concerning Federal deficits. Instead of recognizing that his tax cuts had been a fiscal disaster, Bush claimed in November 2002 that without his tax cuts, the deficit would be worse. In the words of Bush:

We have a deficit because tax revenues are down. Make no mistake about it, the tax relief package that we passed…has helped the economy, and…the deficit would have been bigger without the tax relief package (Quoted in Corn, 2003, 251).

Two months later in January 2003, Bush introduced a new tax-cuts proposal and again argued that his tax cuts would lead to "higher revenues for the government" (Quoted in Corn, 2003, 251). Unfortunately, that is not what the 2003 Economic Report of the President released by Bush's own Council of Economic Advisors indicated. Instead, the Bush's Economic Advisors stated in the Report,

The modest effect of government debt on interest rates does not mean that tax cuts pay for themselves with higher output. Although the economy grows in response to tax reductions, it is unlikely to grow so much that lost tax revenue is completely recovered by the higher level of economic activity (Quoted in Corn, 2003, 251).

The fact that Bush does not follow the Report from his own Council on Economic Advisors is an indicator of the extent to which he is captive to ideology. Ideology has no need of experts, because ideology provides all of the correct answers without study. As a consequence, the United States drifts toward unparalleled fiscal disaster. Meanwhile, in March 2003, the Congressional Budget office issued a report that noted that without Bush's tax and spending plan, the Federal government would have run almost a $900 billion surplus over ten years. The CBO also stated that Bush's tax cut plans were unlikely to improve the economy (Quoted in Corn, 2003, 254-256). In spite of their own negative analysis, however, Congress passed another $320 billion tax cut package in May 2003. The *Financial Times* reacted to the most recent tax-cutting folly with the following:

The long-run costs of financing huge U.S. fiscal deficits, which stretch far into the future, will weigh heavily on future generations. With little of the tax cut having an immediate effect, the necessary short-run economic stimulus will be negligible...The lunatics are now in charge of the asylum. Including sunsetting provisions to cut the ten year cost of the tax measures is an insult to the intelligence of the U.S. people...In response to this onslaught, there is not much the rational majority can do: reason cuts no ice; economic theory is dismissed; and contrary evidence is ignored (Quoted in Corn, 2003, 260).

Bush's 2001 tax cut was the largest in history, and his 2003 cut was the third largest. That being the case, is should be obvious to even the "lunatics" that tax cuts essentially can be expected to produce marginal growth at best, but large deficits most likely. If there is anything else that is certain, it is that they do not seem to create jobs. The American economy lost 236,000 jobs in the first half of 2003 and the unemployment rate stood at 6.4% in June, the highest level in nine years (Corn, 2003, 261). Consequently, to conclude that Bush's tax cuts have been beneficial requires the heaviest of ideological blinders.

Bush and Social Welfare

George W. Bush and the Republican Congress have reflected the conservative ideological opposition to social welfare programs with the reauthorization of TANF and the inclusion in that reauthorization of a provision known as "Superwaiver." The Superwaiver provision would give sweeping authority to the governor of any State to override most Federal laws or rules governing social welfare programs, including the Food Stamp Program and public housing programs. Under Superwaiver, Governors could alter how Federal funds are used for these programs, alter the target population for benefits, and alter the types and amount of benefits provided. Furthermore, Governors could use Superwaivers to shift Federal resources to low-income programs previously funded exclusively with State funds and thus free us the State funds for unrelated purposes and thereby reduce overall funding for low-income programs (Fremstad and Parrott, 2004). These Superwaivers would have no requirement that they have any research objective or even be subject to an independent evaluation; hence, Superwaivers could be used by individual governors to overturn Congressional social welfare decisions in any given State (Fremstad and Parrott, 2004). Superwaiver is obviously not only anti-social welfare, but also consistent with the conservatives' "return authority to the States" ideology.

Exactly how it squares with the National Supremacy Clause of the U.S. Constitution, however, is a bit unclear. The impact of Superwaivers is potentially the equivalent of John C. Calhoun's "Doctrine of Nullification" from the 1830s under which South Carolina claimed the right to "nullify" Federal laws within its borders. Even States' Rights advocate Andrew Jackson in the 1830s correctly perceived that if States had the authority to nullify Federal laws, it would destroy the Federal system and essentially return the U.S. to the unworkable Confederation that was abolished by the Constitution in 1789. Consequently, Jackson threatened to send 200,000 Federal troops to South Carolina unless they renounced their nullification law (Brinkley, 2003). Unfortunately, the ideologically driven Bush Administration is evidently unable to draw such lessons from history. The ideology teaches that "States' Rights" is the correct path and ignores the historical truth that a primary purpose of the writing of the Constitution in the first place was to create National Supremacy since the State Supremacy approach under the Articles of Confederation had not worked. This principle is explained in virtually every Freshman history and government, text, but either Bush has not read it (highly likely), or his ideology filters out the information since it is inconsistent with his ideology.

Bush's assault on the social welfare system also includes a provision introduced in his Budget in 2003 that would reduce social welfare by reducing the number of children that would receive child care assistance by

300,000 children by the year 2009 (Mezey et al., 2004). Between 2002 and 2003, the number of children receiving child care had already dropped by 100,000 due to cutbacks by the Bush administration (Mezey et al., 2004).

While it is true that this measure does reduce social welfare, what is less clear is whether or not it furthers the conservatives' insistence that low-income people find and hold employment. The reduction in child care assistance has occurred in spite of studies that have concluded that child care assistance programs in the last half of the 1990s increased employment and full-time work among TANF recipients (Fremstad, 2004). Given this information, it is difficult to conclude anything other than that Bush's policies reducing child care assistance are in conflict with his administration's policies that favor employment for low-income individuals.

Bush and Healthcare

As a principle, George W. Bush once stated, "Every low-income, working family in America must have access to basic health insurance—for themselves and their children" (Quoted in Corn, 2003, 44). When faced with what to do about the 43.6 million Americans without health insurance, Bush predictably relied on his "supply-side" ideology to provide him with a cure. For Bush, if it doesn't require a military invasion, his standard response to any problem is to implement a tax cut. In Healthcare, his solution was a tax credit for families making under $30,000 a year that would pay up to $2000 toward the cost of a health insurance policy.

Unfortunately, only Bush seems to know where one can get adequate health coverage for a family of four for $2000 a year. Adequate family health insurance coverage is likely to cost approximately $5000 when deductibles and copays are included in the mix. According to the USA Today, it is estimated that Bush's plan would expand coverage to less than 10% of the uninsured Americans (Quoted in Corn, 2003, 45). Once again, Bush's ideology says that tax cuts and the free market correct all problems, but actual data suggests otherwise.

In an obvious contradiction with Bush's anti-government and anti-entitlement ideology, however, in December 2003, President George W. Bush signed into law an expansion of the Medicare program to include prescription drug coverage. Bush announced that the plan would cost approximately $400 billion over the next decade, but subsequent analysis at the Department of Health and Social Security now estimates the cost at over

$550 billion. Evidently, the Department of Health and Social Security had passed that information on to the White House and Office of Management and Budget prior to passage, but Bush announced the lower estimate anyway. Evidently, the information was not passed on to Congress prior to passage because the Chief Administrator of Medicare, a Bush appointee, threatened to fire his Chief analyst if he told Congress of the higher estimates (*Economist*, April 3, 2004). Once again, Bush is inconsistent with his own focus on "morality" if honesty can be considered part of his "morality."

Anyway, this expansion of Medicare is now expected to cost over $550 billion in the next decade and over $1 Trillion for the decade after that (Park et al., 2003). Obviously, this expansion of a Federal government entitlement program is in conflict with Bush's tax cuts that deny the government the revenue to fund expansion of massive redistribution programs; therefore, the passage of the program can only exacerbate the country's budget problem created by the Bush tax cuts. The legislation does, however, reflect conservative laissez-faire ideology in that it includes no provisions aimed at controlling the spiraling costs of prescription drugs.

Bush's Medicare program also reflects the ideological preference for private, rather than governmental provision of services in that it allows beneficiaries to elect to receive all of their Medicare benefits from private managed care plans (primarily HMOs). The Federal government will then provide $14 billion a year in subsidies to the HMOs, thus creating an unlevel playing field in favor of the subsidized HMOs at taxpayer expense. Obviously, it is true that the plan thus favors private providers, but it also includes government intervention into the free market in violation of Bush's laissez-faire ideology.

Bush's plan also reflects his "supply-side" ideology in that it provides for Health Savings Accounts, that will be tax-advantaged savings accounts established to pay out-of-pocket medical expenses. Holders of these accounts will be able to make tax-deductible deposits in them, watch the earnings compound tax-free, and pay no taxes on the funds upon withdrawal as long as they are used for medical expenses (Park et al., 2003). Incredibly, Bush found a way to incorporate his "tax cuts solve everything" ideology even in the expansion of an entitlement program.

Regardless of whether such a tax break has utility or not, it is clear that this tax break, along with Bush's other tax breaks, will certainly contribute to the national debt, in violation of what once was standard conservative "balanced budget" ideology. This is partially due to the fact that Bush's Health Savings

Accounts are different than 401(k)s and traditional IRAs since withdrawals from those accounts are taxed as ordinary income. Under the Health Savings Accounts, however, not only are deposits to be tax deductible and earnings then compounded on a tax-free basis, but withdrawals are also tax-free if used for a medical purpose; hence, the money in the Health Savings Account is *never* taxed if it is used for its intended purpose.

As a final note on Medicare, it should be mentioned that it is expected that Medicare obligations will exceed Medicare revenue over the next seventy-five years by over $8 Trillion. Similarly, Social Security obligations will exceed Social Security revenue over the same time period by over $3.5 Trillion. The cost of making Bush's tax cuts permanent over the same seventy-five years is estimated at $11 Trillion, or almost the estimated cost of the Medicare and Social Security shortfalls (Greenstein and Orszag, 2004).

Bush and Social Security

As a Presidential candidate in 2000, Bush stated, "Social security is…a test of Presidential candidates—a measure of seriousness and resolve" (Quoted in Corn, 2003, 44). Like his approaches to other social programs, Bush's "resolve" concerning Social Security has reflected his conservative anti-government and anti-redistribution ideology. In Bush's own words, "They want the Federal government controlling Social Security like it's some kind of Federal Program" (Quoted in *USA Today*, 2000).

To begin with, Bush's "resolve" has not been to ensure that Social Security will receive adequate funding (it would be difficult to do so and still maintain his beloved tax cuts). In March 2001, Bush pledged that Social Security funds would only be spent on Social Security, yet one year later, the Congressional Budget Office released a report revealing that Bush's budget would use $1.8 trillion in Social Security surpluses to pay for other government programs (Begala, 2002, 34). In other words, the long-term fiscal viability of Social Security was sacrificed in the interest of covering for Bush's ideologically driven tax cuts. Bush himself acknowledged his awareness of the impending doom of Social Security in 2001 while visiting a senior center when he stated, "if we do nothing to reform the system, the year 2037 will be the moment of financial collapse" (Quoted in Corn, 2003, 42). One would think, therefore, since Bush believed that the Social Security trust fund would be bankrupt in 35 years, that he would not be raiding that same trust fund to support his tax cuts. That the tax cuts therefore had a long term detrimental effect on the viability of Social Security should be obvious. Ideology, however, evidently has the power to obscure the obvious.

To address what to do with Social Security, Bush put together a Presidential Commission on Social Security to study the matter. Basic common sense would suggest, of course, that for starters it might be a good idea to quit raiding the Social Security trust fund if one desired to make the program fiscally sound. Ideology, however, does not allow much room for common sense, and Bush ensured that the Commission would not make any recommendation that might threaten his tax cuts; hence, Bush's Press Secretary Arie Fleischer announced, "The commission that the President will announce will, of course, be comprised of people who share the President's view that personal retirement accounts are the way to save Social Security" (Quoted in Begala, 2002, 36). In other words, the outcome of the Commission's "study" of Social Security had been predetermined by stacking the Commission with conservative privatization ideologues. In such an environment, all sides of an issue are unlikely to be weighed, dissenting voices are likely to be absent, and real critical thinking is necessarily compromised. Not surprisingly, in November 2001, the Commission released an outline of three possible plans to privatize Social Security.

Bush's people correctly underlined the fact that the stock market growth over the previous 40 years had well outpaced the "return" on their tax money that people get from Social Security. Bush pointed out that over the long term, the stock market had averaged a 6% return, but the real return that people received from contributing to Social Security was only 2% (Corn, 2003, 43). Bush's people ignore, however, the fact that minimum wage workers could work all their life and contribute their Social Security taxes to an individual retirement account, but still end up destitute if they live for several decades beyond retirement age. In the United States at present, a sixty-year-old man has an average life expectancy of sixteen years, and an 18% chance of living to age ninety. Life expectancy for women at sixty-five is twenty years, and a sixty-year-old American woman has a 31% chance of living to age ninety. In such cases of extended lifespan, it is reasonable to expect that a government redistribution plan would have to be retained to fill the gap for former low-wage earners that outlive their trust funds (*Economist*, March 27, 2004). Bush also conveniently ignored the fact that Social Security's "return" included disability and survivor's benefits which account for approximately a third of Social Security payments. Consequently, the potential "gains" from shifting to a privatization plan were somewhat exaggerated (Corn, 2003, 43).

Bush planned to make the transition to a privatized Social Security system by taking 16% of employee contributions and diverting them from the current trust fund to be invested in private retirement accounts. Obviously, this would have caused a shortfall in the Trust Fund's capability to pay Social Security beneficiaries that are drawing Social Security in the present. Such a diversion would have caused the Trust Fund to be bankrupt in 2023, rather than 2037, unless Social Security benefits were reduced accordingly (Corn, 2003, 43). Consequently, Bush also planned to reduce the costs of Social Security by cutting benefits. Bush's administration essentially planned to do this by indexing Social Security benefits to inflation rather than to growth in wages. Since growth in wages has surpassed the inflation rate in recent decades, the shift would actually result in a reduction of Social Security benefits. Bush also proposed raising the age of Social Security eligibility (which has already been raised to age 67 beginning in 2009) and thus reducing Federal obligations (Begala, 2002, 38-39). Even Bush's chief economic advisor at the time, Larry Lindsay, admitted in *Newsweek*, "Reductions in the guaranteed amounts of benefits that will go to plan participants are absolutely obvious, so I will say it" (Quoted in Corn, 2003, 43). These measures, if implemented, most certainly therefore would have reduced Social Security Benefits, and therefore government in general, in a manner consistent conservative "less government" and "anti-socialism" ideology. Bush's simplistic ideology teaches that tax cuts are good, privatization is good, and government is bad; hence Bush's tax cuts and plans to privatize Social Security are intrinsically good, and all data and warning signals to the contrary may be ignored.

Whether or not Bush's Social Security proposals were in the interest of the common good, however, became moot by the end of 2002 due to what simply became known as "the Enron scandal." Enron was a corporate giant in the energy industry with close connections to the White House. Enron contributed over $1.3 million to Bush and the Republican Party during the Presidential campaign of 2000 and Enron CEO Ken Lay served on Bush's transition team and interviewed candidates for the Federal Energy Regulatory Commission (Begala, 2002, 100, 107). Enron was obviously viewed by the White House as a "model" company and Ken Lay was obviously respected by Bush as an honest and capable manager when the story broke that Enron had over-reported its earnings and was, in fact, bankrupt. Thousands of Enron employees lost their life savings in worthless Enron stock that had been provided by the company as the corporate contribution to the employee's retirement accounts. One of the most outrageous misdeeds in the Enron scandal was that the company prevented employees from selling the Enron stock in their retirement portfolios while the firm was in the process of becoming insolvent, but the Company's top executives dumped over $1 billion worth of their own shares. During this same time period, Enron CEO Ken Lay even advised employees to purchase more Enron stock, while he sold approximately $50 million worth of his own Enron stock (Corn, 2003, 176). The Enron scandal proved once again that market investments are not always secure. In the aftermath of the Enron disaster, support in Congress for privatization of Social Security eroded and the Bush plan to privatize Social Security has not yet been realized.

Bush and Education

Education is an area of public policy that traditionally has been primarily a State concern, so one might expect a conservative President that favor's "State's Rights" to do nothing with education policy except for allow the States to run their own programs. Bush, however, like other conservative Presidents before him over the last three decades, continued Federal involvement in public education. The centerpiece of Bush's Federal education program is called the No Child Left Behind Act. When Bush signed the Act, Bush stated,

The new role of the Federal government…is to set high standards, provide resources, hold people accountable, and liberate school districts to meet the standards…We're going to spend more on our schools, and we're going to spend it wisely (Quoted in Begala, 2002, 48).

A month after the President signed the bill into law, however, Bush cut the funding for the program, so instead of "spending more on education" as Bush had promised, Bush's Federal education budget proposal for 2003 was the smallest increase in education funding in seven years (2.8%) and barely enough to keep up with inflation (Begala, 2002, 48). The marginal spending increase may be inconsistent with Bush's statement when he unveiled the No Child Left Behind Act, but it is certainly consistent with the "less government" and "low taxes" mantra of contemporary conservative ideology.

Bush's budget proposal also froze or reduced funding for a number of important Federal Education programs. Included was a freeze on funding for the Teacher Quality initiative, a program that helps States reduce class sizes and do a better job of training teachers, and the 21st Century Community Learning Centers program, a program that provides safe, healthy places for children to learn after school. Bush's budget also cut funding 14% for Safe and Drug-Free Schools Act, a program designed to build safe schools by reducing drugs and violence, and Bush's budget also provided less than half the funding allowed for the Individuals with Disabilities Education Act (IDEA) that provides funding to States to help with the education of special needs children. Bush's budget also proposed cutting $122 million from Federal technology education programs. Similarly, Pell Grants were frozen at the previous year's maximum level of $4000. In 1976, a Pell Grant covered 84% of the cost of attending a public University, but in 2003 it was only 40% (Begala, 2002, 49-53). These cuts followed Bush's 2001 proposal for a 19% reduction in spending on libraries at the same time his wife, former school librarian Laura Bush, was engaging in a campaign to boost America's libraries, calling them "community treasure chests, loaded with a wealth of information available to everyone, equally" (Quoted in Moore, 2002, 104). While Laura Bush may be correct in her assertion, it appears that thanks to her husband's anti-government ideology, there will be less in these "treasure chests" and fewer people that can read and enjoy those treasures in the future due to cuts in funding for education. Evidently, George Bush's "less government is better" ideology extends even to public education and libraries.

Bush and Foreign Policy

Perhaps nowhere has a policy area been more driven by ideological abstraction than the foreign policy area of the George W. Bush Administration. Consequently, there is perhaps no policy area where the results have been more controversial and deadly. Furthermore, the ramifications of the policies that the Bush administration has set in motion may take generations to reverse should the American people decide to pursue different directions.

Since Bush had no previous foreign policy experience and his education in foreign affairs must be considered quite limited, foreign policy is an area where Bush must rely both on his famous "instincts" and his trusted foreign policy advisors. Bush's foreign policy advisors, with the exception of

Secretary of State Colin Powell, have proven to be largely a group of ideologues that subscribe to an ideology termed as "neoconservatism" espoused and formulated by a conservative Washington Think Tank known as the Project for the New American Century (PNAC). The group associated with the PNAC includes Vice President Dick Cheney, Defense Secretary Donald Rumsfeld, and Undersecretary of Defense Paul Wolfowitz, as well as former Vice President Dan Quayle, publishing magnate and former Presidential candidate Steve Forbes, and the President's own brother and Florida Governor, Jeb Bush.

According to the PNAC in their own "Statement of Principles" (PNAC, 1997), American foreign policy under the Clinton Administration had been "adrift" and had abandoned the "sound" principles of Ronald Reagan. PNAC argues for increases in military spending and an active role for the U.S. in promoting its interests abroad. Importantly, however, PNAC argues that the "history of the 20th Century should have taught us that it is important to shape circumstances before crises emerge and to meet the threats before they become dire." Translated, what this means is that the PNAC believes that the great errors of the 20th Century are that fascism, Nazism, and Communism were allowed to exist and grow unchecked until they wreaked havoc on the world and grew to such proportions that they could only be eliminated by tremendous and costly effort. The "lesson" that should be learned in the eyes of the PNAC is that tyrants cannot be "appeased" as the Allies attempted to do with Adolph Hitler in 1938, but must be thwarted at the outset.

In furtherance of this thinking, the PNAC argues that the U.S. must "challenge regimes hostile to our interests and values" (PNAC, 1997). In other words, the PNAC argues for Bush's policy that became known as "preemption," or the idea that the U.S. should take the initiative in overthrowing unfriendly and undemocratic governments, militarily if necessary, and replacing them with pro-U.S., capitalist, democratic regimes. The "anti-American" and "undemocratic" rogue State of Iraq under Saddam Hussein would be a perfect example of the kind of regime the PNAC argues that the U.S. should militarily overthrow and replace. To fail to do so would be to repeat the error of 1938 and "appease" a tyrant, most probably leading to disastrous consequences.

That President Bush was persuaded by the arguments of these "neocons" is obvious since he launched what he himself termed as a preemptive war to oust Saddam Hussein from Iraq and bring "freedom and democracy" to the Iraqi people. That the ideology has a few flaws is also obvious since things in

Iraq clearly have not gone according to the well-laid plans of the neocons, Iraq does not appear closer to "freedom and democracy" than they were under Saddam Hussein, security in Iraq appears to be more fragile than it was prior to the invasion, and there is no evidence to suggest that the U.S. is safer from terrorism after the war than it was before it. Instead, the U.S. army is subject to daily terror attacks by Iraqi insurgents, and over 2400 Americans have died in the fighting at this writing. Evidently, reality has again proven to be more complex than ideologically driven policies created by a conservative Washington think tank.

Ideology and Bush's Foreign Policy Failures

Ever since the tragedies of the 9/11/01 terrorist attacks on the United States, Americans have been forced to ask the question; what went wrong? For conservative ideologues, of course, the answers are simple and easily conjured by ideology without investigation. The problem is that the Clinton administration did not pay any attention to terrorism, was "asleep at the wheel," did not vigilantly pursue Osama Bin Ladin, and left President Bush without the necessary information to prevent the attacks. In short, the 9/11/01 terrorist attacks are directly the result of what Clinton either did or did not do, and no blame could be placed on the Bush administration, who had not even been in office a full eight months. This perspective, however, does not hold up to sound analysis. There is much blame to spread around for the 9/11/01 terrorist attacks, but at least part of the blame should be directed to the ideological constraints of the Bush administration.

First of all, one of Bush's most trusted foreign policy advisors is National Security Advisor Condoleezza Rice. Dr. Condoleeza Rice is Ph.D. in political science and well read in international relations theory. During the 1980s, one of the most important international relations theories in political science was that of Kenneth Waltz (1978). Waltz (1978, 97) argued, "students of international relations make distinctions between international political systems only according to the number of their great powers." In Waltz's view, only the great powers in international relations are important and smaller powers, such as Iraq, or nonstate actors, such as al Qaeda, may be ignored. A decade later, international relations scholars Robert Keohane and Joseph Nye (1989), essentially challenged Waltz's contentions, arguing that nonstate actors were becoming increasingly important in international relations and could not be ignored.

Either Rice did not keep up with the more current readings among international relations scholars, or she discarded the newer theories as lacking merit, because in an article she wrote in Foreign Affairs (2000), Rice argued that a foreign policy was required that "separates the important from the trivial" and she then chastised the Clinton administration for their failure to do that. China and Russia, Rice asserted, were what were really important and Clinton had "frittered away" American power and prestige by devoting too much time to what she viewed as "second or third-tier" concerns. In Rices' view, terrorism needed attention only insofar as it was used by rogue States to advance their interests.

According to Daniel Benjamin and Steven Simon, director and senior director for counterterrorism on Clinton's National Security Council, Clinton's National Security advisor Sandy Berger explicitly told Rice when they handed her the files on al Qaeda that "You're going to spend more time during your four years on terrorism generally and al-Qaeda specifically than any other issue" (Benjamin and Simon, 2002, 328). Rice, however, was not persuaded. Instead, Rice dismissed the Clinton administration's focus on terrorism as "empty rhetoric that made us look feckless" (*Washington Post*, January 20, 2002).

Richard Clarke (2004), who was the National Coordinator for Security, Infrastructure Protection, essentially concurs with Benjamin and Simon's overview of Rice's priorities. Clarke explains,

As I briefed Rice on al Qaeda, her facial expression gave me the impression that she had never heard the term before…Rice looked skeptical…I realized that Rice, and her deputy, Steve Hadley, were still operating with the old Cold War paradigm (Clark, 2004, 229-230).

Instead, the Bush administration came into office with a belief that China posed an immediate and long-term threat to the U.S. Bush himself criticized the Clinton Administration for viewing China as a "strategic partner" instead of a "strategic competitor." As a consequence, Bush's top priority, and the security issue he had spoken of most frequently, was the construction of a national missile defense system that would have nothing to do with defense against terrorism (Benjamin and Simon, 2002, 329). In furtherance of Bush's goal of providing a check on China's power, Bush approved a multibillion dollar weapons sale to Taiwan (Benjamin and Simon, 2002, 330).

Concerning Iran, a country that has sponsored terrorism since the Islamic

Revolution of 1979, Bush himself has referred to as part of the "Axis of Evil," and has had a hand in numerous terrorist attacks on the U.S. including the Khobar Towers bombing in Saudi Arabia in 1996 and the truck bombing of the marine compound in Lebanon in 1983 that killed 241 Americans (Baer, 2002), Bush was committed to normalizing trade relations (Benjamin and Simon, 2002, 330). This clearly indicates that Bush was not so concerned about terrorism. In fact, Bush even said so himself in an interview with Bob Woodward before he evidently realized that such candor could have serious negative political fallout (Woodward, 2002).

Bush's inattention to terrorism was reflected in numerous other policies pursued by his administration in the eight months leading up to 9/11/01 as well. In the area of finance for terrorist groups, the Clinton administration had pursued policies through the G-7 multilateral Financial Action Task Force and the Organization for Economic Cooperation and Development that would encourage countries with loose banking regulations into tightening their laws to make them more difficult for money launderers. The Bush administration, however, opposed such measures as "coercive" and unnecessary regulations of business that were contrary to American interests (*Time*, 2001, 73). The Clinton Administration also pushed for the creation of a National Terrorist Asset Tracking Center, but no funding for the Center was provided under the Bush Administration (Wechsler, 2001).

The idea that the Bush Administration did not give tracking money for terrorism a high priority is reinforced by Richard Clarke (2004), who stated,

When the Bush administration came into office, I wanted to raise the profile of our efforts to combat terrorist financing, but found little interest. The President's economic advisor, Larry Lindsey, had long argued for weakening U.S. anti-money laundering laws in a way that would undercut international standards (Clarke, 2004, 196).

According to Clark (2004, 196), the Bush administration distrusted everything from the Clinton Administration and anything multilateral in nature. The distrust of the Clinton Administration is surely related to Bush's Traditional Conservative ideology that divides the world into good and evil, black and white, and with us, or against us. It should be noted that Clinton defeated Bush's father for the Presidency in 1992; hence, in Bush's conception, may qualify as an evil enemy. Multilateralism, of course, was vehemently denounced by the neoconservatives in the PNAC think tank. In the neoconservative's ideology, multilateralism erodes America's sovereignty and therefore leads to a weak America. This argument can be traced back at least as far as the opposition to the Versailles Treaty and the League of Nations after WWI. In the words of Senator Albert Beverage in 1919, "The League of Nations is the work of amiable old grannies...who would emasculate America's manhood" (Quoted in Jones, 1996). Finally, the proposed regulations on banking interfered with the free market and introduced greater governmental regulation of capitalism in violation of the tenets of the Reaganesque Classic Liberalism to which Bush subscribes. In the final analysis, since Bush's ideology taught him that nonstate actors are not a real threat, such interference into the free market could not be justified.

Attorney General John Ashcroft showed that the Justice Department was expecting no terrorist attacks when he proposed cutting $65 million from Clinton's Federal grant program to local governments that assisted communities in buying equipment such as decontamination suits and radios that might be needed for dealing with response to a terrorist attack. Ashcroft also declined to support the FBI's request for $58 million that would have provided for the hiring of 400 counterterrorism agents, analysts, and translators (*New York Times*, February 28, 2002).

All in Bush's administration, however, were not so oblivious to the terror threats. Between May and August 2001, the FBI three times notified 18,000 State and local law enforcement agencies and the FAA contacted every airline and airport with "credible, but not specific" terrorism threats (Benjamin and Simon, 2002, 342). In July, Egyptian President Hosni Mubarak informed the U.S. that his intelligence service had received information that al-Qaeda planned to attack President Bush at the annual G-7 meeting held that month in Genoa, Italy. The Italians mounted antiaircraft guns at the Genoa airport and the air space around the city was closed, and the G-7 meeting passed without incident, but Bush had been given another warning.

Bush's reaction to that warning, as well as his reaction to the memo from Richard Clarke to Condoleezza Rice entitled "Bin Laden Plans Attacks on America" was to depart on August 4, 2001, for a vacation at Crawford Ranch. How Bush could nonchalantly go on vacation after receiving such threats is illustrative of the fact that his ideology taught him that al Qaeda was not a threat; consequently, he was unable to grasp the gravity of the danger in spite of the facts. Bush's ideological information filter is therefore perhaps as much to blame for the 9/11/01 terrorist attacks as any other government failure.

Bush and Iraq

Besides being distracted by the focus on Great Power competition, however, Bush and important actors within his administration were also distracted from al Qaeda by what can only be described as an obsession with Iraq. Unremembered by most Americans, Saddam Hussein sent a hit team into Kuwait in March 1993 to attempt to assassinate George H.W. Bush who was in Kuwait on a speaking engagement two months after his term ended in the White House. Bush's obsession therefore might possibly be best explained as a personal vendetta instead of an ideological tangent. Only George W. Bush knows his true motive, and he is unlikely to publicly admit to such pettiness, but the motives of his subordinates, who are unlikely to be so strongly driven by any such revenge factor, appear to be driven by the neoconservative "preemption" ideology of the PNAC think tank.

In support of the notion that it is the "preemption ideology" that drove Bush's Iraq policy, Richard Clarke (2004, 231-232) discusses an April 2001 Deputies Committee meeting on terrorism where he stressed the threat of al Qaeda to the other Deputies. According to Clarke,

Paul Wolfowitz, Donald Rumsfeld's deputy at Defense, fidgeted and scowled. (Stephen) Hadley asked him if he was all right. "Well I just don't understand why we are beginning by talking about this one man bin Laden," Wolfowitz responded.

When Clarke responded that al Qaeda posed an immediate and serious threat to the U.S., Wolfowitz replied, "Well, there are others that do that as well, at least as much. Iraqi terrorism for example" (Quoted in Clarke, 2004, 231). Clarke then responded that he knew of no Iraqi terrorism directed at the United States since 1993, to which Wolfowitz replied that "Just because the FBI and CIA have failed to find the linkages does not mean they don't exist." Wolfowitz then announced that he resented any comparison between the Holocaust and "this little terrorist in Afghanistan."

In this exchange with Clarke, Wolfowitz clearly takes the ideological, "don't confuse me with the facts, path." The fact that Iraq was not behind al Qaeda terrorist attacks on the U.S. was inconsistent with Wolfowitz' PNAC goal of using the U.S. military to launch "preemptive strikes" against rogue States and replace them with democratic regimes favorable to the U.S. The focus on al Qaeda was also inconsistent with the ideology of Condoleeza

Rice, an ideology that Wolfowitz may have shared, that stresses the importance of focusing on great powers only and ignores nonstate actors such as al Qaeda.

The exchange between Clarke and Wolfowitz was virtually repeated by Secretary of Defense Donald Rumsfeld at a Principals Committee meeting on al Qaeda on September 4, 2001, that Clarke had "urgently"called for eight months prior. According to Clarke, he, CIA director George Tenet, and Secretary of State Colin Powell, laid out an aggressive strategy against al Qaeda. In the words of Clarke (2004, 238),

Rumsfeld, who looked distracted throughout the session, took the Wolfowitz line that there were other terrorist concerns, like Iraq, and whatever we did on this al Qaeda business, we had to deal with the other sources of terrorism.

Rumsfeld, like Wolfowitz, obviously had been reading his PNAC "preemption Bible" and evidently did not want to be confused with any facts. His plan, from the beginning, apparently had been to invade Iraq. According to former Treasury Secretary Paul O'Neill, on January 30, 2001, ten days in to Bush's administration, Bush met with the Principals of his National Security Council for the first time. In this meeting, during a discussion of the problems between Israel and the Palestinians, Bush turned to Condoleezza Rice and asked her what was next on the agenda. Rice's response was, "How Iraq is destabilizing the region." In what O'Neill then describes as a "scripted exchange," Rice had CIA director George Tenet unveil a photograph of a possible chemical or biological weapons factory in Iraq. Tenet did mention, however, that there was "no confirming intelligence as to the materials being produced" (Quoted in Suskind, 2004, 73). By the end of the meeting, O'Neill explains that Bush directed Colin Powell to draw up a new sanctions regime, and Donald Rumsfeld and Hugh Shelton were to examine military options and explain how it might look to use U.S. ground forces in Iraq to support insurgents to topple Saddam Hussein. CIA director George Tenet was charged with investigating how the U.S. could improve intelligence on Iraq (Suskind, 2004, 75).

One would assume after the 9/11/01 terrorist attacks, however, that Rumsfeld's obsession and focus on Iraq would have abated and been replaced with an obsession with al Qaeda; however, it appears that the Defense Secretary retained his obsession with Iraq even after the 9/11/01 terrorist attacks. According to O'Neill, Rumsfeld raised the question of invading Iraq just two days after the attacks on September 13, even though he knew that al Qaeda, not Saddam Hussein, was behind the attacks (Suskind, 2004, 184). According to O'Neill, it was clear from NSC meetings that any connection between Saddam and al Qaeda was unlikely. In O'Neill's words,

Saddam Hussein had been slaughtering Islamic fundamentalists for years—al Qaeda hated him as much as they did the United States. Saddam was no fool—he'd been tamping down fundamentalists in his country for two decades; the last thing he'd do was arm them, if he had any arms to give (Quoted in Suskind, 2004, 279).

Rumsfeld had to be well-aware of these conclusions, but they were evidently ignored due to the over-riding ideology of preemption. Once again, ideology had little use for contradictory information. O'Neill argues, therefore, that Bush's decision to invade Iraq was based on the ideology of preemption, and "the ideology was not subject to penetration by facts." Unfortunately, O'Neill concludes that the ideology itself is on a "collision course with reality" (Quoted in Suskind, 2004, 280, 305, 307) and O'Neill added, "trust me, they haven't thought this through" (Suskind, 2004, 328). O'Neill is most certainly correct since all ideologies are on a collision course with reality and ideology does not "think things through" or it would not be considered ideology in the first place.

Bush, for his part, said he ordered the invasion of Iraq to eliminate the Iraqi's "weapons of mass destruction" and liberate the Iraqi people from the "murderous" regime of Saddam Hussein, although Bush did also argue that the U.S. had to strike rogue States before they had the chance to strike the United States. This assertion, of course, was straight from the PNAC's ideological handbook. Bush planned to then install a pro-American democratic regime in Iraq and Saddam Hussein's regime was quickly toppled in a couple of months. On May 1 2003 Bush landed in a fighter jet on an aircraft carrier and declared the American military mission "accomplished" and his war in Iraq to be over. Evidently, no one told him that a war is not over unless *both* sides agree to quit fighting.

The result of Bush's ideologically driven folly is that Iraq is less stable and more dangerous than it was before the U.S. invasion, terror attacks on the U.S. are no less likely, Iraq is not anywhere near approaching democracy, and a military dictatorship is still killing Iraqi people. To make matters worse, at a press conference in the Rose Garden with Canada's new Prime Minister, Paul Martin, in May 2004, Bush asserted, "gone are Saddam Hussein's torture chambers and rape rooms" (*Economist*, May 8, 2004, 34). Since picture proof hit the American media the previous week in April 2004 demonstrating that those "torture chambers and rape rooms" are still in use, once again, the only difference appears to be that they are no longer Saddam Hussein's, but George W. Bush's. The biggest difference in Iraq in general after over a year of American occupation appears to be that the military dictator oppressing, torturing, and killing Iraqi people is no longer named Saddam Hussein, but George W. Bush. If there is anywhere that the PNAC and the neoconservatives have proven to be correct it is that it is folly to repeat the mistakes of the 20th Century and allow ideology to run amuck. Unfortunately, the ideology that has run amuck is their own.

Bibliography.

Aaron, Henry, and William B. Schwartz. *The Painful Prescription: Rationing Hospital Care*. Boston, Beacon Press, 1984.

Adelson, Joseph, and Robert O'Neil. "Growth of Political Ideas in Adolescence: The Sense of of Community." In Roberta S. Sigel Ed. *Learning About Politics: A Reader in Political Socialization*. New York: Rando+m House, 1970.

Aiken, Henry D. *The Age of Ideology: The Nineteenth Century Philosophers*. New York: Mentor, 1956.

Alexander, Charles C. *The Ku Klux Klan in the Southwest*. Lexington, KY: University of Kentucky Press, 1965.

American Civil Liberties Union. "ACLU Submits Statement Before House Anti-Gay Marriage Hearing." Washington D.C.: *ACLU*, May 22, 1996.

_____. "ACLU Says that Clinton Panders to Bigotry With Announcement That He Will Sign Ban on Same-Sex Marriage." Washington, D.C.: *ACLU*, May 22, 1996.

_____. "ACLU Criticizes Allies for Jumping Ship on Gay Marriage." Washington, D.C.: *ACLU*, July 11, 1996.

_____. "Testimony Regarding S. 1740-Defense of Marriage Act." Washington, D.C.: *ACLU*, July 11, 1996.

_____. "ACLU Condemns House Passage of Anti-Gay Marriage Bill, Says Measure is Unconstitutional and Bad Public Policy." Washington, D.C.: *ACLU*, July 12, 1996.

_____. "ACLU Background Briefing: Congress Considers Anti-Gay Marriage Bill and Employment Non-Discrimination Act." Washington, D.C.: *ACLU*, August 6, 1996.

_____. "ACLU Blasts Senate Passage of Anti-Gay Marriage Ban." Washington, D.C.: *ACLU*, September 10, 1996.

_____. "Statewide Anti-Gay Marriage Law." Washington, D.C.: *ACLU*, January, 6, 1998.

Anderson, Ronald, and John F. Newman. "Societal and Individual Determinants of Medical Care Utilization in the United States." In S.J. Williams, Ed. *Issues in Health Services*. New York: Wiley and Sons, 1990.

Andrews, Pat. *Voices of Diversity*. Guilford, CT: Dushkin, 1993.

Attarian, John. "The Entitlement Time Bomb." *The World and I*. November, 1996.

Bacon, Kenneth H. "AARP Now Championing Healthcare for All, Scrambles to Prove it's More than a Paper Tiger." *Wall Street Journal*. December 27, 1989.

Baer, Robert. *See No Evil*. New York: Three Rivers Press, 2002.

Bane, M.J., and D. Ellwood. *Welfare Realities: From Rhetoric to Reform*. Cambridge, MA: Harvard University Press, 1994.

Bardach, Eugene, and Robert Kagan. *Going by the Book: The Problem of Regulatory Unreasonableness*. Philadelphia: Temple University Press, 1982.

Bayer, Ronald, and Daniel Callahan. "Medicare Reform: Social and Ethical Perspectives." *Journal of Health Politics, Policy, and Law*. 10 (3) 1985.

Beck, Allen. "Survey of State Prison Inmates." Washington, D.C.: U.S. Department of Justice, Bureau of Justice Statistics, March, 1995.

Begala, Paul. *It's Still the Economy Stupid*. New York, Simon and Schuster, 2002.

Bell, Daniel. *The End of Ideology: On the Exhaustion of Political Ideas in the Fifties*. New York: Free Press, 1960.

Bell, P.M.H. *The Origins of the Second World War in Europe*. London and New York: Longman, 1986.

Bellah, Robert, Richard Madsen, William Sullivan, Ann Swidler, and Steven M. Tipton. Habits of the Heart: *Individualism and Commitment in American Political Life*. Berkley, CA: University of California Press, 1985.

Bennett, Ralph Kinney. "Tour Risk Under the Clinton Health Plan." *Reader's Digest*. March, 1994.

Benjamin, Daniel, and Steven Simon. *The Age of Sacred Terror*. New York: Random House, 2002.

Berlet, Chip. "Dances with Devils." *Political Research Associates*. www.publiceye.org., 1998.

Billig, Michael. *Fascists: A Social Psychological View*. New York: Academic Press, 1979.

Blumstein, Alfred. "Prisons." In James Q. Wilson and Joan Petersilia Eds., *Crime*. San Francisco: Institute for Contemporary Studies.

Bosso, Christopher J. "Environmental Groups and the New Political Landsdcape." In Kraft and Vig eds. *Environmental Policy*. Fourth Edition. Washington, D.C.: Congressional Quarterly Press, 2000.

Boston Globe. March 21, 2001.

Breckenridge, Adam C. "The History of the Constitution of the United States." In Bruce Stinebricker Ed. *Annual Editions: American Government 02/03.* Guilford, CT: Dushkin/McGraw-Hill, 2002.

Brinkley, Alan. *American History: A Survey.* 11th Edition. Boston, MA: McGraw-Hill, 2003.

Brown, Lawrence D. "The Managerial Imperative and Organizational Innovation in Health Services." In Eli K. Ginzberg, Ed. *The U.S. Healthcare System: A Look to the 1990s.* Totowa, NJ: Rowman and Allenheld, 1985.

Bryce, James. *The American Commonwealth.* 1888.

Butz, Arthur R. *The Hoax of the Twentieth Century: The Case Against the Presumed Extermination of European Jewry.* Chicago: Theses and Dissertations Press, 2003.

Callahan, Daniel. *Setting Limits: Medical Goals in an Aging Society.* New York: Simon and Schuster, 1987.

Carson, Gerald H. "Who Put the Borax in Dr. Wiley's Butter." In Kenneth G. Alfers, C. Larry Pool, and William Mugleston eds. *Perspectives On America, Volume 2: Readings in United States History Since 1877.* New York: Forbes Custom Publishing, 1997.

Center for Budget and Policy Priorities. "Number of Americans Without Helath Insurance Rose in 2002." October 8, 2003.

_____. "Poverty Increases and Median Income Declines for Second Consecutive Year." September 29, 2003.

Chalmers, David M. *Hooded Americanism: The History of the Ku Klux Klan.* New York: Doubleday, 1965.

Clear, Todd, and George F. Cole. *American Corrections.* Second Edition. Pacific Grove, CA: Brooks/Cole, 1990.

Conason, Joe, and Gene Lyons. *The Hunting of the President: The Ten Year Campaign to Destroy Bill and Hillary Clinton.* New York: Bedford/St. Martin's 2000.

Congressional Budget Office. "Budget and Economic Outlook: Fiscal Years 2002-2011." January 1, 2001.

Congressional Quarterly Weekly Report. "Administration of Justice Escapes Deep Spending Cuts in New Reagan Budget Plan." February 13, 1983.

Corn, David. *The Lies of George W. Bush.* New York: Crown, 2003.

Cram, Ralph Adams. *The End of Democracy.* New York: Ayer, 1937.

Crispino, Ralph J. "The EPA Dilemma." In Theodore and Theodore Eds. *Major Environmental Issues Facing the 21st Century.* Upper Saddle River, NJ: Prentice-Hall, 1996.

Csikszentmihalyi, Mihaly, and Reed Larson. *Being Adolescent: Conflict and Growth in Teenage Years.* New York: Basic Books, 1984.

Denver Post. March 15, 2001.

De Toqueville, Alexis. *Democracy in America.* New York: HarperCollins, 1835

Dilulio, John. "The Federal Role in Crime Control." In James Q. Wilson and Joan Petersilia Eds. *Crime.* San Francisco: Institute for Contemporary Studies, 1995.

Dobelstein, Andrew. *Moral Authority, Ideology, and the Future of American Social Welfare.* Boulder, CO: Westview Press, 1999.

Dunn, Charles W., and J.David Woodard. *American Conservatism from Burke to Bush: An Introduction.* Lanham, MD.: Madison Books, 1991.

Eatwell, Roger. The Nature of the Right, 2: The Right as a Variety of Styles of Thought." In Roger Eatwell and Noel O'Sullivan Editors, *The Nature of the Right.* Boston, MA: Twayne, 1989.

Ebenstein, William, and Alan O. Ebenstein. *Introduction to Political Thinkers*. Fort Worth, TX: Harcourt Brace, 1992.

Economist. "Inequality: For Richer, For Poorer." November 5, 1994, 19-21.

_____. "Honor Laws." June 21, 2003.

_____. November 1, 2003.

_____. "New Fuel for the Culture Wars." March 5, 2004.

_____. "Forever Young." March 27, 2004.

_____. "A Matter of Trust." April 3, 2004.

_____. April 10, 2004.

_____. "Lexington: A House Divided." May 8, 2004

Egan, Timothy. "Triumph Leaves No Targets for Conservative Talk Shows." *New York Times*. January 1, 1995.

Ellerbe, Helen. *The Dark Side of Christian History*. Orlando, FL: Morninstar and Lark, 1995.

Etzioni, Amitai. "Has the ACLU Lost Its Mind?" *Washington Monthly*. October, 1994, 9-11.

Farmer, Brian R. *American Domestic Policy: Substance and Process*. Lanham, MD: University Press of America, 2003.

Ferry, Barbara. "New Mexico Congressman Linked to 'Wise Use' Movement." *States News Service*. June 5, 1997.

Fingerhut, Lois, and Joel C. Kleinman. "International and Interstate Comparisons of Homicide Among Young Males." *Journal of the American Medical Association*. 263 (24) June, 1990.

Fowler, Robert Booth, and Jeffrey R. Orenstein. *An Introduction to Political Theory*. New York: HarperCollins, 1993.

Franken, Al. *Lies and the Lying Liars Who Tell Them: A Fair and Balanced Look at the Right*. New York: E.P. Dutton, 2003.

Franklin, Daniel. "Act Now—There's Still Time to Stop the Revolution." *The Washington Monthly*. September, 1995.

Freeden, Michael. *Ideology: A Very Short Introduction*. Oxford and New York: Oxford University Press, 2003.

Fremstad, Shawn. "Recent Welfare Reform Research Findings: Implications for TANF Reauthorization and State TANF Policies." *Center on Budget and Policy Priorities*. January 30, 2004.

Fremstad, Shawn, and Sharon Parrott. "Superwaiver Provision in House TANF Reauthorization Bill Could Significantly Weaken Public Housing, Food Stamps, and Other Low-Income Programs." *Center on Budget and Policy Priorities*. March 23, 2004.

Friedman, Milton. *Capitalism and Freedom*. Chicago: University of Chicago Press, 1962.

Forst, Brian. "Prosecution and Sentencing." In James Q. Wilson and Joan Petersilia Eds. *Crime*. San Francisco: Institute for Contemporary Studies, 1995.

Forst, Brian, and Kathleen Brosi. "A Theoretical and Empirical Analysis of the Prosecutor." *Journal of Legal Studies*. 6, 1977.

Glamour, June, 2000.

Gilliard, Darrell K. *Prisoners in 2002*. Washington, D.C.: Bureau of Justice Statistics. May, 2003.

Goodman, John C. *The Regulation of Medical Care: Is the Price Too High?* Washington, D.C.: Cato Institute, 1980.

Goodwin, Doris Kearns. *No Ordinary Time: Franklin and Eleanor Roosevelt: The Home Front During World War II*. New York: Touchstone, 1995.

Gould, Lewis L. *Progressives and Prohibitionists: Texas Democrats in the Wilson Era*. Austin: University of Texas Press, 1973.

Grant, Madison. *The Passing of the Great Race, or, the Racial Basis of European History*: Manchester, NH: Ayer, 1970.

Greenstein, Robert. "What the Trustees' Report Indicates About the Financial Status of Social Security. *Center on Budget and Policy Priorities*. March 31, 2004.

Greenstein, Robert, and Edwin Park. "Health Savings Accounts in Final Medicare Conference Agreement Pose Threats Both to Long-Term Fiscal Policy and to the Employer-Based Health Insurance System." *Center on Budget and Policy Priorities*. December 1, 2003.

Greenstein, Robert, and Peter Orszag. "Misleading Claims About New Social Security and Medicare Projections." *Center on Budget and Policy Priorities*. April 2, 2004.

Grunhut, M. *Penal Reform*. London: Oxford University Press, 1948.

Hamby, Alonso. *Beyond the New Deal*. New York: St. Martin's Press, 1973

Hardball with Chris Matthews. August 11, 1998.

Harwood, Richard. *Did Six Million Really Die? The Truth at Last*. Uckfield, East Sussex, U.K.: Historical Review Press, 1974.

Hasenfeld, Y., and J. Rafferty. "The Determinants of Public Attitudes Toward the Welfare State." *Social Forces*. 67, 1989.

Hayek, Friedrich Von. *The Road to Serfdom*. Chicago: University of Chicago Press, 1944.

Heclo, Hugh. "Poverty in Politics." In S. Danziger, G.D. Sandefur, and D. Weinberg Eds. *Confronting Poverty: Prescriptions for Change*. Cambridge, MA: Harvard University Press, 1994.

Henly, Julia R., and Sandra K. Danziger. "Confronting Welfare Stereotypes: Characteristics of General Assistance Recipients and Postassistance Employment." *Social Work Research*. December 20, 1996.

Herrnstein, Richard J. and Charles Murray. *The Bell Curve: Intelligence and Class Structure in American Life*. New York: Touchstone, 1996.

Hersh. Seymour M. "Target Qaddafi." *New York Times Magazine*. February 22, 1987.

Hess, Karl. *Community Technology*. New York: Harper and Row, 1979.

Hoffman, Bruce. "Holy Terror: The Implications of Terrorism Motivated by a Religious Imperative." *Studies in Conflict and Terrorism*. 18: 271-284, 1995.

Hoffman, Peter, and Barbara Stone-Meierhoefer. "Post-Release Arrest Experiences of Federal Prisoners: A Six Year Follow-Up." *Journal of Criminal Justice*. 7, 1979.

Hoover, Kenneth. *Ideology and Political Life*. Second Edition. Belmont, CA: Wadsworth, 1994.

Huntington, Samuel. "Conservatism as an Ideology." *American Political Science Review*. 51 1957, 454-473.

Hyman, Herbert H. *Political Socialization*. Glencoe: The Free Press, 1959).

Ingersoll, David E., Richard K. Matthews and Andrew Davison. *The Philosophic Roots of Modern Ideology*. Upper Saddle River, New Jersey: Prentice-Hall, 2001.

Interpol. *International Crime Statistics*. March, 2001.

Ivins, Molly, and Lou Dubose. Shrub: *The Short but Happy Political Life of George W. Bush.* New York: Vintage, 2002.

Janda, Kenneth, Jeffrey M. Berry, and Jerry Goldman. *The Challenge of Democracy: Government in America.* Third Edition. Boston, Houghton Mifflin, 1992.

Jones, Howard. *Quest for Security: A History of U.S. Foreign Relations.* New York: McGraw-Hill, 1996.

Justice Assistance News. Washington, D.C.: U.S. Department of Justice, November 2, 1981.

Karger, Jacob, and David Stoesz. *American Social Welfare Policy.* New York: Longman, 1998.

Katz, M. *The Underserving Poor.* New York: Pantheon, 1989.

Kellstedt, Lyman A., and Corwin E. Smidt. "Doctrinal Beliefs and Political Behavior: Views of the Bible." In David C. Leege and Lyman A. Kellstedt Eds. *Rediscovering the Religious Factor in American Politics.* Armonk, NY: M.E. Sharpe, 1993.

Kellstedt, Lyman A., and John C. Green. "Knowing God's Many People: Denominational Preference and Political Behavior." In David C. Leege and Lyman A. Kellstedt Eds. *Rediscovering the Religious Factor in American Politics.* Armonk, NY: M.E. Sharpe, 1993.

Kemper, Vicki, and Viveca Novak. *Common Cause Magazine.* January-March, 1992.

Keohane, Robert, and Joseph S. Nye. *Power and Interdependence.* Cambridge, MA: Harper-Collins, 1989.

Kinsey, Alfred. *Sexual Behavior in the Human Male.* Bloomington, IN: Indiana University Press, 1948, 1998.

Kirk, Russell. "Libertarians: Chirping Sectaries." *The Heritage Lectures:*

Proclaiming a Patrimony. Washington, D.C.: The Heritage Foundation,
Kneese, Allen V., and Charles L. Schultze. *Pollution, Prices, and Public
Policy*. Washington, D.C.: Brookings Institution, 1975.

Koh, Harold Hongju. "Rights to Remember." *The Economist*. November 1,
2003.

Koon, Richard L. *Welfare Reform: Helping the Least Fortunate Become Less
Dependent*. New York: Garland, 1997.

Kosterlitz, Julie. "Itching for a Fight?" *National Journal*. January 15, 1994.

"Kraft, Michael E., and Norman J. Vig. "Environmental Policy from the
1970s to 2000: An Overview." In Kraft and Vig, Eds. *Environmental Policy*.
4th Edition. Washinton, D.C.: Congressional Quarterly Press, 2000.

Kristol, Irving. *Two Cheers for Capitalism*. New York: New American
Library, 1983.

LaHaye, Tim. *The Battle for the Mind*. Old Tappan, NJ: Fleming H. Revell
Co., 1980.

Lane, Robert E. *Political Life*. Glencoe, New York: The Free Press, 1959.

Lav, I.J., E. Lazere, R. Greenstein, and S. Gold. "The States and the Poor:
How Budget Decisions Affected Low Income People in 1992." Washington,
D.C.: Center on Budget and Policy Priorities.

Loconte, Joe. "I'll Stand Bayou." *Policy Review*. May/June, 1998 30-34.

Lasswell, Harold. *Politics: Who Gets What, When, How*. New York:
Meridian Books, 1958.

Levy, Leonard. "The Framers and Original Intent." In George M. McKenna
and Stanley Feingold eds. *Taking Sides:Clashing Views on Controversial
Political Issues*. Eighth Edition. Guilford, CT: Dushkin, 1993.

Lindsay, James. "Apathy and Interest: The American Public Rediscovers

Foreign Policy After September 11th." In James M. Lindsay Ed., *American Politics After September 11th*. Cincinnati, OH: Atomic Dog, 2003.

Lindsay, James. "Chronology of America's War on Terrorism." In James M. Lindsay Ed., *American Politics After September 11th*. Cincinnati, OH: Atomic Dog, 2003.

Lipset, Seymour Martin. *Political Man*. Garden City, NY: Doubleday, 1967.

_____.*The First New Nation*. Garden City, NY: Doubleday, 1967.

Loconte, Joe. "I'll Stand Bayou." *Policy Review*. May/June, 1998.

Lynch, James. "Crime in International Perspective." In James Q. Wilson and Joan Petersilia Eds. *Crime*. San Francisco: Institute for Contemporary Studies, 1995.

Machan, Tibor. *The Libertarian Alternative*. Chicago: Nelson Hall, 1974.

Manchester, William. *The Last Lion: Winston Spencer Churchill*. Boston: Little, Brown, 1983.

Manning, D.J. *Liberalism*. New York: St. Martin's, 1976.

Martinson, Robert. "What Works? Questions and Answers about Prison Reform." *Public Interest*. 35 Spring, 1974.

Marx, Karl. *Capital: A Critique of Political Economy*. New York: Penquin, 1992.

Maxwell, William, and Ernest Crain. *Texas Politics Today*. Seventh Edition. Belmont, CA: West Publishing, 1995.

_____. *Texas Politics Today*. Tenth Edition. Belmont, CA: Wadsworth, 2002.

_____. *Texas Politics Today*. Eleventh Edition. Belmont, CA: Wadsworth, 2003.

McKinlay, John B., and Sonja M. McKinlay. "The Questionable Contribution of Medical Measures to the Decline of Mortality in the United States in the Twentieth Century." In Stephen J. Williams Ed. *Issues in Health Services*. New York: Wiley and Sons, 1980.

McQueen, Michel. "Voters, Sick of Current Health-Care System, Want Federal Government to Prescribe Remedy." *Wall Street Journal*. June 28, 1991.

Mencken, H.L. *A Carnival of Buncombe*. New York: John Hopkins University Press, 1996.

Mezey, Jennifer. Sharon Parrott, Mark Greenberg, and Shawn Fremstad. "Reversing Direction on Welfare Reform: President's Budget Cuts Child Care for More than 300,000 Children." *Center on Budget and Policy Priorities*. February 10, 2004.

Miller, Mark Crispin. *The Bush Dyslexicon: Observations on a National Disorder*. New York: Norton, 2000.

Moore, Michael. *Stupid White Men*. New York: HarperCollins, 2001.

Mosse, George. *The Crisis of German Ideology: Intellectual Origins of the Third Reich*. New York: Grosset and Dunlap, 1964.

Muccigrosso, Robert. *Basic History of Conservatism*. Melbourne, FL: Krieger, 2001.

Muller, Jerry Z. *The Other God that Failed: Hans Freyer and the Deradicalization of German Conservatism*. Princeton, NJ: Princeton University Press, 1987.

Muller, Jerry Z. *Conservatism: An Anthology of Social and Political Thought from David Hume to the present*. Princeton, NJ: Princeton University Press, 1997.

Murray, Charles. *Losing Ground*. New York: Basic Books, 1986.

Murrin, John R. *Liberty, Equality, Power*. Fort Worth: Harcourt Brace, 1996.

Mussolini, Benito. "The Doctrine of Fascism," in John Somerville and Ronald E. Santoni, eds. *Social and Political Philosophy*. Garden City, NY: Doubleday, 1963).

Nakane, Chie. *Japanese Society*. Berkeley, CA: University of California Press, 1986.

Nash, Gary B., Julie Roy Jeffrey, John R. Howe, Peter J. Frederick, Allen F. Davis, and Allan M. Winkler. *The American People: Creating a Nation and a Society*. Fourth Edition. New York: Longman, 1998.

National Women's Political Caucus. May 26, 1987.

Natural Resource Defense Council. "Rewriting the Rules: The Bush Administration's Assault on the Environment." April 22, 2002.

New York Post. March 17, 1990.

New York Times. "Clinton Plan Alive Upon Arrival." October 3, 1993.

_____. February 4, 2002.

_____. February 24, 2002.

_____. February 28, 2002.

Nietzsche, Friedrich. *Thus Spake Zarathustra*. New York: Penguin, 1969.

Nock, Albert J. *The Theory of Education in the United States*. New York, Arno Press, 1931.

_____, *Our Enemy the State*. New York: Arno Press, 1936, 1972.

Northwest Arkansas Times. "Human Dignity Resolution Fails." 11/4/98

Nozick, Robert. *Anarchy, State, and Utopia*. New York: Basic Books, 1974.

NYPost.com/millenium/mill. 2003.

Observer. September 29, 1987.

OECD. *International Crime Victims Surveys*. March, 2002.

Packer, H. *The Limits of Criminal Sanction*. Palo Alto, CA: Stanford University Press, 1968.

Palumbo, Dennis J. *Public Policy in America: Government in Action*. Second Edition. Fort Worth: Harcourt Brace, 1994.

Paine, Thomas. *Common Sense*. Dover, DE: Dover Publications, 1776, 1997.

Paniccia, Domonic. "The Environmental Movement." In Theodore and Theodore Eds. *Major Environmental Issues Facing the 21st Century*. Upper Saddle River, NJ: Prentice-Hall, 1996.

Park, Edwin, and Robert Greenstein. "The AARP Ads and the New Medicare Prescription Drug Law." *Center on Budget and Policy Priorities*. December 11, 2003.

Park, Edwin, Melanie Nathanson, Robert Greenstein, and John Springer. "The Troubling Medicare Legislation." *Center on Budget and Policy Priorities*. December 8, 2003.

Pear, Robert. "Health Spending Rises to Record 15% of Economy. *New York Times*. January 9, 2004.

People For the American Way Foundation. "Anti-Gay Politics and the Religious Right." Washington, D.C.: *People for the American Way*, 2000.

Petersilia, Joan, Susan Turner, James Kahan, and Joyce Peterson. *Granting Felons Probation: Public Risks and Alternatives*. Santa Monica Ca: Rand Corporation, 1985.

Poliakov, Leon. *The Aryan Myth*. New York: New American Library, 1974.

Pollack, Andrew. "Medical Technology Arms Race Adds Billions to the Nation's Bill. *New York Times*. April 29, 1991.

Quinton, Anthony. *The Politics of Imperfection: The religious and Secular Traditions of Conservative Thought in England from Hooker to Oakeshott*. London: Routledge, 1978.

Rand, Ayn. *The Virtue of Selfishness*. New York: New American Library, 1961.

_____. *Conservatism: an Obituary*. 1962.

_____. *Capitalism: The Unknown Ideal*. New York: Signet Books, 1966.

Rankin, Robert, and David Hess. "Reinventing Welfare." *Wisconsin State Journal*. June 15, 1994.

Reagan, Michael. *Curing the Crisis: Options for America's Healthcare*. Boulder, CO: Westview Press, 1992.

Reinhardt, Uwe. "Book Review of Rosemary Stevens, *In Sickness and in Wealth*." *New York Times*. August 20, 1989.

Rhodes, Steven. Valuing Life: Public Policy Dilemmas. Boulder, CO: Westview Press. 1980.

Rice, Condoleeza. "Promoting the National Interest." *Foreign Affairs*. January-February, 2000.

Rokeach, Milton. *The Open and Closed Mind: Investigations into the Nature of Belief Systems and Personality Systems*. New York: Basic Books, 1972.

Rosengren, William R. *Sociology of Medicine: Diversity, Conflict and Change*. New York: Harper and Row, 1980.

Rosenthal, Elisabeth. "Health Problems of Inner City Poor Reach Crisis Point." *New York Times*. December 24, 1994.

Rossiter, Clinton. *Conservatism in America*. 2nd Edition. Cambridge, MA:

Harvard University Press, 1982.

Rothbard, Murray. *America's Great Depression*. New York: New York University Press, 1975).

Sale, K. *The Green Revolution*. New York: Hill and Wang, 1993.

Sanders, Bernard. "What's Really Going on with the Economy." *USA Today Magazine*. March, 1997.

Schaeffer, Eric. "Clearing the Air: Why I Quit Bush's EPA." *Washington Monthly*. July/August, 2002.

Schudson, Michael. "America's Ignorant Voters." *The Wilson Quarterly*. Spring, 2000, 16-22.

Schumaker, Paul, Dwight C. Kiel, and Thomas Heilke. *Great Ideas/Grand Scheme*. New York: McGraw-Hill, 1996.

_____. *Ideological Voices: An Anthology in Modern Political Ideas*. New York: McGraw-Hill, 1997.

Schwartz, William B. "Do Advancing Medical Technologies Drive Up the Cost of Healthcare?" *Priorities*, Fall, 1992.

Serafini, Marilyn Werber. "Welfare Reform, Act 2." *National Journal*. June, 2000.

Shabecroff, Philip. *A Fierce Green Fire*. New York: Hill and Wang, 1993.

Shapiro, Isaac, and Joel Friedman. Tax Returns: A Comprehensive Assessment of the Bush Administration's Record on Cutting Taxes." *Center on Budget and Policy Priorities*. April 23, 2004.

Sinclair, Upton. *The Jungle*. New York: See Sharp Press, 1906, 2003.

Singer, J.L., and D. G. Singer. *Television, Imagination and Aggression: A Study of Preschoolers*. Hillsdale, NJ: Erlbaum, 1981.

Skidmore, Max. *Ideologies: Politics in Action.* Second Edition. Fort Worth, TX: Harcourt Brace, 1993.

Skocpol, Theda. *Protecting Soldiers and Mothers.* Cambridge, MA: Harvard Univeristy Press, 1992.

Sloan, John Henry. "Handgun Regulations, Crime, Assaults, and Homicide." *The New England Journal of Medicine.* November 10, 1998.

Smith, B.D. and J.J. Vetter. Theoretical Approaches to Personality. Englewood Cliffs, NJ: Prentice-Hall, 1982.

Somerville, John, and Ronald Santoni. *Social and Political Philosophy: Readings from Plato to Gandhi.* New York: Anchor, 1963.

Sorel, G. *Reflexions on Violence.* Glencoe, IL: Free Press, 1969.

Specter, Michael. "Unhealthy Care for the Poor." *Washington Post National Weekly Edition.* July 15-21, 1991.

Spencer, Herbert. "The Survival of the Fittest," in *Social Statics.* New York: D. Appleton, 1851.

Squire, Peverill, James M. Lindsay, Cary R. Covington, and Eric R.A.N. Smith. *Dynamics of Democracy.* Third Edition. Cincinnati, OH: Atomic Dog, 2001.

Stanfield, Rochelle. "The New Federalism." *National Journal.* January 28, 1995.

Steinbruner, John. *The Cybernetic Theory of Decision.* Princeton, NJ: Princeton University Press, 1974.

Stillman, Richard J. *Preface to Public Administration: A Search for Themes and Direction.* New York: St. Martin's Press, 1991.

Stockman, David. *The Triumph of Politics.* New York: Random House, 1987.

Storey, John W. *Texas Baptist Leadership and Social Christianity, 1900-1980.* College Station, TX: Texas A&M University Press, 1986.

Suskind, Ron. *The Price of Loyalty: George W. Bush, the White House, and the Education of Paul O'Neill.* New York: Simon and Schuster, 2004.

Swoboda, Frank. "Major Firms, Unions Join National Health Insurance Bid." *Washington Post.* March 14, 1990.

Talk. September, 1999.

Territo, Leonard, James Halstead, and Max Bromley. *Crime and Justice in America.* St. Paul, MN: West Publishing, 1989.

Thompson, Frank J. *Health Policy and the Bureaucracy: Politics and Implementation.* Cambridge, MA: MIT Press, 1981.

Thompson, James J. Jr. *Tried as by Fire: Southern Baptists and the Religious Controversies of the 1920s.* Macon, GA: Mercer University Press. 1982.

Tucille, Jerome. Radical *Libertarianism: A Right Wing Alternative.* New York: MacMillan, 1970.

Time. October 22, 2001.

Tinder, Glen. *The Political Meaning of Christianity.* Baton Rouge, LA: Louisiana State University Press, 1989.

Toner, Robin. "Gold Rush Fever Grips Capital as Healthcare Struggle Begins." *New York Times.* March 13, 1994.

Tweedie, Jack. "When Welfare Ends." *State Legislatures.* October/November, 1998.

United Nations. *Human Development Report 2003.* New York and Oxford: Oxford University Press, 2003.

United States Census Bureau. "The Official Statistics." U.S. Government

Printing Office. Washington, D.C.: September 9, 1998.

United States Department of Energy. "OEPA Environmental Law Summary: Clean Air Act." *Office of Environmental Policy and Assistance*. Washington, D.C.: January 25, 1996.

United Stated Department of Health, Education, and Welfare. *Health in America 1776-1976*. Washington, D.C.: Government Printing Office, 1976.

United States Department of Justice. "Crime and Victims Statistics." Washington, D.C.: Bureau of Justice Statistics, 2003.

United States General Accounting Office. "Waste Water Dischargers are Not Complying with EPA Pollution Control Permits." Washington, D.C.: *General Accounting Office*, 1983.

_____. "Water Pollution: Many Violators have not Received Appropriate Federal Attention." Washington, D.C.: *General Accounting Office*, 1996.

United States Office of Management and Budget. "Budget of the United States Government." Washington, D.C.: Government Printing Office, 1976.

_____. "Budget of the United States Government." Washington, D.C.: Government Printing Office, 1986.

_____. "Budget of the United States Government." Washington, D.C.: Government Printing Office, 1999.

USA Today. November 3, 2000.

Vachss, A.H., and Y.Bakal. *The Life-Style Violent Juvenile*. Lexington, MA: Lexington Press, 1979.

Wall Street Journal. October 13, 1993.

Waltz, Kenneth. *Theory of International Politics*. New York: Random House, 1978.

Waltzman, Nancy. "Socialized Medicine Now-Without the Wait." *The Washington Monthly*. 23 (10) October, 1991.

Washington Post. February 28, 1994.

_____. March 14, 2001.

_____. January 20, 2002.

Wechsler, William F. "Follow the Money." *Foreign Affairs*. July-August, 2001.

Welch, Michael R., David C. Leege, Kenneth D. Wald, and Lyman A. Kellstedt. "Are the Sheep Hearing the Shepherds? Cue Perceptions, Congregational Responses, and Political Communication Processes." In David C. Leege and Lyman A. Kellstedt Eds. *Rediscovering the Religious Factor in American Politics*. Armonk, NY: M.E. Sharpe, 1993.

Wells, Donald. *Environmental Policy*. Upper Saddle River, NJ: Prentice-Hall, 1996.

Wheeler, James O. and Peter O. Muller. *Economic Geography*. New York: John Wiley and Sons, 1986.

Wheless, Joseph. *Is it God's Word?* Kila MT. Kessinger, 1997.

KessWhite, Jonathan. *Terrorism: An Introduction*. Belmont, CA: Wadsworth, 2001.

White, Morton. *The Age of Analysis: The Twentieth Century Philosophers*. New York: Mentor, 1956.

Wilson, James Q. *Thinking About Crime: A Policy Guide*. Second Edition. New York: Basic Books, 1983.

_____. "Crime and Public Policy." In James Q. Wilson and Joan Petersilia Eds. *Crime*. San Francisco: Institute for Contemporary Studies, 1995.

Wilson, James Q., and John DiIulio. *American Government*. 6th Edition. Lexington, MA: D.C. Heath, 1995.

Woods, Roger. "The Radical Right: The Conservative Revolutionaries in Germany." In Roger Eatwell and Noel O'Sullivan Editors, *The Nature of the Right*. Boston, MA: Twayne, 1989.

Woodward, Bob. *Bush at War*. New York: Simon and Schuster, 2002.

World Bank. *World Development Indicators*. Washington, D.C.: World Bank, 1998.

www.epa.gov/globalwarming/climate/index.html

Zastrow, Charles. *Social Work and Social Welfare*. Sixth Edition. Pacific Grove, CA: Brooks/Cole, 1996.